EXPECTATIONS

Language and Reading Skills
for Students of ESL

EXPECTATIONS

Language and Reading Skills
for Students of ESL

KENNETH J. PAKENHAM
English Language Institute,
University of Akron

Prentice Hall Regents, Englewood Cliffs, NJ 07632

Library of Congress Cataloging-in-Publication Data

Pakenham, Kenneth J.
   Expectations: language and reading skills for
students of ESL.

   Includes index.
   1. English language—Text-books for foreign speakers.
I. Title.
PE1128.P237 1986   482.2'4   85–24372
ISBN 0-13-294414-6

My thanks go to my colleagues in the E.L.I., University of Akron, for their interest, support, and active help during the writing of this book, and to the many students of ESL whose use of the emerging text helped shape its final form.

Cover designer: Ben Santora
Manufacturing buyer: Harry P. Baisley
Illustrations by Amy Franks

 © 1986 by Prentice-Hall, Inc.
A Simon & Schuster Company
Englewood Cliffs, New Jersey 07632

Printed in the United States of America

10   9   8   7   6   5

ISBN 0-13-294414-6   01

Prentice-Hall International, Inc., *London*
Prentice-Hall of Australia Pty. Limited, *Sydney*
Editora Prentice-Hall do Brasil, Ltda., *Rio de Janeiro*
Prentice-Hall Canada Inc., *Toronto*
Prentice-Hall Hispanoamericana, S.A., *Mexico*
Prentice-Hall of India Private Limited, *New Delhi*
Prentice-Hall of Japan, Inc., *Tokyo*
Prentice-Hall of Southeast Asia Pte. Ltd., *Singapore*
Whitehall Books Limited, *Wellington, New Zealand*

Contents

To the Teacher

The goal of this book is to equip adult students of ESL with some of the linguistic knowledge and reading skills needed for the comprehension of texts of a general academic nature. It is intended for use with near-beginning, low-proficiency students who have had the equivalent of approximately sixty hours of global-skills instruction and who are familiar with the Roman alphabet. It can also be used with "false beginners," students who may have had more classroom experience of ESL but whose reading proficiency is still low.

An entry-level knowledge of some basic English vocabulary and structure is presupposed for students who are to work with the book. This knowledge is specified in Appendix 3.

APPROACH

The book is based on a number of general beliefs about the nature of the reading process and its relationship to linguistic skills. The beliefs are as follows:

1. Learning to understand a second language will proceed more quickly than learning to produce it.
2. Linguistic knowledge (i.e., grammar and vocabulary) is necessary for efficient reading, but it is not sufficient.
3. The development or mobilization of reading skills can run concurrently with the acquisition of linguistic knowledge.
4. The ability to formulate expectations for the form and content of text still to be read is central to efficient reading.
5. The possession of some background knowledge will facilitate reading.

The activities presented in this book will reflect one or more of these beliefs.

GENERAL OUTLINE

The book consists of seven units and a brief Introductory Unit. Each unit focuses on one general topic, with the topics alternating between issues of international interest and issues more directly related to life in the United States.

Each unit consists of two sections: (1) a vocabulary study and preparatory reading section and (2) a main reading section. The first section defines, exemplifies, and offers practice in vocabulary items likely to be encountered in general academic, pre-technical English. Approximately forty items are introduced, in five groups. The section includes five short reading passages; the passages are intended to show the new vocabulary items in wider contexts and to establish some background knowledge which will be helpful for the understanding of the main reading of each unit.

The main reading section includes a longer reading passage which uses the structures and vocabulary introduced and practiced earlier in the unit. It also includes exercises in main idea recognition, detailed comprehension, and coherence recognition. Pre-reading exercises are provided as well; these promote the comprehension of unknown vocabulary from context and the development of expectations for the content of the upcoming main reading passage.

Appendix 1 consists of grammar study sections for each unit. They explain one or more points of English structure and provide exercises in the understanding of these structures for reading.

As the book proceeds, the readings become longer. In addition, sentence structure becomes more sophisticated and varied, reflecting the structural points introduced in preceding units.

GUIDELINES FOR USE

Reading teachers will devise many ways to effectively use the material in this text. However, since the book departs somewhat from the format of existing reading texts, a number of suggested guidelines for its use are provided. First I have given some general suggestions about the sequencing of activities within the book and within each unit. Then I have outlined general guidelines for the division of activities between in-class and homework assignments.

1. Since each unit builds on the vocabulary and structure of preceding units, the unit-by-unit sequence of the book should be followed. The Introductory Unit, consisting of a short grammar study section (in Appendix 1) and a vocabulary study section, is intended to introduce students to some of the less common features of the book in order to reduce the load of new activities that students will have to master in Unit One.
2. Teachers should complete the vocabulary study and preparatory reading section in each unit before beginning the main reading. This will allow students to become familiar with the vocabulary and general subject matter of the main reading.
3. Teachers may use or omit the grammar section of each unit, as they see fit. If teachers choose to use this section, it can be presented before the introduction of the new vocabulary. Alternatively, some teachers may wish to postpone consid-

eration of the grammatical structures until students have encountered these structures in their reading of the short passages in the vocabulary study and preparatory reading section.

4. In each vocabulary study and preparatory reading section, teachers can have students work on preliminary familiarization with a set of words before reading the appropriate short passage. Alternatively, focused vocabulary work could be postponed until the students have encountered the new items in the shorter reading passage.

The vocabulary exercises (Same or Different, Expectations, and Vocabulary Quiz) are best left until the students have familiarized themselves with the vocabulary items in question. In these exercises, the vocabulary items of Parts A and B are practiced together, as are the items from Parts C, D, and E. The exercises are designed to offer reinforcement and consolidation of preliminary learning.

Note, however, that the items in the Vocabulary Quiz exercises are arranged to follow the order of their introduction. This allows teachers, if they wish, to assign the appropriate part of these exercises earlier—for example, immediately after students have had their first exposure to the items in a given group.

5. The Expectations exercises in the main reading sections (which begin in Unit Two) should be completed before any intensive reading of the passage is undertaken. The Vocabulary in Context can also be done prior to the main reading, or it can be postponed until the given words are encountered in the main reading.

The sequence of the Main Ideas Check and the Comprehension Check is flexible. However, it should be pointed out that the Main Ideas Check states the main ideas and asks students to assign them to the correct paragraphs. The knowledge gained by doing this exercise before the Comprehension Check may help students, especially during the first weeks of the class. The Paragraph Reading exercises deal with information which will be fairly familiar to students after the main reading. Consequently, these exercises are best done as the final activity in the unit.

In general, the book is intended to provide copious amounts of reading or reading-related activities, both for in-class work and homework. In-class work can be done with the entire class, but it is probably more profitably pursued in small-group or individualized work sessions where feedback from the teacher is tailored to each student's needs. The following suggestions may be useful:

1. Teachers are encouraged to present the grammar points in their own way and with their own examples. The first three parts of each section (Introduction, Examples, and Explanation) of Appendix 1 are really intended for the students' reference after initial presentation and practice of the structures in question. Note that the goal is the ability to understand the structures, not to produce

them. Since the goal is a more modest one than the goal of a typical structure class, more material can be presented, material which has its place in the reading class but which would not be encountered in the early stages of a course aimed at productive mastery of structure.

2. The Same or Different and Expectations exercises in the vocabulary study and preparatory reading sections are probably best reserved for in-class work, where valuable feedback can be given promptly and in individualized form, if necessary. Most of the other activities in this section lend themselves equally well to in-class work and to homework. The exception is vocabulary memorization, which is best reserved as a homework activity.

3. It is recommended that the Vocabulary in Context and the Expectations exercises in the main reading section be done in class. This will eliminate, in the case of the former, possible dictionary use. In the Expectations exercises, it will allow the students to learn the point of an exercise which may be very unfamiliar to them and enable the teacher to offer immediate guidance and feedback. The other activities in this section are suitable both for in-class work and for homework. This allows teachers to vary the assignment of activities. Note that in all the comprehension questions, students are asked to specify the place (or places) in the text where they find the answers to questions. This is intended to preempt guessing and to emphasize the text as the source of information requested.

A separate Teacher's Manual is available to accompany this book. It contains more specific suggestions for the use of the materials in the book, as well as supplementary exercises and keys.

Introductory Unit

Grammar for this unit: Actions in the past
You will find information and practice on this grammar point in
Appendix 1, Introductory Unit.

Vocabulary Study and Preparatory Reading

PART A

to **seem** (verb)

DEFINITION ·to seem to be something: to give the idea of something

EXAMPLES 1. Today it is 70°F, but it doesn't *seem* so warm. It *seems* quite cold. There is a strong wind from the north.
2. Things far away from you *seem* very small.

accident (noun)

DEFINITION an accident: something bad happens to you. This is an *accident.*

EXAMPLES 1. There are car *accidents* every day. People drive too fast and don't take enough care on the roads.
2. A person falls down the stairs and is hurt. This is an *accident.*

maybe/perhaps (adverb)

DEFINITION maybe: not sure about something
perhaps: maybe

EXAMPLES 1. Robert: Hi, Mike, are you coming to the soccer game with us?

Mike: *Maybe.* I have to do some work for tomorrow, so I'm not 100% sure.

2. John: Hi, Mike. Where's Robert?

Mike: I don't know for sure. *Perhaps* he's in the cafeteria. It's lunch time.

to **arrive** (verb)

DEFINITION to arrive: to get to a place; to finish a journey

EXAMPLES 1. I want to meet you at the airport. When does your plane *arrive?*

2. The party begins at nine o'clock, but Mike has to work this evening. He can't *arrive* before eleven o'clock.

to **leave** (irregular verb)
left (past tense)

DEFINITION to leave: 1. to go away from a place or from a person
2. not to take something with you

EXAMPLES 1. Tomorrow we have to get up early. Our plane *leaves* at 8:30 A.M.

2. I can't find my English book. Maybe I *left* it at home.

trouble (noun)

DEFINITION trouble: difficulty

EXAMPLES 1. This math class is giving me a lot of *trouble.* It is very difficult for me.

2. I am having *trouble* with my car. It doesn't start on cold mornings.

important (adjective)

DEFINITION important: We have to pay attention to something; it matters a lot.

EXAMPLES 1. Here is some *important* information about your journey to Washington. The plane leaves at 8:30, not at 9:00.

2. Tomorrow is an *important* day for me. I begin a new job tomorrow.

way (noun)

DEFINITION a way: 1. how to do something
2. how to get to a place

EXAMPLES 1. What is a good *way* to learn English?
Go to the U.S., take classes there, and live with Americans.
2. Mike: Can you tell me the *way* to the library?
Jane: Go down this street for one block. The library is on your right.

to **continue** (verb)

DEFINITION to continue: to go on with something

EXAMPLES 1. After an hour in New York, we *continued* our journey from London to San Francisco.
2. The students read two pages of the story on Monday; on Tuesday they *continued* the story; on Wednesday they finished it.

Now read this passage and answer the questions about it. Also write the numbers of the lines where you found the answers.

1   Every year millions of people travel by plane without any diffi-
2   culty. I don't fly very often, but I always seem to run into trouble.
3   Trouble seems to like me; it goes with me like a friendly dog! Last
4   year, for example, I wanted to come home from a winter vacation
5   in Miami, Florida. I had to take a plane to Atlanta and then take
6   another plane home. We left Miami on a Sunday morning. The
7   weather there was warm and sunny. We arrived in Atlanta at
8   12:30 P.M., but then it began to snow. In the next three hours, 10
9   inches of snow fell, and the plane could not leave. After twenty-
10   four hours at the Atlanta airport, I was able to continue my
11   journey. I arrived home and went to work. "You look tired," the
12   people at work said. "You need a vacation!"
13   This year I had to go to Washington, D.C., for an important
14   business meeting. For the plane journey, I wore sports clothes; they
15   were old, but I felt comfortable in them. My good clothes for the
16   meeting were in my suitcase. That was a very intelligent idea! I
17   arrived in Washington, but my suitcase didn't. Maybe it went to
18   London or perhaps to San Francisco. I don't know, but it didn't
19   arrive in Washington with me! I went to my important meeting in
20   my tennis clothes. Now that is not a good way to do business!
21   People in Washington wear suits to business meetings, not shorts
22   and tennis shoes. My meeting did not go well. That was two weeks
23   ago. Now I am home again, and I am still waiting for my suitcase!

1. When did the writer have trouble last year? Line(s) _____
   a. On his way to Miami
   b. On the plane from Miami to Atlanta
   c. On his way home from Miami

2. Why did the writer have to wait in Atlanta? Line(s) _____
   a. The weather became bad, and his plane could not leave.
   b. All the planes were full; he could not get a ticket.
   c. He could not find his suitcase.

3. T F The writer had to wear tennis clothes to his business Line(s) _____
   meeting in Washington.

4. T F The writer was happy with his meeting in Washing- Line(s) _____
   ton; it went well.

5. What trouble did the writer have on his trip to Washington? Line(s) _____
   a. He got on the wrong plane.
   b. The plane was late, and he was late for his important meeting.
   c. Someone did not put his suitcase on the Washington plane.

PART B

strange (adjective)

DEFINITION strange: You don't know things or people; you don't see them
often. For you, they are *strange*.

EXAMPLES 1. For many people from other countries, American football is
a very *strange* game. It is called football, but the players
keep the ball in their hands.
2. Many drivers from the U.S. and Europe feel *strange* in
Britain. They have to drive on the left side of the road, not
the right.

result (noun)

DEFINITION a result: 1. something happens because of another thing
2. the news of a test or a game

EXAMPLES 1. My friend has a lot of trouble with his right leg. This is *the
result* of a car accident last year.
2. The students were happy with *the results* of their test.
Everyone got over 80%.

to **take place** (irregular verb)
took place (past tense)

DEFINITION to take place: to happen

EXAMPLES 1. The soccer World Cup *took place* in Spain in 1982. It *took place* in Argentina in 1978.
2. The Olympic Games *take place* every four years.

real (adjective)
really (adverb)

DEFINITION real: true
really: 1. truly
2. very

EXAMPLES 1. Some people don't like to tell their *real* age. They want to be young.
2. Robert: Mike, do you *really* want to go to the game tonight? It's very cold.
Mike: No. Let's forget it and go another night.
3. I'm *really* tired. I have to go to bed.

suitable (adjective)
unsuitable (adjective)

DEFINITION suitable: right for someone or something
unsuitable: not right

EXAMPLES 1. This apartment is *unsuitable* for my brother and his family. It has only one bedroom and it is not near any schools. (He has three children.)
2. This book is not *suitable* for our class. It is too difficult.

cause (noun)
to **cause** (verb)

DEFINITION to cause something: to make something happen
a cause: a reason

EXAMPLES 1. The bad weather *caused* a lot of road accidents.
2. In our class, we are studying the *causes* of World War II. We are asking the question, Why did the war begin?

nearly (adverb)
almost (adverb)

DEFINITION nearly: not 100%, but very close
almost: nearly

EXAMPLES 1. The classroom is *nearly* full. There are only one or two free chairs.
2. It's *almost* three o'clock. (Maybe three or four minutes before three.)

clear (adjective)

DEFINITION clear: You can understand or see something easily.

EXAMPLES 1. Good teachers can give *clear* examples to their students. From the examples, the students can understand the rule.
2. Student: Can you please explain this rule to me again? It's not really *clear* to me.

Now read this passage and answer the questions about it. Also write the numbers of the lines where you found the answers.

1   To people from other countries, baseball seems a very strange
2 game. Its rules are not clear, and it is not really a "world" game,
3 like soccer. But there are other strange things about baseball. One
4 is the name of the top team: the top baseball team in North Amer-
5 ica is called the "World Champions." The "World Series" is the
6 name of the seven games between the top two teams. But how can
7 it be a *World* Series; how can the top teams be *World* Champions?
8 Only teams from the U.S. and Canada play in this *World* Series!
9   The World Series takes place in October every year. There can
10 be up to seven games in the series. The first team with four wins
11 becomes the World Champions. The teams play two games in the
12 home city of one of the teams; then they leave that city and play
13 the next two or three games in the home city of the other team.
14 The last two games take place in the first city.
15   For many Americans, October is not a suitable month for the
16 World Series. "Baseball is a summer game," they say. "We need
17 good weather for these important games." They are right. In some
18 cities—Chicago, Montreal, Toronto, Detroit, New York, Cleveland,
19 Pittsburgh—October is almost winter and the weather can be very
20 cold. The cold can cause trouble for the players. In one game of a
21 World Series it began to snow; the players couldn't keep the ball in
22 their hands and made a lot of mistakes in the game.
23   But for the people at the games, the weather isn't really impor-
24 tant. They come to the games in warm weather and in cold
25 weather. The important thing for them is a good result—a win for
26 their team.

1. When does the World Series of baseball take place?   Line(s) _____
   a. In the United States and Canada
   b. In October every year
   c. Between the top two teams of North America
   d. No, it does not take place every year.

2. T F   Teams from many countries of the world play in the   Line(s) _____
           World Series.

3. T F   People from other countries do not really understand   Line(s) _____
           baseball.

4. T F   Baseball players like cold weather.   Line(s) _____

5. Here are the results of the first four games in the 1976 World Line(s) _____
   Series. Cincinnati played New York.

   Game 1: Cincinnati, 5–New York, 1
   Game 2: Cincinnati, 4–New York, 3
   Game 3: Cincinnati, 6–New York, 2
   Game 4: Cincinnati, 7–New York, 2

   How many games did they have to play in this World Series?
   a. Four
   b. Seven
   c. Five

Exercises for Parts A and B

SAME OR DIFFERENT?

Read the two sentences in each example. Do they express the same ideas, or do they express different ideas? Write *S* for sentences with the same ideas; write *D* for sentences with different ideas.

   Remember: You can express the **same** ideas with **different** words and **different** grammar!

1. a. How can I learn English fast?   _____
   b. What is a good way for me to learn English fast?

2. a. The bad weather caused the accident.   _____
   b. The accident was the result of the bad weather.

3. a. I didn't really understand the professor's explanation.   _____
   b. The professor's explanation was very clear to me.

4. a. I am having a lot of trouble with this math class.   _____
   b. This math class is really important for me.

5. a. Mike felt really tired, but he continued to work. ———
   b. Mike stopped working; he felt really tired.

6. a. There was snow on the field, but the game took place. ———
   b. They did not play the game; there was snow on the field.

7. a. Tomorrow's game means a lot to our team. ———
   b. The game tomorrow is very important for our team.

8. a. It's very hot today; it's almost 95°F. ———
   b. Today is very hot; it's nearly 95°F.

EXPECTATIONS

Read the first sentence in each of these examples. Think about the ideas in it. What ideas can you expect in the next sentence? From (a), (b), and (c), choose the sentence or sentences that can follow the first sentence. Together the sentences have to have a clear meaning.

1. There were a lot of people at the baseball game last night.
   a. It was a very important game.
   b. The stadium was almost full.
   c. The weather was really bad last night.

2. Mike does not want to go to the soccer game with us today. That's very strange.
   a. He does not really like soccer.
   b. Last year he went to every game with us.
   c. He has an important test tomorrow.

3. I am not really sure about Mike's address.
   a. Perhaps Robert can tell you; he and Mike are very good friends.
   b. He lives at 151 Main Street.
   c. It's Apartment 2, 55 Market Street.

4. These light clothes are not suitable for the winters in this part of the country.
   a. You really need them for the cold weather.
   b. They're all right for the summer, but you need different clothes for the cold weather.
   c. It gets really cold here.

5. My brother is not a good driver.
   a. He was very happy about the result.
   b. He had three accidents last year.
   c. Two days this week he almost caused an accident.

Choose the right word for each example. Use each word only once.
Remember: Read the whole example. Then choose!

strange	cause	arrive	suitable
trouble	important	maybe	clear
continue	take place	real	way
almost	result	seem	leave

1. Robert _____s unhappy to me. Perhaps he is having difficulties with his classes.

2. We fly from London at 8 A.M., British time, and we _____ in New York at 9:30 A.M., U.S. time. The journey takes about six hours.

3. John: Where is Robert today? He wasn't in class.

   Mike: I don't really know. He didn't feel well last night, so _____ he's staying home today.

4. Can you help me, please? I'm trying to get to the hospital, but I don't know the _____.

5. Mike wants to sell his old car. It is giving him a lot of _____. It doesn't start in cold or wet weather.

6. Snow on the roads _____d a number of accidents. Drivers could not stop, and they ran into other cars.

7. We were really happy with the _____ of the soccer game. Our team won 3–1!

8. This room is not _____ for our class. We need a television and tables for our work. The room does not have any.

9. Let's get home fast. It's _____ time for the big soccer game on television.

10. It's very _____. I don't understand it. John is very good in math, but he is having a lot of difficulty with this math class.

The Discovery of America

Grammar for this unit: Relative clauses
You will find information and practice on these grammar points in
Appendix 1, Unit 1.

Vocabulary Study and Preparatory Reading

PART A

opinion (noun)

DEFINITION   an opinion: an idea, a belief
in my opinion: I think . . .

EXAMPLES   1. Mike: What's your *opinion* of Dr. Smith, our math professor?
John: He's a good teacher. He can explain things well,
and he doesn't go too fast.
2. Ali: What did you think of our reading class today?
Carlos: Well, in my *opinion*, the teacher talked too much.
We didn't read enough.

to **discover** (verb)
discovery (noun)

DEFINITION   to discover: to find something that no one knows
discovery: 1. the action of discovering
2. the thing which you discover

EXAMPLES   1. A British scientist *discovered* penicillin in 1936. It was a
very important *discovery* for doctors.
2. In the opinion of many people, Columbus *discovered* America.

truth (noun)

DEFINITION   truth: true facts; something which is true

EXAMPLES   1. You can't believe this person. There's no *truth* in anything he says.
2. Sometimes the *truth* can hurt a person. So sometimes people don't want to tell the *truth*.

origin (noun)
original (adjective)

DEFINITION   origin: beginning
original: first
originally: at the beginning

EXAMPLES   1. There are many words in modern English that *originally* come from the Latin language. There are also words that have their *origins* in Greek and Arabic.
2. The *original* people of America are the Indians. They came to America 25,000 years ago.

settler (noun)
settlement (noun)

DEFINITION   settler: a person who goes to live in a new country
settlement: a small town which settlers build

EXAMPLES   1. The first English *settlers* came to America in 1607.
2. They built a small *settlement* in Virginia.

to **realize** (verb)

DEFINITION   to realize something: to understand

EXAMPLES   1. I was driving home, and I didn't see my exit on the highway. After a minute, I *realized* my mistake, but I had to drive six miles to the next exit.
2. There was ice on the road, but the driver didn't *realize* it. He had an accident.

to **reach** (verb)

DEFINITION   to reach somewhere: to arrive at a place, to get to a place

EXAMPLES   1. Columbus wanted to find a new way to China and the East Indies. But he never *reached* Asia.
2. Our journey was long and difficult. But after twenty-four hours we *reached* London, and we were able to rest there.

to **decide** (verb)
decision (noun)

DEFINITION   to decide: to think about something and to choose to do something
decision: a choice

EXAMPLES   1. Maria: Why did you *decide* to come to this university,
Mayumi?
Mayumi: Well, a friend of mine was here two years ago.
He liked it, and he told me about it.
2. Carlos: Well, Ali, do you want to take this apartment or
not?
Ali: That's a difficult *decision*. The apartment is
really comfortable, and it isn't too expensive. But
it's a long way from the university. I don't know.
Let's think about it for an hour or so.

Now read this passage and answer the questions about it. Also write the numbers of the
lines where you found the answers.

1	Christopher Columbus was not the first person to discover
2	America. But his journey is important. After it, the first European
3	settlers began to arrive in the New World. There is one very
4	strange thing about the story of Columbus. He discovered America
5	by accident. Originally he wanted to discover a new way by sea to
6	Asia; he did not expect to find a new continent. His ships landed in
7	the West Indies, but in his opinion, the lands that he reached were
8	part of Asia. For some years, Columbus continued to believe this;
9	he did not realize his mistake. In his opinion, Cuba was Japan or
10	part of China, the islands of the Caribbean were the East Indies,
11	and Panama was Malaya. Almost until his death, he believed this.
12	In the last years of his life, he began to realize the truth: The lands
13	which he discovered were not in Asia; they were part of a new
14	continent that lay between Asia and Europe and Africa.

1. T F   Columbus reached the part of the world that he   Line(s) _____
wanted to reach.

2. T F   Columbus wanted to discover the new continent of   Line(s) _____
America.

3. T F   According to Columbus, the new lands that he   Line(s) _____
reached were part of Asia.

4. T F   Columbus was not the first person to reach America.   Line(s) _____

5. T F Columbus reached a new continent, but he never   Line(s) _____
          realized this.

PART B

to **explore** (verb)
explorer (noun)

DEFINITION to explore: to travel through a place to discover new things
            explorer: a person who goes to new places to learn about them

EXAMPLES 1. Columbus reached America in 1492. But he did not try to
             explore the new continent.
          2. European *explorers* began to travel in Africa in the nine-
             teenth century. They discovered many interesting things
             and places.

group (noun)

DEFINITION a group: a number of persons or things which belong together

EXAMPLES 1. Scientists divide blood into a number of *groups* or types. I
             am in blood *group* B.
          2. Sometimes teachers do *group* work in class. Two or three
             students sit together and work together.

according to (preposition)

DEFINITION according to X: X says . . .
                           X shows . . .
                           X thinks . . .

EXAMPLES 1. Maria: How are Professor Brown's classes, Mayumi?
             Mayumi: Well, *according to* Mike, he's a very good teacher,
                     and his classes are interesting. Mike took a class
                     with him last year.
          2. *According to* the television program I saw last night, about
             one person in every ten has no work.

century (noun)

DEFINITION a century: one hundred years, for example 1800–1900

EXAMPLES 1. We are now living in the twentieth *century*.
          2. In the fourteenth *century* no Europeans lived in America.
             But after Columbus, many explorers began to cross the
             Atlantic.

to **design** (verb)
design (noun)

DEFINITION   to design something: to make a plan for something (a new
                          building, a new car, a new plane)
             a design: 1. a plan
                       2. how people built something

EXAMPLES   1. The *designs* of cars today are very different from the *de-
              signs* of cars thirty years ago.
           2. The people who *designed* this house made a big mistake.
              All the windows are on the north side, so the rooms never
              get any sun!

native (noun and adjective)

DEFINITION   a native: one of the original people of a country
             native: describes something which belongs naturally to a
                     place or to a person

EXAMPLES   1. In America there was often a lot of trouble between the
              settlers and the *natives*. The Indians did not want to lose
              their lands.
           2. According to some scientists, there were no horses in
              America before 1500. Horses are not *native* to America.
              The Spanish brought the first horses with them in the
              sixteenth century.

doubt (noun)
to **doubt** (verb)

DEFINITION   to doubt: not to believe, not to be sure
             doubt: an unsure feeling about something

EXAMPLES   1. Bob caused the accident. There's no *doubt* about that. He
              was driving too close to the car in front.
           2. Carlos: Is Mike coming to the party tonight?
              Ali: I *doubt* it. He has an important test tomorrow.

to **connect** (verb)
connection (noun)

DEFINITION   to connect X and Y: to bring X and Y together
             connection: something that brings X and Y together

EXAMPLES   1. Interstate highways *connect* many cities of the United
              States.

2. Look at these two sentences. There is no *connection* between them. Their ideas do not belong together.
   (a) Mike likes soccer.
   (b) Washington, D.C., is the capital of the U.S.

Now read this passage and answer the questions about it. Also write the numbers of the lines where you found the answers.

1	When did the first people from the Old World (Europe, North
2	Africa, and the Middle East) come to the New World (North and
3	South America)? Different scientists give different answers to this
4	question. One group of these scientists are called "isolationists."
5	According to them, the first visitors were the Vikings in the elev-
6	enth century. The next explorers were Columbus and the men who
7	came after him at the end of the fifteenth and at the beginning of
8	the sixteenth century. But these scientists have to explain a num-
9	ber of strange facts which perhaps show early connections between
10	America and the Old World. First, some of the buildings of the
11	New World look very like buildings in the Old World. People in the
12	Middle East built pyramids 4,000 years ago. There are also pyra-
13	mids in Mexico and Peru. Their design is very like the design of
14	some of the pyramids in the Middle East. There are two possible
15	explanations: (1) In two different parts of the world, perhaps two
16	different groups of people by accident decided to build the same
17	type of building. Or (2) perhaps one culture brought the idea to the
18	other. A second strange fact that the isolationists have to explain is
19	this: The cotton and banana plants which the sixteenth-century
20	explorers found in the New World were not native to America.
21	They originally came from the Old World; scientists have little
22	doubt about this. But did the sea carry these plants to America? Or
23	did someone bring them?

1. T F   All scientists give the same answer to the question, When did the first people from the Old World reach America?   Line(s) _____

2. T F   According to this passage, the first people from the Old World arrived in America in the fifteenth century.   Line(s) _____

3. T F   The cotton and banana plants of America did not originally come from there.   Line(s) _____

4. T F   The pyramids of the Middle East are very different from the pyramids of Mexico and Peru.   Line(s) _____

The Discovery of America   **15**

5. T F   According to some scientists, the Vikings were the   Line(s) _____
           first Europeans in America. But there is some doubt
           about this.

Exercises for Parts A and B

SAME OR DIFFERENT?

Read the two sentences in each example. Do they express the same ideas, or do they express different ideas? Write *S* for sentences with the same ideas; write *D* for two sentences with different ideas.

   Remember: You can express the **same** ideas with **different** words and **different** grammar!

1. a. The police don't really believe the driver's story of the accident.   _____
   b. The police don't doubt the truth of the driver's story of the accident.

2. a. English is not Ali's native language, but he speaks it well.   _____
   b. Ali's first language is not English, but he can speak it well.

3. a. Our plane reached Paris at 6:30 A.M., after a seven-hour journey   _____
      from New York.
   b. The flight from New York took seven hours, and we arrived in
      Paris at 6:30 in the morning.

4. a. You can find bananas in many parts of Central and South Amer-   _____
      ica, but they originally came from Africa.
   b. Bananas are native to many parts of Central and South Amer-
      ica, but you can find them in Africa also.

5. a. Europeans began to explore America at the beginning of the six-   _____
      teenth century.
   b. European explorers began to come to America about 1500.

6. a. In Columbus's opinion, Cuba was Japan. He never discovered his   _____
      mistake.
   b. According to Columbus, Cuba was Japan. He realized the truth
      years later.

7. a. At the beginning there was no trouble between the North Ameri-   _____
      can Indians and the first English people who came to live in
      America.
   b. At the beginning the natives and the first English settlers in
      North America lived together without difficulties.

8. a. According to Indian stories, a small group of white people reached South America long before 1500. _____
   b. There are Indian stories which tell about a small number of white people who arrived in South America long before the sixteenth century.

EXPECTATIONS

Read the first sentence in each of these examples. Think about the ideas in it. What ideas can you expect in the next sentence? From (a), (b), and (c), choose the sentence or sentences that can follow the first sentence. Together the sentences have to have a clear meaning.

1. According to one group of scientists, no explorers from the Old World reached America before the eleventh century.
   a. In their opinion, people from Egypt settled in America 3,000 years ago.
   b. In their opinion, the Viking journeys of about A.D. 1080 were the first to the New World.
   c. They believe the stories about Egyptian explorers who brought their culture to America around 2500 B.C.

2. The person who designed this house did a number of strange things that I don't understand.
   a. He decided to build the kitchen on the second floor beside the bathroom.
   b. He planned to have a large living room with a window which looks out to the garden.
   c. It has three bedrooms, two bathrooms, a kitchen, a living room, and a study.

3. People who decided to settle in America often had trouble in their native countries.
   a. Some of them could not find work at home.
   b. Some of them could not practice their religion.
   c. Some of them were rich and famous in their home countries.

4. Scientists often do not believe stories about people who lived long ago.
   a. In their opinion, parts of the stories are perhaps true, but you cannot discover these parts.
   b. According to them, the stories do not have much truth in them.
   c. The stories are about things which really took place and about people who really lived.

5. Ali planned to finish his English classes after one semester, but then he decided to continue with English for another six months.
   a. He realized his need for more English.
   b. He understood a lot of English.
   c. He clearly did not know enough English for his studies.

Choose the correct word for each empty space. Use each word only once.
Remember: Read to the end of each example. Then decide!

explore	doubt	reached	decided
original	connection	discover	truth
designed	decision	groups	settlement
natives	according to	century	realized

1. "I don't believe you. You're not telling the _____."

2. Vikings from Iceland and Greenland _____ America in the eleventh century, about 400 years before Columbus.

3. The Vikings built a small _____ in Newfoundland. It had about six houses.

4. Columbus wanted to _____ a new way by sea to Asia. But he never found it.

5. In 1960 a scientist discovered the old Viking settlement in Newfoundland. None of the _____ buildings were still standing, but he found their floors and parts of their walls under the ground.

6. The _____ caused a lot of trouble for the new Viking settlers. They did not want the settlers in their land. After some years, the Vikings returned to Greenland.

7. Yes, I believe Mike's story. It's true. I have no _____ about it.

8. Today, we are living in the twentieth _____.

9. _____ some history books, Columbus discovered America. But many people do not believe this.

10. This red car looks very like that other car over there. Perhaps the same person _____ both types of car.

PART C

to **destroy** (verb)

> DEFINITION to destroy something: to break 100%
>
> EXAMPLES 1. There was a bad fire in the city last night. It *destroyed* an apartment building. Now sixty people have no homes.
> 2. American and British planes *destroyed* many German towns during the Second World War.

interested (adjective)

> DEFINITION to be interested in something: to want to know about it, to want to learn about it
>
> EXAMPLES 1. My brother is very *interested* in different languages and cultures. He travels to many different countries on his vacations.
> 2. I don't want to go to that movie. I'm not *interested* in it.

to **describe** (verb)
description (noun)

> DEFINITION to describe something: to give a picture of it in words
> a description: a picture in words
>
> EXAMPLES 1. I am reading a very interesting book. It *describes* a journey through the Himalayas.
> 2. Policeman: Can you give me a *description* of the man who took your purse?
> Woman: He was tall and young, with red hair. He wore jeans and a white shirt.

ancestor (noun)

> DEFINITION an ancestor: a person in your family a long time ago
>
> EXAMPLES 1. According to scientists, the early *ancestors* of American Indians came from Asia 25,000 years ago.
> 2. A lot of Americans study the history of their families. They want to learn about their *ancestors*.

to **remain** (verb)
remains (plural noun)

> DEFINITION to remain: to stay; to continue to be
> remains: parts of a thing that still exist (the other parts are not there any more)

EXAMPLES 1. Nearly everyone in the class finished the test early and left. Only Maria *remained* to the end of the hour.
2. Scientists found the *remains* of a 1,000-year-old town near here. The houses are not standing anymore, but the scientists are discovering many interesting facts about life here 1,000 years ago.

ancient (adjective)

DEFINITION ancient: from a very long time ago; very old

EXAMPLES 1. *Ancient* history is usually the history of 2,000 years ago or more.
2. The scientists of *ancient* Egypt knew many things about the world. For example, 4,000 years ago, an Egyptian scientist worked out the distance around the earth.

civilization (noun)

DEFINITION civilization: 1. life with laws, science, schools, towns, cities, and so on
2. a country that has a life like this for its people

EXAMPLES 1. In the opinion of some people, Europeans brought *civilization* to America. But there were already great *civilizations* in that part of the world in the sixteenth century.
2. In fact, the Europeans destroyed the *civilizations* which they discovered in America.

to **contain** (verb)

DEFINITION to contain X: to have X inside something

EXAMPLES 1. I bought an interesting book yesterday. It *contains* all the prices which people pay for used cars.
2. This bottle *contains* 100 aspirin. Keep it away from children.

Now read this passage and answer the questions about it. Also write the numbers of the lines where you found the answers.

1   After Columbus, other Spanish explorers and soldiers dis-
2   covered great Indian civilizations in Central and South America:
3   the Inca civilization in Peru, the Chibcha civilization in Colombia,
4   and the Aztec civilization in Mexico. The ancient stories of these
5   civilizations contained descriptions of white men who were not like

6   any American Indian. They had light hair and wore beards. Ac-
7   cording to the old stories, they arrived many centuries before. They
8   brought with them the information which the ancestors of the Indi-
9   ans used to build their civilizations and cultures. In Peru, Spanish
10 soldiers found the remains of old buildings which stood there long
11 before the Inca civilization. According to the natives, white people
12 with beards built them. The Spanish soldiers destroyed these great
13 Indian civilizations, and for centuries no one asked questions about
14 their origins. But in the twentieth century, scientists found old
15 paintings that showed men with beards. People became interested
16 in the strange white men with beards. How can we explain them?
17 According to some scientists, the men were from the Old World.
18 Their original home was possibly the Middle East. They arrived in
19 America possibly before 1000 B.C.

1. T F   According to this passage, the Spanish explorers built   Line(s) _____
           great civilizations in Central and South America.

2. T F   The Indians of America knew nothing about white men   Line(s) _____
           before the arrival of the Spanish.

3. T F   According to some Indian stories, white men arrived   Line(s) _____
           in America hundreds of years before Columbus.

4. T F   From the sixteenth century to the twentieth century,   Line(s) _____
           people were interested in the origins of the stories
           about the men with beards.

5. T F   Scientists know *only* from native stories about the   Line(s) _____
           strange men with beards in America.

6. T F   The Incas of Peru were not the only American Indi-   Line(s) _____
           ans who had a great civilization in the sixteenth cen-
           tury.

PART D

definite (adjective)

DEFINITION   definite: sure, without doubt

EXAMPLES   1. Mike wants to sell his car to me. I didn't say yes or no. But
              I have to give him a *definite* answer tonight.
           2. Bob: Is Ali coming to the soccer game with us?
              Mike: It's not *definite*. He has a test next week. So maybe
                    he needs time to study.

to **sail** (verb)
sailor (noun)
sail (noun)

DEFINITION   to sail: to travel by ship or boat
sailor: a person who works on a ship
a sail: a piece of cloth which catches the wind; then the wind
drives the boat

EXAMPLES 1. Magellan, a sixteenth-century *sailor* from Portugal, was
the leader of the first men to *sail* around the world.
2. Many years ago, ships did not have engines. They only had
sails. But sometimes in good weather, they could move
quite fast.

skill (noun)
skillful (adjective)

DEFINITION   skill: ability to do something well
skillful: able to do something well

EXAMPLES 1. Carlos is a really *skillful* soccer player. He's good enough
to play for the university team.
2. The people of the ancient world had wonderful *skills*. They
could build and sail boats that crossed the oceans. They
could find their way across the oceans by the stars.

danger (noun)
dangerous (adjective)

DEFINITION   a danger: something bad which can perhaps happen
dangerous: not safe

EXAMPLES 1. A red light on the road usually means "Stop" or "*Danger*."
2. Cigarettes are *dangerous*. They can make you very ill.

available (adjective)

DEFINITION   something is available: you can get it or use it

EXAMPLES 1. I wanted a two-bedroom apartment, but there were none
available in my building at the time. So I took a one-
bedroom apartment.
2. Henry Ford's first car was *available* in only one color—
black!

material (noun)

DEFINITION material: a general word for anything which you use to make another thing

EXAMPLES 1. The *materials* which we use for summer clothes must be light and cool.
2. Building *materials* are becoming very expensive, so the price of houses is going up.

wood (noun)

DEFINITION wood: material of a tree

EXAMPLES 1. Furniture is usually made of *wood*.
2. Until the middle of the nineteenth century, ships were all made of *wood*. Now all big ships are made of steel.

unlike (adjective and preposition)

DEFINITION unlike X: not like X, different from X

EXAMPLES 1. *Unlike* my last car, this car is giving me a lot of trouble. (My last car gave me no trouble.)
2. *Unlike* almost everyone else in the world, the British drive on the left side of the road.

Now read this passage and answer the questions about it. Also write the numbers of the lines where you found the answers.

1   According to one group of scientists, the Vikings were defi-
2   nitely the first people from Europe or from the Mediterranean to
3   cross the Atlantic to America. But according to another group of
4   scientists, people from the Old World definitely reached parts of
5   America before the Viking journeys of the eleventh century. In
6   their opinion, the Phoenicians and the ancient Egyptians had the
7   skills which were necessary for long journeys of exploration.
8   Thor Heyerdahl, a famous explorer of our time, wanted to test
9   the ideas of these scientists. He studied old pictures of Egyptian
10   boats and the remains of a boat that scientists found beside a
11   pyramid in Egypt. He designed and built a new boat which was
12   like these ancient boats. Unlike the boats of the Vikings and other
13   people, Heyerdahl's boat was not made of wood. It was made of
14   papyrus reeds. (Papyrus reeds are river plants that the ancient
15   Egyptians used to make paper.) This was the only material that

16	was easily available for boats in ancient Egypt. Heyerdahl named
17	his boat *Ra* after the sun-god of ancient Egypt. On May 25, 1969,
18	he sailed from Safi on the west coast of Morocco. The first journey
19	did not go well. There was a mistake in the design of the boat.
20	After eight weeks and 2,700 miles, the boat began to break up.
21	Heyerdahl decided not to continue the journey and got the six men
22	with him out of danger. The next year Heyerdahl built another
23	papyrus boat, the *Ra II,* and began the same journey. This time the
24	boat was strong enough for the Atlantic. The *Ra II* reached Barba-
25	dos in fifty-seven days.
26	So did the ancient Egyptians or Phoenicians reach America in
27	the same sort of ship 4,000 years ago? Heyerdahl's journey cannot
28	give a definite yes to this question. But one thing is clear: The
29	Egyptians and Phoenicians had the necessary skills in boat build-
30	ing and in sailing for a journey across the Atlantic.

1. What was the scientific idea which Thor Heyerdahl wanted to test?   Line(s) _____
   a. Perhaps the Vikings reached America in the eleventh century.
   b. Perhaps the ancient Egyptians or Phoenicians reached America.
   c. Perhaps American Indians traveled by boat to the Old World.

2. T F   The Viking boats were made of wood.   Line(s) _____

3. T F   Wood was easily available for boats in ancient Egypt.   Line(s) _____

4. T F   Clearly the boats which the ancient Egyptians sailed were strong enough to cross the Atlantic.   Line(s) _____

5. T F   The ancient Egyptians or Phoenicians reached America about 4,000 years ago. The second journey of Heyerdahl's boat leaves no doubt about this.   Line(s) _____

6. T F   Both of Heyerdahl's journeys ended very well.   Line(s) _____

PART E

to **move** (verb)
movement (noun)

DEFINITION   to move: to take something to another place; not to stay in the same place
movement: the act of moving

1. There is no wind tonight. Even the leaves on the trees are not *moving*.
2. I am not a good sailor. The *movement* of a ship on the sea makes me sick.

a **great deal** of (phrase)

DEFINITION a great deal of: much, a lot

EXAMPLES 1. I'm having a *great deal* of trouble with my car. I spent $500 on it only last month, and now it's in the garage again!
2. My friend Kate earns a *great deal* of money in her new job, but she doesn't like it. She stays in an office all day, and she doesn't meet people.

leather (noun)

DEFINITION leather: material which we make from the skin of animals

EXAMPLES 1. Shoes made of *leather* are very expensive. Shoes of other materials are not too expensive.
2. The seats of this Rolls Royce are covered with *leather*.

knowledge (noun)

DEFINITION knowledge: the things that a person knows

EXAMPLES 1. Many people want to learn English. A good *knowledge* of English is important in many jobs.
2. Ancient scientists had a great deal of *knowledge* about the world. They knew some things which people did not know 3,500 years later.

primitive (adjective)

DEFINITION primitive: early and without knowledge of science or other things

EXAMPLES 1. *Primitive* man, 40,000 years ago, used only stones for tools.
2. The Inca culture was not a *primitive* culture. The Incas built a great civilization.

tool (noun)

DEFINITION a tool: something which you use for a special job

EXAMPLES 1. I could not fix my car. I did not have the right *tools*.
2. Today electric *tools* make some jobs very easy. For example, electric saws cut wood very fast.

equipment (noun)

DEFINITION equipment: a general word for tools or other things that you need for something

EXAMPLES 1. You need a lot of *equipment* for American football. But for running, you only need shoes, a shirt, and shorts.
2. I have to buy some new skiing *equipment* this year. I need new boots and new skis. My old ones are nearly fifteen years old!

to **calculate** (verb)
calculation (noun)

DEFINITION to calculate: to work with numbers to find the answer to a question
calculation: working with numbers

EXAMPLES 1. I would like to take a vacation in Europe next year. But maybe I won't have enough money. First I need to *calculate* the cost of the trip. Then I can decide.
2. I had a math test yesterday. I made a stupid mistake in one of my *calculations*. I'm angry with myself!

Now read this passage and answer the questions about it. Also write the numbers of the lines where you found the answers.

1   In the opinion of many Americans and Europeans, we only
2 began to really explore our world in the sixteenth century. Accord-
3 ing to them, the sailors of the ancient world did not explore distant
4 parts of the world; they did not have the necessary knowledge or
5 skills for long sea journeys. However, the people who have this
6 opinion are forgetting two important facts of history.
7   First, sometimes early scientists have an idea which is correct,
8 but scientists in later centuries do not believe it. For example,
9 about 270 B.C., a Greek scientist had an idea which we all believe
10 today: The earth moves around the sun. But for the following 1,600
11 years scientists did not believe this. In their opinion, the sun
12 clearly moved around the earth. They discovered the truth again
13 only in the fifteenth century!
14   The second fact of history that many people forget is this:
15 Ancient does not mean primitive. For example, the ancient Egyp-
16 tians knew a great deal about the stars; they used this knowledge
17 to find their way across the oceans. Two thousand years ago a
18 Greek scientist who lived in Egypt calculated the distance around
19 the earth. The results of his calculations were close to the real

20   distance we know today! So the ancients had a great deal of scien-
21   tific knowledge. They also had skills which equaled the skills of
22   today. For example, 1,300 years ago and before, fishermen in Ire-
23   land built their boats of wood and leather. Today some fishermen
24   in Ireland still make boats of the same design. They use tools and
25   materials which are not very different from the tools and materials
26   which their ancestors used. Why? The ancient design of the boats
27   was good, and with skillful sailors, these boats can sail in all kinds
28   of weather.

29   Clearly long before the sixteenth century, people had the skill,
30   the knowledge, and the equipment which were necessary for long
31   journeys by sea. The world did not have to wait until the sixteenth
32   century for its first explorers!

1. T F   According to the writer, we only began to really ex-   Line(s) _____
          plore the world in the sixteenth century.

2. T F   In the history of science, people sometimes have to   Line(s) _____
          discover a fact a second time.

3. T F   The ancient Egyptians had very little knowledge   Line(s) _____
          about the stars.

4. Why does the writer use the example of the Greek scientist   Line(s) _____
who calculated the distance around the world?
  a. He wants to show the primitive knowledge of ancient sci-
    entists.
  b. He wants to give an example of something which later sci-
    entists did not believe.
  c. He wants to give an example of scientific knowledge which
    was available to early explorers.

5. According to the writer, why do Irish fishermen still use boats   Line(s) _____
like the boats which their ancestors used 1,000 years ago?
  a. The design of the boats is very good.
  b. The necessary materials are easily available.
  c. They don't have the money for expensive boats.

6. People from the ancient world sailed around Africa. They even   Line(s) _____
reached America.
    In your opinion, how does the writer of the passage feel
about these ideas?
  a. In his opinion, they are possible.
  b. He does not believe them.
  c. In his opinion, ancient explorers did not have the skills
    which were necessary for long journeys like these.

Exercises for Parts C, D, and E

SAME OR DIFFERENT?

Read the two sentences in each example. Do they express the same ideas, or do they express different ideas? Write *S* for sentences with the same ideas; write *D* for sentences with different ideas.

Remember: You can express the **same** ideas with **different** words and **different** grammar!

1. a. In some countries, people could not get any wood; they built their boats with other materials.
   b. Wood was not available in some countries; people used other materials to build boats.

2. a. I asked Mike to our party, but he didn't give me a definite answer.
   b. I asked Mike to our party. He said, "Maybe I can come; maybe I can't. I don't know."

3. a. Many foreign students want to remain in the U.S. for quite a long time.
   b. Many foreign students don't want to stay in the U.S. for a long time.

4. a. Four hundred years ago the journey across the Atlantic to the New World was very dangerous.
   b. Four hundred years ago there was no danger in the journey across the Atlantic to the New World.

5. a. The student gave the police a description of the car that caused the accident.
   b. The student described the car that caused the accident to the police.

6. a. Mike has very little knowledge of ancient history.
   b. Mike knows a great deal about ancient history.

7. a. Unlike Ali, Carlos is really interested in baseball.
   b. Ali is really interested in baseball, but Carlos isn't.

8. a. Some American Indians had great civilizations in the fifteenth century.
   b. Some American Indians lived quite primitive lives in the fifteenth century.

9. a. The ancestors of today's native Americans came from Asia, perhaps 25,000 years ago. _____
   b. Native Americans originally came from Asia, perhaps 25,000 years ago.

10. a. We don't want to move to a new apartment this year. _____
    b. For this year we want to remain in our present apartment.

11. a. We need Mike for our soccer team; he is a very skillful player. _____
    b. We need Mike for our soccer team; he has a lot of skill.

12. a. Europeans discovered the Inca civilization of Peru. _____
    b. Europeans destroyed the Inca civilization of Peru.

EXPECTATIONS

Read the first sentence in each of these examples. Think about the ideas in it. What ideas can you expect in the next sentence? Choose the sentence or sentences that can follow the first sentence. Together the sentences have to have a clear meaning.

1. This is a good book for people who are interested in the early history of America.
   a. It describes life in America in the twentieth century.
   b. It gives a great deal of information about the lives of the natives before the arrival of the Europeans.
   c. It contains descriptions of the early civilizations that our ancestors found here.

2. John is not a very skillful or careful driver.
   a. He pays a great deal of attention to the other people who are using the road.
   b. He sails a small boat on the weekends.
   c. A drive with him can be a little dangerous.

3. Wood was not easily available to the ancient Egyptians.
   a. They used wood for all the boats which they built.
   b. They had to find other materials to build their boats.
   c. There was a great deal of wood in the country, and they used it for their boats and buildings.

4. The rent on our apartment is going up too high.
   a. We want to move to another apartment.
   b. We don't want to remain here.
   c. Do you know any cheap apartments that are available for rent?

5. The early explorers who tried to get to the top of Mount Everest were not able to reach it.

   a. They only remained on top of the mountain for two hours.

   b. Some of them even died on the mountain.

   c. They did not have the good equipment that is available today.

6. These shoes are really comfortable.

   a. I can't wear them for more than an hour.

   b. They are made of very soft leather.

   c. I'd like to buy another pair.

7. The ancient Egyptian civilization was not a primitive culture.

   a. Its scientists understood a great deal about the stars and the movement of the earth around the sun.

   b. The tools which remain from this time are all very primitive.

   c. Its people lived in small groups and showed no interest in scientific knowledge.

8. Did people from the Old World reach America before the Vikings in the eleventh century? Scientists cannot give a definite answer to this question.

   a. Some years ago scientists in Mexico found the remains of an old boat that without doubt came from Africa. It is nearly 2,500 years old.

   b. According to all scientists, the Vikings were without doubt the first people to reach America from the Old World.

   c. The Vikings built a settlement which scientists found in 1960; but other people who perhaps came to America earlier left nothing.

VOCABULARY QUIZ

Choose the correct word for each empty space. Use each word only once.
Remember: Read to the end of each example. Then decide!

sailor	contained	material	equipment
primitive	movement	destroyed	definite
moved	interested	tools	description
skills	unlike	wood	dangerous
available	knowledge	calculated	remain

1. I did not have anything to wear for my vacation. On the journey the airline

   lost the suitcase that _____ all my clothes!

2. A fire _____ the Smiths' home last month. The family lost everything.

3. Someone stole Maria's car. She called the police and gave them the license number of the car and a _____ of it.

4. Mike is very _____ in computers. He takes every computer science course he can find in the university.

5. "Please, do not get up. _____ in your seats. The plane is still moving."

6. "Don't cross the road here. It's _____. There is at least one accident here every month."

7. Some years ago ships were all made of _____. But today most ships are made of steel.

8. Tickets for the soccer game are still _____. You can get them at the stadium.

9. The Vikings were very good _____s. From Norway, they traveled in their open ships to England, France, Iceland, and Greenland. They even reached North America.

10. _____ Ali, Carlos has no interest in baseball. Ali goes to a game every week; Carlos never goes to any games.

11. Maria: I would like to learn to ski, but the _____ is very expensive. You need boots and skis.

    Carlos: You don't have to buy them. You can rent them.

12. In the opinion of many people in the sixteenth century, the sun _____ around the earth. They did not want to believe scientists who had different ideas.

13. The houses which people built 40,000 years ago were very _____.

14. Mike wants to fix his car. But he doesn't have any _____. He had to borrow them from his brother.

15. My _____ of Spanish is not very good. I can only speak and understand a few words.

Main Reading

Pre-Reading Exercises

VOCABULARY IN CONTEXT

In this exercise, we try to find the meaning of new words. But we do not use a dictionary. We get help from the other words and ideas in the sentences.

Read each example to the end. Do *not* stop in the middle. Pay attention to the words in italics. They are words that you already know. Then try to guess the meaning of the new word in boldface type. The words in italics can help you.

1. Did people from Europe reach America before the Vikings? We *cannot be* 100% **certain** *about the answer* to this question. *Perhaps* people from ancient Mediterranean civilizations sailed to America 2,000 years ago, but we *cannot be sure.*

   To be certain means _____.
   a. to be interested
   b. to be sure
   c. to be skillful

2. Last winter my father's car stopped on the highway. There was a lot of snow at the side of the road, and my father could not drive the car out of it. A police car stopped, and the policemen *helped* get the car out of the snow. My father *was able to continue his journey.* Afterward, in a letter to the newspaper, he *thanked the policemen* for *their* **assistance.**

   Assistance means _____.
   a. money
   b. driving
   c. help

3. On his journey across the Atlantic, Thor Heyerdahl was *not alone.* He had **companions** with him from different countries.

   A companion is _____.
   a. a person who goes with another person
   b. a scientist who studies life in the sea
   c. a type of small boat

4. Thor Heyerdahl *tried* to cross the Atlantic on a boat made of papyrus reeds. He was *not* **successful.** The boat began to break up, and Heyerdahl had to stop the journey. But a year later, in a second boat, he was **successful.** He *safely reached* the West Indies.

To be successful means _____.

    a. to be able to do the thing that you wanted to do
    b. to plan to do something that is very difficult
    c. to begin to do something that is difficult

5. Did any Europeans reach North America before Columbus? For many years, no one could answer this question. Then in 1960 **archaeologists** *discovered* an *old settlement* in Newfoundland. *They studied* the tools they found there; the tools were of Viking *origin.*

    An archaeologist is _____.

    a. an ancient tool which people used long ago
    b. a person who makes tools and other equipment
    c. a person who studies the remains of old civilizations

6. Last *winter* we had some very **unusual** weather. For a few days in *February* it became *very warm.* It reached *70°F!* People were very *surprised.* **Usual** temperatures for February are about *28°F.*

    *Un*usual means _____.

    a. strange
    b. warm
    c. good

    Usual describes something _____.

    a. which causes difficulties for people
    b. which happens often and which people expect
    c. which many people like

7. Thor Heyerdahl *tried to cross* the Atlantic in a boat made of papyrus reeds. But he was *not successful.* He had to **give up** 200 miles from the Bahamas. The boat was beginning *to break up,* and the people on it were *in great danger.* Heyerdahl decided to *try again* later.

    To give up something means _____.

    a. to continue to do something
    b. to stop doing something
    c. to decide to do something

8. There is some *doubt* about the **health** of the president. According to some people, he is *not* in *good* **health.** He is *sick* often and cannot work. Last month he was in the *hospital* for a week. He does *not* look *well,* either.

    Health means _____.

    a. how well or how sick a person is
    b. how intelligent a person is
    c. how successful a person is at work

9. Often we can*not* give *definite* answers to questions about history. We often don't have enough information, so we cannot be **completely** *sure* about our answers. *For example,* there is still some *doubt* about the first Europeans in America.

> Completely means _____.

> a. in the past
> b. difficult
> c. 100%

10. In 1492, Columbus was *not trying* to find a new continent. He *wanted* to *discover* a new way by sea to Japan, China, and India. *This* was his original **goal.**

> Goal means _____.

> a. a long journey across the ocean
> b. something that a person wants to do
> c. a boat that can cross the ocean

11. After the *accident,* a small plane took the **injured** *driver* to the hospital. But *his injuries* were *too bad,* and the doctors were *not able* to *help* him.

> Injured means _____.

> a. young
> b. fast
> c. hurt

Who Really Discovered America?

1   In August 1492, Christopher Columbus sailed from Spain with   1
2 a group of three small ships. They sailed south and west into the
3 Atlantic. Columbus wanted to find a new way to reach Japan,
4 China, and India. That was his original goal. On October 12, 1492,
5 the ships reached the Bahama Islands in the Atlantic Ocean. But
6 for Columbus, the islands which he discovered were not part of any
7 New World. In his opinion, they were parts of China and Japan.
8 Some years afterward, however, people realized the truth: For Eu-
9 ropeans, this was a new continent—America. Columbus became
10 famous, and he is still famous today. For many people, he is the
11 man who discovered America.
12   But Columbus was not the first person to reach America. Ac-   2
13 cording to many scientists, the people who really discovered Amer-
14 ica came from Asia, not from Europe. They first arrived here about

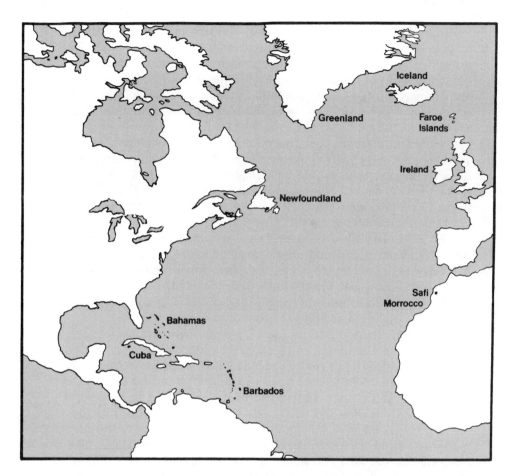

Journeys of Exploration Across the Atlantic

15   25,000 years ago. Unlike Columbus, they did not have to cross the
16   sea. At that time a piece of land connected Siberia and Alaska. The
17   people were able to walk from Siberia to Alaska. Slowly these
18   people moved into all parts of North America and down into Cen-
19   tral and South America. They were the ancestors of the Indians, or
20   native Americans, whom European explorers and settlers found in
21   the New World. Some of these Indians built great civilizations long
22   before the arrival of Columbus.

23   Columbus was not even the first European to come to America.   3
24   For many years, scientists were interested in a number of old Vik-
25   ing stories about the New World. According to these stories, the
26   Vikings sailed west from Greenland and built settlements in a new
27   land that they called Vinnland. The stories gave scientists an idea:

Perhaps the Vikings reached North America long before Columbus! In 1960 an archaeologist discovered the remains of an old settlement in Newfoundland. The design of the houses was very like the design of the houses in old Viking settlements in Iceland and Norway. Archaeologists also found tools and pieces of kitchen equipment which were clearly of Viking origin. According to their calculations, people lived in the settlement in the eleventh century, 400 years before Columbus! The Vikings did not stay long in America. Probably they had a great deal of trouble with the natives, and life in Vinnland became just too dangerous. But we now know one thing without doubt: The old stories about Viking settlements in America contain some truth. The Vikings really did reach America long before Columbus.

In 1973, Tim Severin, a professor who was interested in history and exploration, read an old book. It is in Latin, and it tells the story of a journey to a strange New World about 400 years before the Vikings. It describes the journey of St. Brendan. Brendan was an Irish priest who traveled by sea to England, Scotland, France, Iceland, and perhaps to other places.

Professor Severin had an idea: Perhaps there was some truth in the story of Brendan's voyage to this wonderful country in the west! Perhaps Brendan really reached North America in the sixth century! Severin found some other people who were very interested in his idea. With their assistance, he designed and built a very unusual boat. It was like the boats that the old Latin book described. It was made of wood and leather only. These were the only materials which were available in Ireland 1,300 years ago. The boat was 36 feet long and 8 feet across; it had two sails. It seemed very primitive, but Severin planned to sail it across the Atlantic.

With four companions, Severin left Ireland in May 1976, but they quickly ran into bad weather and other problems. On the second day one of the men hurt his arm. It began to cause him a lot of pain, so Severin and the others decided to land. They did not want to endanger the health of their friend. They landed their injured companion on the north coast of Ireland and sent him to the hospital. Then they continued their journey. The wind and the movements of the sea carried the boat north, past Ireland and Scotland to the Faroe Islands, and then on to Iceland. This part of the journey ended three months later, in July 1976. Severin decided not to continue the journey that year. The weather was bad, and in the sea around Greenland there was a great deal of ice which could quickly destroy their light boat. But Severin and his friends did not give up. They waited until the spring and left Iceland in May 1977. After a very dangerous journey through bad

72	weather and fields of ice, they reached Newfoundland at the end of
73	June.
74	So did Brendan the Navigator reach America 300 years before
75	the Vikings? We still cannot be completely certain. There are no
76	signs of Irish settlements in North America. The successful journey
77	of Severin and his friends does not give us a definite answer, but
78	their success shows one thing clearly: The Irish sailor-priests of the
79	sixth century had the knowledge and the skills which were neces-
80	sary for a journey to America. Perhaps they were the first Europe-
81	ans to reach America.

7

MAIN IDEAS CHECK

Each paragraph of this passage has its own main idea. All of the main ideas of the paragraphs are connected with the subject of the passage. Here are the main ideas for the paragraphs. Connect each paragraph with its main idea. Write the number of the paragraph opposite the correct main idea.

PARAGRAPH   IDEA

_____   An old book tells the story of an Irish priest who sailed to a new land 1,300 years ago.

_____   We cannot give a definite answer to the question, Did anyone reach America before the Vikings?

_____   The first people in America originally came from Asia.

_____   Columbus discovered the New World really by accident.

_____   A professor decides to test the story of the Irish priest.

_____   The Vikings were in the New World long before Columbus. This is certain.

_____   Severin's leather boat successfully sailed across the Atlantic to America.

COMPREHENSION CHECK

1. T F   Christopher Columbus reached America in August   Line(s) _____
            1492.

2. Why did Columbus sail across the Atlantic in 1492?   Line(s) _____
    a. To find the new continent of America
    b. To discover a new way to Asia
    c. To build settlements in America

3. Who really discovered America?   Line(s) _____

   a. Christopher Columbus
   b. People from Norway who built a settlement in Newfound-
      land
   c. A priest from Ireland who sailed to America 1,300 years
      ago
   d. People who crossed from Siberia to Alaska thousands of
      years ago

4. The ancestors of the Indians who live in America   Line(s) _____

   a. originally came from Asia.
   b. originally came across the Atlantic with Columbus.
   c. originally came from Greenland with the Vikings.

5. What did the Vikings call the new land they discovered?   Line(s) _____

   a. America
   b. Vinnland
   c. Greenland
   d. Newfoundland

6. T F   Maybe the Vikings came to America. But we are not   Line(s) _____
          sure about this.

7. The old settlement that scientists found in Newfoundland in   Line(s) _____
   1960

   a. definitely belonged to the Vikings.
   b. perhaps belonged to some North American Indians.
   c. was perhaps of Viking origin.

8. Brendan was   Line(s) _____

   a. a professor who was interested in history and exploration.
   b. a Viking who sailed to America before Columbus.
   c. an Irish priest who perhaps reached America in the sixth
      century.

9. T F   The boat that the explorer made for his journey was   Line(s) _____
          very different from the boat Brendan probably used.

10. T F   The professor's boat never reached America. He   Line(s) _____
          gave up in Iceland.

11. The book that tells the story of Brendan is in   Line(s) _____

   a. Latin.
   b. English.
   c. Irish.

12. Who is or was Tim Severin?   Line(s) _____
    a. An Irish sailor who perhaps reached America 1,300 years
       ago
    b. A Viking sailor who built a settlement on Newfoundland
       in the eleventh century
    c. A present-day explorer who sailed to America in a boat
       made of wood and leather

13. T F   Brendan reached America in the sixth century. Scien-   Line(s) _____
            tists are now sure about this.

PARAGRAPH READING

These sentences form a paragraph, but they are not in the correct order. Put the sentences into their correct order. The first sentence is already in the correct place.

To help you: Write each sentence on a card. Then use the cards for the exercise.
You can quickly change the order of the cards. You can test different orders in this way.

__1__   For many years people said, "Columbus was the first European to reach
         America."

_____   Tools and kitchen equipment which the archaeologists found there were
         also clearly of Viking origin.

_____   Their successful journey shows this possibility: Perhaps other people from
         Europe reached America even before the Vikings.

_____   But some years ago, in 1960, archaeologists discovered the remains of an
         ancient settlement in Newfoundland.

_____   So for some years, people said, "The Vikings were definitely the first Eu-
         ropeans in America."

_____   Then, some years after this discovery, a group of men sailed to Newfound-
         land in a boat which was like the boats in sixth-century Ireland.

_____   The design of the houses in the settlement was very like the design of
         Viking houses in Greenland, Iceland, and Norway.

The Population Explosion

Grammar for this unit: Future actions
Word families in English
You will find information and practice on these grammar points in
Appendix 1, Unit 2.

Vocabulary Study and Preparatory Reading

PART A

problem (noun)

DEFINITION a problem: a difficulty, or a question which you have to
answer

EXAMPLES 1. I'm having *problems* with my car. It doesn't start in cold
weather.
2. Bob: I don't have a car, and I need to be at the airport at
seven o'clock tomorrow morning.
Mike: That's no *problem*. I can take you there.

solution (noun)
to **solve** (verb)

DEFINITION a solution: the answer to a question or a problem
to solve a problem: to find the answer to a problem

EXAMPLES 1. After the test, the professor gave the *solutions* to the questions in the test. The students studied the *solutions* and
tried to understand their mistakes.
2. I was able to *solve* the math problem that the professor
gave us. But it was very difficult. I worked on it for three
hours!

serious (adjective)

DEFINITION   serious: important or dangerous (Something which is serious needs your attention.)

EXAMPLES   1. Jim's illness is *serious*. He will have to stay in the hospital for some weeks.
2. Some countries have *serious* problems. They do not have enough food for their people.

to **produce** (verb)
product (noun)

DEFINITION   to produce: to make something
product: a thing which a person makes

EXAMPLES   1. This factory *produces* 500 cars a day. But there are some factories which make 600 or 700 a day.
2. Americans buy a lot of *products* from other countries, for example, televisions and cameras from Japan.

method (noun)

DEFINITION   a method: a way to do something

EXAMPLES   1. What is a good *method* to learn new words? One good way is to read a lot and to learn a small number of words every day.
2. Many years ago, people heated their homes with open fires. Now we have *methods* which give us more heat.

modern (adjective)

DEFINITION   Modern: modern describes something which is new and which belongs to the present.

EXAMPLES   1. Years ago planes were very slow, small, and uncomfortable. *Modern* planes can carry 300 passengers in comfort and can fly at 500 miles an hour.
2. I live in a *modern* apartment building. It opened in 1982.

energy (noun)

DEFINITION   energy: the strength to do work; for example, to make heat, to drive machines

EXAMPLES   1. Electricity is a type of *energy*.
2. Our bodies make *energy* for us from the food that we eat.

to **increase** (verb)

DEFINITION   to increase: to go up in number or in other ways

EXAMPLES   1. The price of butter *increased* by 10% last month. It went up from $1.80 to $2.00 a pound.
2. The number of foreign students in the U.S. *is increasing* every year. More and more students want to study here.

Now read this passage and answer the questions about it. Also write the numbers of the lines where you found the answers.

1   There are many problems in our modern world. One very seri-
2   ous problem is energy. We get a great deal of energy we need from
3   coal, gas, and oil. However, the amount of energy which we use is
4   increasing every year, and we only have enough coal, gas, and oil
5   for the next twenty or thirty years. How will we live without the
6   energy which these things give us? Scientists are looking for solu-
7   tions to this problem. They are looking for new methods to produce
8   energy. For example, they are working with new ways to produce
9   energy from the light and heat of the sun. They are also working
10   with plans which will produce energy from the movements of the
11   oceans. All of the new methods which scientists are finding are still
12   very expensive, but perhaps they will help solve our energy prob-
13   lems in the future.

1. T   F   In fifty years there will surely be enough oil for the world.   Line(s) _____

2. T   F   The amount of energy which the world uses every year is going up.   Line(s) _____

3. T   F   The new methods to produce energy will be enough to solve all our energy problems.   Line(s) _____

4. T   F   The new methods that scientists are finding to produce energy are quite cheap.   Line(s) _____

5. T   F   We are not producing a lot of energy from the movements of the oceans.   Line(s) _____

PART B

to **fail** (verb)
failure (noun)

DEFINITION   to fail: not to be successful
a failure: something or someone that is not successful

1. Maria *failed* her driving test. She did not stop the car at a red light. She will have to take the test again.
2. George wants to be a writer, but his first book was a *failure*. Only twenty-five people bought it. He is going to try again; perhaps his next book will be successful.

to **improve** (verb)

DEFINITION to improve: 1. to become better
2. to make something better

EXAMPLES 1. According to the television, the weather will *improve* tomorrow. The rain will stop, and the weather will be warm and sunny.
2. The professor could not read the student's writing. "Please try to *improve* your handwriting," he said. "Then I will be able to read your work and give you a grade."

to **depend** on (verb)

DEFINITION to depend on X: to need the help of X for something (X decides something.)

EXAMPLES 1. Young animals *depend on* their mothers for food.
2. Bob: What will we do next weekend?
Mike: That *depends on* the weather.

government (noun)

DEFINITION government: the people who decide the laws of a country

EXAMPLES 1. In many countries the people can choose a new *government* every four or five years.
2. The *government* of the United States meets in Washington, D.C.

effect (noun)

DEFINITION an effect: a result that one thing produces in another thing

EXAMPLES 1. The bad weather last year in Florida had an *effect* on the price of oranges. The price of Florida oranges went up.
2. I had the flu last week, and I still feel the *effects* of it. I get tired quickly; I have little energy; I have no appetite.

welfare (noun)

DEFINITION welfare: the assistance and money which the government gives to people who have no work

EXAMPLES 1. Fifty years ago in the U.S. there was no *welfare*. People who had no work did not get any money or help from the government.
2. A lot of people today are on *welfare*. They have no jobs, and they get money for their rent and food from the government.

population (noun)

DEFINITION population: the number of people who live in a place

EXAMPLES 1. The *population* of the U.S. is about 230 million.
2. The *population* of some U.S. cities is falling. In 1970 the number of people in Pittsburgh was 550,000. Now it is 460,000.

Now read this passage and answer the questions about it. Also write the numbers of the lines where you found the answers.

1   In many countries there is always a part of the population
2   which does not have any work. About forty years ago, some govern-
3   ments began to give welfare to people who had no jobs. The govern-
4   ments thought: "Welfare will help these people. It will solve their
5   problems." Welfare now exists in many countries, but welfare
6   alone cannot solve the problems of people who have no work. Yes,
7   it can improve their lives in one way. It gives them enough money
8   for food, housing, and clothes. But it can also have a negative effect
9   on them. After years without work, a person will perhaps think: "I
10   am a failure." People learn to depend on the money they get from
11   the government. They sometimes forget how to work. Their chil-
12   dren often do not see any reason to work, lose interest in school,
13   and perhaps will get into trouble with the police. Clearly, welfare
14   can help people who have no work, but new jobs are also an impor-
15   tant part of the solution to the problem.

1. T F   Government welfare began in the twentieth century.   Line(s) _____

2. T F   Welfare solves all the problems of people who have no   Line(s) _____
work.

3. T F   Welfare can have good and bad effects on the lives of   Line(s) _____
people who cannot find jobs.

4. T F   There are no problems for the children of people who   Line(s) _____
do not work for a long time.

5. T F   In the future, welfare alone will not solve all the   Line(s) _____
problems of people who have no work.

Exercises for Parts A and B

SAME OR DIFFERENT?

Read the two sentences in each example. Do they express the same idea, or do they express different ideas? Write *S* for sentences with the same ideas; write *D* for sentences with different ideas.

Remember: You can express the **same** ideas with **different** words and **different** grammar!

1. a. Carlos tried to find an apartment near the university, but he   _____
      was not successful.
   b. Carlos failed to find an apartment near the university.

2. a. In some countries there is no welfare for people who have no   _____
      work or who cannot work.
   b. In some countries people who have no work or who cannot work
      get money from the government.

3. a. The math course which I am taking this semester is giving me   _____
      some problems.
   b. I'm taking a math course this semester, and I'm having some
      trouble with it.

4. a. Ali and Carlos are going to a movie this evening. Bob isn't going   _____
      with them; he doesn't have the energy.
   b. Bob doesn't want to go to the movies with Ali and Carlos this
      evening; he's too tired.

5. a. The population of some U.S. cities is falling.   _____
   b. In some U.S. cities the population is increasing.

6. a. Some governments are trying to solve the problem of hunger in   _____
      the world.
   b. Some governments are looking for solutions to the problem of
      world hunger.

7. a. The new jobs program had no effect on the number of people who   _____
      were out of work.
   b. The new jobs program failed to bring down the number of people
      without work.

8. a. Modern scientists are looking for ways to produce energy from   _____
      the sun.
   b. Today scientists are trying to find methods to use the sun for
      energy.

Read the first sentence in each of these examples. Think about the ideas in it. Then choose the sentence or sentences that can follow it.

1. According to the radio, the weather will improve for tomorrow's soccer game.
   a. The rain will stop, and it will get quite warm.
   b. We are going to have high winds and temperatures below zero.
   c. It'll be dry and sunny, with a light wind from the west.

2. In the U.S. the population of some northern industrial cities is falling.
   a. In 1960 the population of Pittsburgh was 650,000 people. In 1980 it was 475,000.
   b. The population of Houston, Texas, is increasing by 1,000 new families every week.
   c. People are moving to southern cities which have more job possibilities.

3. I am having serious problems with the math course I am taking this semester.
   a. A week ago we had our first test, and I failed it.
   b. I like the professor's method of teaching; his classes are always very clear.
   c. My grades improved from C to B+ from the first to second test.

4. The number of people who depend on welfare is falling.
   a. The car industry is having serious problems, and workers are losing their jobs.
   b. The government's work program is already having an effect.
   c. Four months ago, 10% of the workers in this city didn't have jobs. Now 8.5% have no work.

5. In 1979 the government failed to find a solution to the problem of increasing prices.
   a. In that year prices went up by 18%.
   b. From January to December 1979 the price of a small car stayed the same.
   c. The effect of the government's program was to bring down the cost of food and many other products.

VOCABULARY QUIZ

Choose the correct word for each empty space. Use each word only once.
Remember: Read to the end of each example. Then decide!

problem	serious	improve	population
solution	produce	modern	depend
energy	method	increase	solve
welfare	fail	government	effect

1. My brother doesn't like _____ music; his favorite music is the music of the nineteenth century.

2. We don't have enough oil and gas for the future, so scientists are looking for other ways to produce _____.

3. I like this professor's _____ of teaching. She doesn't talk all the time, and the students don't just sit and listen. She often gives us _____s which we can solve with the information which she gives us in other classes.

4. A student whom I know well has a problem with his eyes. It is quite _____. He has to go into the hospital next week.

5. Many students who already know a little English come to the U.S. for English classes. They want to _____ their English for their studies.

6. The _____ of the United States is increasing. In 1973 it was about 210 million people; in 1981 it was over 226 million.

7. Richard Nixon tried to become president of the U.S. in 1960, but he _____ed. John Kennedy was president from 1960 until his murder in 1963.

8. An increase in the price of oil will have a(n) _____ on the price of many other things. For example, oil prices go up, and then food prices go up.

9. In many countries there's a system of _____. It's for people who are poor or have no work. It gives them money for food and rent.

PART C

size (noun)

DEFINITION   size: how big or small something (or someone) is

EXAMPLES   1. My shoes are not comfortable. They are not big enough. I bought the wrong *size*.
2. We liked the apartment which we saw yesterday. It was clean and in a good part of the city. But the *size* was not right for us. The rooms were too small, and there was only one bedroom.

to **grow** (irregular verb)
grew (past tense)

DEFINITION   to grow: to become big, or to help something (plants etc.) become big and healthy

EXAMPLES   1. Plants usually cannot *grow* without water and light. They need these things to be healthy.
2. My friends have a large garden behind their house. They *grow* a lot of food for themselves there.

to **limit** (verb)

DEFINITION   to limit: to keep something small

EXAMPLES   1. Our apartment is small. We'll have to *limit* the number of people we ask to our party.
2. According to some scientists, salt can be bad for you. People often *limit* the salt which they eat.

to **be born** (verb)
birth (noun)

DEFINITION   to be born: to come into the world, to begin to live

EXAMPLES   1. My sister had a baby yesterday. He *was born* at 2:00 A.M. My sister and her husband are very happy.
2. My *birth*day is next week. I'm going to have a party.

to **accept** (verb)

DEFINITION   to accept: 1. to take something that someone wants to give to you
2. to believe something

EXAMPLES   1. Mary asked me to the party, and I *accepted* the invitation. I went to the party, and I really enjoyed it.
2. Six hundred years ago, many people said, "The world is flat." But others, like Columbus and Magellan, did not *accept* this idea. "We can sail round the world," they said.

to **control** (verb)
control (noun)

> DEFINITION to control something: to be able to decide something
>
> EXAMPLES 1. There was ice and snow on the road. The driver could not *control* his car, and it went off the road.
> 2. Birth *control,* or family planning, is how to plan or limit the number of children who are born.

to **agree** with (verb)
to **disagree** with (verb)

> DEFINITION to agree with something or someone: to accept the opinions or ideas of another person
>
> EXAMPLES 1. "Let's take this apartment," said Mike, but Bob did not *agree*. "No," he said. "Let's look at some other apartments. This apartment is not big enough."
> 2. Many people do not like the things that the government is doing. For example, the government wants to spend a lot of money on the army. But many people *disagree* with this idea. "Let's spend the money on hospitals," they say.

Now read this passage and answer the questions about it. Also write the numbers of the lines where you found the answers.

1   The population of the world is growing quickly. The growth is
2   very fast in some countries which already do not have enough food
3   for their people. The governments of many of these countries are
4   trying to limit the number of babies being born. They say: "Stop
5   after two children! Small is beautiful! Two children is a good size
6   for your family!" These governments have programs which show
7   poor people modern methods of birth control. But not everyone
8   agrees with these programs. The people who are against the gov-
9   ernment programs say things like: "Governments cannot control
10 the lives of people. They cannot decide the size of families. There is
11 enough food in the world for everyone." Clearly, not everyone ac-
12 cepts birth control as a solution to the problem of population, and
13 many birth control programs are failures.

1. T   F   Some countries that have food problems do not have   Line(s) _____
enough people.

2. T F   Some governments are teaching methods of birth con-   Line(s) _____
trol to their people.

3. T F   Some governments want to limit the number of peo-   Line(s) _____
ple who get married.

4. T F   Everyone accepts birth control as a solution to the   Line(s) _____
population problems of the world.

5. T F   Not all government programs of birth control are suc-   Line(s) _____
cessful.

PART D

disease (noun)

DEFINITION   a disease: an illness or a sickness (often serious)

EXAMPLES   1. Smallpox is a *disease* which in the past killed many people
every year. But now doctors can control it. Last year no
one died of smallpox.
2. This plant has a *disease*. The green leaves are becoming
black and falling off.

to **cure** (verb)
a **cure** (noun)

DEFINITION   to cure: 1. to stop a disease or illness
2. to bring someone back to good health

EXAMPLES   1. Scientists are still looking for *a cure* for the common cold.
2. The man became very ill, but the doctor was able *to cure*
him. The man went back to work yesterday.

medicine (noun)
medical (adjective)

DEFINITION   medicine: the science of how we can cure diseases

EXAMPLES   1. My sister is studying *medicine*. She wants to be a doctor.
2. People over the age of twenty-five should have a *medical*
examination every year. Then their doctor can discover
any problems early.

to **develop** (verb)
developing (adjective)

DEFINITION   to develop: 1. to grow or to become better
2. to cause something to become better

EXAMPLES 1. *Developing* countries are countries which were poor and which did not have many schools, hospitals, or good farms years ago. Now they are building these things.

2. Some engineers are *developing* a car which will use electricity, not gasoline. But they still have to solve many problems.

imagination (noun)
to **imagine** (verb)

DEFINITION to imagine: to make a picture in your head of something you cannot really see

EXAMPLES 1. How will life be in the year 2080? We don't know, but we can try to *imagine* it.

2. This author writes very exciting stories. He has a good *imagination*.

research (noun)

DEFINITION to do research into something: to study something (to discover new facts about it)

EXAMPLES 1. Scientists are doing *research* into energy from the sun. They are trying to make machines that will use the sun's heat to heat buildings during the winter.

2. We spend a lot of money for medical *research* every year. Scientists, of course, still do not know all the answers, but they discover new things every year.

progress (noun)

DEFINITION to make progress: to improve

EXAMPLES 1. Two months ago Carlos did not know any English, but he is making good *progress*. Now he can understand a lot of English, and he can hold short conversations in English.

2. Maria is still in the hospital, but she's making *progress*. She will be able to leave the hospital tomorrow.

Now read this passage and answer the questions about it. Also write the numbers of the lines where you found the answers.

1 One hundred years ago, there were many diseases which doc-
2 tors could not cure. These diseases, for example, smallpox and chol-
3 era, killed large numbers of people in many countries every year.
4 But medical science made great progress in 100 years, and devel-
5 oped ways to control or cure many of these dangerous diseases. But

6	doctors still say: "There are still thousands of questions which		
7	medical scientists have to answer." The doctors are right. We are		
8	spending a great deal of money for medical research, but we still do		
9	not have a cure for the common cold. Every year, scientists dis-		
10	cover new diseases that they cannot cure. There are some people		
11	who imagine a world without disease in the near future, but		
12	clearly these people do not understand the problems which medical		
13	science still has to solve.		

1. T F   Medicine made no progress in the last 100 years.   Line(s) _____

2. T F   Today doctors can help people with diseases which killed people in the past.   Line(s) _____

3. T F   In a short time we will live in a world without diseases.   Line(s) _____

4. T F   We have cures for all the diseases that troubled people in the nineteenth century.   Line(s) _____

5. T F   Diseases which doctors cannot cure appear every year.   Line(s) _____

PART E

an **advertisement** (noun)
a **commercial** (noun)

DEFINITION   an advertisement: words and pictures which try to sell a product. (You can see advertisements in magazines, in books, and in newspapers.)
a commercial: an advertisement on the radio or television

EXAMPLES   1. *Advertisements* do not always tell the truth about the product that they are trying to sell.
2. In the opinion of many people, there are too many *commercials* in the middle of interesting television programs.

to **worry** about (verb)
worried (adjective)

DEFINITION   to worry: to have problems and to think about them

EXAMPLES   1. Maria is ill and in the hospital. Her friends are *worried* about her. But the doctors say, "Don't *worry!* It's not serious! Maria will be better in two or three days."
2. I am taking my driving test tomorrow. I am *worried* about it. I can't drive very well.

to **suggest** (verb)
suggestion (noun)

DEFINITION   to suggest: to put an idea into a person's mind

EXAMPLES   1. "Let's have our classes in the evenings," said one student. But the other students in the class did not like this *suggestion*.
2. Last night we all wanted to go out. Mike *suggested* a movie. But we could not find an interesting film, so we went to a disco.

goods (noun)

DEFINITION   goods: a general word for things which people make and sell (Goods are things which you can move.)

EXAMPLES   1. Americans are buying many *goods* from Japan, for example, radios, televisions, stereos, and cameras.
2. *Goods* from the U.S. are very expensive in Japan, so not many people buy American products there.

to **support** (verb)

DEFINITION   to support something or someone: to give the help, money, or food that it needs to continue or to live

EXAMPLES   1. In many countries, people who cannot *support* their families get help from the government.
2. Some parts of Africa cannot *support* the numbers of animals that live there. There is not enough food and water, so some governments are moving large numbers of animals to other parts of the country.

unpleasant (adjective)
pleasant (adjective)

DEFINITION   pleasant: nice or friendly

EXAMPLES   1. Our vacation was great. The hotel and food were excellent, and the weather was very *pleasant*. It did not rain, and it did not get too hot.
2. The people who help customers in stores always have to be nice and friendly. Customers will not come back to stores which have *unpleasant* assistants.

resources (noun)

DEFINITION   resources: the things which can make a person or a country rich

EXAMPLES   1. Oil is the main natural *resource* of Kuwait and Saudi Arabia.
2. A country also has other *resources*. It has the energy and intelligence of the people who live there.

Now read this passage and answer the questions about it. Also write the numbers of the lines where you found the answers.

1	In the U.S. most people get their news and information about
2	the things that are happening in the world from television. They
3	believe the things they hear and see on television. Probably most of
4	the information is true, and we can believe it. But will we always
5	be able to believe the information which television gives us?
6	Television stations depend on the support of advertisers who
7	buy time for commercials on their programs. The companies who
8	advertise their goods on television are often very rich, so now some
9	people in the U.S. are worried about one unpleasant possibility:
10	Perhaps advertisers with great resources will be able to control the
11	television stations. Then they will be able to choose the news and
12	information that we can hear; perhaps they will not give us any
13	news or information which will be bad for them. They will perhaps
14	only suggest ideas to us which agree with their own ideas, and we
15	will hear no voice which disagrees with them. This possibility is
16	real; some television companies already belong to big companies,
17	and the interests of these companies are not always the same as
18	the interests of the people of this country.

1. T F   We will always be able to believe the news which we see on television. The writer is certain about this.   Line(s) _____

2. T F   Most people in the U.S. get their news of the world from newspapers.   Line(s) _____

3. T F   Not everyone in the U.S. is happy with the developments that they see in commercial television.   Line(s) _____

4. T F   According to the writer, companies will never be able to choose the kind of news and information we can hear.   Line(s) _____

5. T F   In the future, perhaps we will not be able to hear   Line(s) _____
           ideas that disagree with the ideas of the people who
           own the television stations.

Exercises for Parts C, D, and E

SAME OR DIFFERENT?

Read the two sentences in each example. Do they express the same ideas, or do they express different ideas? Write *S* for sentences with the same ideas; write *D* for sentences with different ideas.

Remember: You can express the **same** idea with **different** words and **different** grammar!

1. a. The student is making progress in his English.   _____
   b. The student's English is improving.

2. a. My father agrees with my ideas about television.   _____
   b. My father does not accept my ideas about television.

3. a. This country has many different natural resources.   _____
   b. This country produces a lot of different goods.

4. a. There are still many diseases that modern medicine cannot   _____
      cure.
   b. Modern medicine still cannot cure any serious illnesses.

5. a. There was ice on the road. The driver could not control his car,   _____
      and it went off the road.
   b. The car went off the road; the driver lost control of it on the icy
      road.

6. a. Scientists are doing research into ways to produce energy from   _____
      the movements of the sea.
   b. Scientists are studying methods to make energy from the move-
      ments of the ocean.

7. a. The apartment which we saw yesterday was not the right size   _____
      for us.
   b. The apartment which we visited yesterday was too modern for
      us.

8. a. The number of American married couples who use modern   _____
      methods of birth control is growing.
   b. More and more married Americans are using modern methods
      of birth control.

9. a. We had a very pleasant vacation last summer. _____
   b. We did not really enjoy our vacation last summer.

10. a. Many developing countries get support from the U.S. and Euro- _____
    pean countries.
    b. The U.S. and European countries help many developing coun-
    tries.

11. a. Students who are learning English need to learn a lot of words. _____
    b. Students of English need to develop a good vocabulary in
    English.

12. a. Many married people want to limit the size of their families. _____
    b. Many married people want to have a large number of children.

EXPECTATIONS

Read the first sentence in each of these examples. Think about the ideas in it. Then
choose the sentence or sentences that can follow it.

1. Birth control programs are failing in some developing countries.
   a. The people in these countries like small families.
   b. Good hospitals and doctors are the reason for the success of the programs.
   c. Sometimes these countries have religions that do not accept birth control.

2. Some industrial countries, for example, Japan, have few natural resources.
   a. They have to buy all their coal, gas, and oil from other countries.
   b. They buy all the goods which their people use from other countries.
   c. They depend on other countries for the raw materials which their industries need.

3. The government is very worried about a new disease that appeared in the
   U.S. last year.
   a. It is spending a lot of money for research into methods of birth control.
   b. Medical researchers still do not know its cause.
   c. The disease killed 2,000 people last year, and doctors cannot cure or control
   it.

4. There are no commercials on public television in the U.S.
   a. The advertisements come only at the beginning and end of each program,
   not in the middle.
   b. Companies can buy time to advertise their products.
   c. Companies cannot advertise their products, but their names appear before
   or after the programs which they support.

5. According to his doctors, the patient is making good progress.

   a. Three days ago he was seriously ill. Now he is out of danger.
   b. The new medicine the doctors are giving him is not having an effect.
   c. The doctors see no improvement, and they are very worried.

6. Scientists are doing a great deal of research into ways to solve the problem of hunger in the world.

   a. They are trying to find cures for diseases that still kill a lot of people.
   b. They are trying to find ways to control diseases that kill plants and farm animals.
   c. They are developing plants which will grow without a lot of attention from the farmer.

7. The population of the world is growing too quickly.

   a. Somewhere in the world, a baby is born every two seconds.
   b. Diseases which are not dangerous in the U.S. still kill a lot of people in developing countries.
   c. One solution that people suggest for this problem is to start birth control programs in developing countries.

8. The government's work program is not having the effect that the government hoped.

   a. It is not spending enough money for research into diseases which still cause problems for us.
   b. The number of people who are out of work is growing not falling.
   c. It is winning a lot of support from people who usually disagree with the government.

VOCABULARY QUIZ

Choose the correct word for each empty space. Use each word only once.
Remember: Read to the end of each example. Then decide!

resource	worried	improve	unpleasant
product	agree	medicine	develop
limit	born	size	disagree
research	advertise	control	grow
accept	progress	suggest	cure

1. The population of some U.S. cities is falling, but in other cities the population is _____ing. Houston, Texas, gets 500 new families every week. People are moving there from cities in the north.

2. Carlos liked the shirt that he saw in the store, but it was not the correct _____. It was too small for him. It was a 15, and Carlos takes a 16.

3. You cannot drive at eighty miles an hour on highways in the U.S. There is a law which _____s your speed to fifty-five miles an hour. Police stop drivers who go too fast.

4. Last week the professor _____ed a new job in a university in West Germany. He is going to begin in September of this year.

5. Ali does not _____ with the ideas of his history professor. In Ali's opinion, the professor's ideas are wrong.

6. Maria is in the hospital. She is making good _____. She will be able to leave the hospital at the end of the week.

7. Scientists are doing a lot of _____ into diseases that we still cannot control. They are looking for answers to the problems that still exist.

8. In the 1960s and 1970s, American cars used too much gasoline. Now the auto makers are _____ing solutions to this problem.

9. A doctor's job is to _____ disease and help sick people.

10. Scientists are making great progress in _____ every year. They are discovering cures for diseases which were once very dangerous.

11. Stores _____ the goods which they want to sell on television. We see the commercials, and perhaps we will decide to buy something.

12. The three friends had nothing to do on Friday evening. Ali _____ed a movie, and Adnan and Carlos agreed. They went to see a new space movie.

13. I am very _____ about my math test tomorrow. I missed some classes last week, and I don't understand some of the questions that the teacher gave for homework.

14. This is a very rich country. It has lots of natural _____s; it has coal and oil and good farming land.

15. The weather last week was very _____. It was cold, there was a strong wind, and it rained a lot. Maybe it will improve this week.

Main Reading

Pre-Reading Exercises

VOCABULARY IN CONTEXT

Read each example to the end. Do not stop in the middle. Pay attention to the words in italics. They are words that you already know. Then try to guess the meaning of the new word in boldface type. The words in italics will help you.

1. This country does *not* have *enough food* for its people. Without help from other countries, thousands, perhaps millions, of people will *die* of **starvation** and *disease*.

   Starvation means _____.
   a. fights and wars
   b. diseases
   c. no food

2. With **irrigation,** we *can* now *grow* plants in *dry* parts of the world which *did not produce* any *food* fifteen or twenty years ago.

   Irrigation means _____.
   a. the machines that help farmers in their work
   b. new plants that scientists are developing
   c. water that you bring from far away

3. Scientists are doing a lot of *research* into *new plants* and *farming methods*. They can grow plants in water. They are developing plants which grow very fast. They can cure many diseases that attack plants. **Agricultural** scientists will continue to find *ways* that will help *farmers*.

   Agricultural scientists are _____.
   a. scientists who do research into diseases
   b. scientists who study farming problems
   c. scientists who work with water

4. Agricultural progress costs a lot of money. So the governments of *rich* countries will have to help the *poor* countries. Without the help of the **wealthy** nations, the *poor* countries will not be able to use the products and methods which scientists develop.

   Wealthy means _____.
   a. new
   b. agricultural
   c. rich

5. Sometimes wealthy countries send agricultural scientists to developing countries. The scientists teach modern farming **techniques** to the native farmers. The *old ways* of farming often do not produce enough food, and sometimes they have a bad effect on the land.

   Techniques means ———.
   a. ways of doing something
   b. equipment and tools
   c. accidents

6. Every day we have to **transport** large numbers of people *to* their work and *back home* again in the evening.

   To transport means ———.
   a. to keep
   b. to feed
   c. to move

7. John did not feel well, so he went to see his doctor. The doctor said, "Your problem is **overwork.** Take a vacation. You need to *rest* and *relax.*"

   Overwork means ———.
   a. this is not the right job for you
   b. too much work
   c. not enough work

   So overpopulation means ———.
   a. not enough people
   b. too many people
   c. you are above the people; you can give them orders

8. **Poverty** is a big *problem* in the modern world. In many countries, people do *not* earn *enough money* even to buy food for their families.

   Poverty means ———.
   a. people are poor
   b. people do not have schools
   c. people do not have work

9. In 1492, Columbus reached the new continent of America, but he **refused** to *believe* this. He wanted to reach China. *According to Columbus*, the islands which he reached in the Caribbean were really part of China, *not* part of a new continent.

   To refuse means ———.
   a. to try to do something
   b. not to want to do something
   c. to begin to do something

10. The country is having **economic** problems. Prices are *increasing by 70%* every year. A lot of people are *out of work.* Every day some more companies *fail* and *go out of business.*

   Economic means ____.
   a. connected with the government of the country
   b. connected with money and business
   c. connected with history

11. The new industry will bring a number of **benefits** to the city. It will give *jobs to 2,000 people* who are out of work; it will *bring visitors* to the city and *improve* the city's economy.

   Benefits means ____.
   a. dangerous diseases
   b. serious problems
   c. good effects

12. Many poor people are without food or **shelter.** They are living *outside on the streets* or *in the parks.* We will have to find **shelter** for these *homeless* people before the beginning of winter.

   Shelter means ____.
   a. something to eat
   b. medical help
   c. a place to live

EXPECTATIONS

Let's try to get some ideas about the article that we are going to read. But let's try to get them *now—before* we begin to read the whole article. We can call these ideas *Expectations.* They can help us with the article later.

   Read the title of the article carefully. Think about it. It gives us information about the ideas which we can expect in the article. Look up the word *exploding* in your dictionary. Then read the ideas that appear below. We can expect *some* of these ideas in the article. The others are ideas which we don't expect. Choose the ideas which you expect (YES), and the ideas which you don't expect (NO). Here's an example:

   Scientists are discovering a lot of new things about space.   YES (NO)

Well, the title says nothing about space research, so we do not expect this idea in the article. Now continue:

1. The number of people in the world is increasing very quickly.   YES   NO

2. An increase in population will be good for the world.   YES   NO

3. The article will talk a lot about the progress that medical science is making.   YES   NO

4. An increase in the world's population will cause difficulties.   YES   NO

5. The article will talk about the large numbers of people who are taking vacations in other countries.   YES   NO

6. The article will talk about answers to the problems that overpopulation causes.   YES   NO

Your job is to get an idea of the passage that you are going to read. The title will help you with this. Also the first sentence of a paragraph can sometimes help you. It sometimes will give you a clear idea of the ideas that a paragraph will contain.

Look at the first sentence of Paragraph 2 (line 9). Read only this first sentence and then stop. Choose the ideas which you expect and the ideas which you don't expect in this paragraph.

1. We will read about the size of the population increase.   YES   NO

2. We will read about the bad effects of overpopulation.   YES   NO

3. The problems that overpopulation causes are not really serious.   YES   NO

Sometimes a paragraph will introduce ideas for a number of paragraphs. Paragraph 3 does this. Read it quickly and choose the idea(s) which you can expect in the paragraphs which follow Paragraph 3.

1. We will read about the negative effects of overpopulation.   YES   NO

2. We will read about possible solutions to the problem of overpopulation.   YES   NO

3. We can expect only one solution to the problem of overpopulation.   YES   NO

Sometimes we can divide a long article into a number of small parts. This can also help our reading. Let's try to divide this article. Look at the title again. According to the title, how many parts can you expect in this article?

Well, the title talks about (1) *problems* and (2) *solutions*. So perhaps the article will have two parts. One part will talk about the problems that overpopulation causes. The other part perhaps will talk about the solutions.

Now read the first sentences of Paragraphs 2–9. Then answer these questions.

1. What paragraph(s) will talk about the problem?   ——

2. What paragraph(s) will talk about possible solutions?   ——

Now let's look at the part which talks about solutions. Read the first sentence of Paragraph 4 again. What ideas do you expect in Paragraph 4?

1. Overpopulation is a big problem in developing countries. YES NO

2. Birth control is one possible solution to overpopulation YES NO

3. The paragraph will describe family-planning programs. YES NO

Now read the first sentence of Paragraph 5. What ideas do you expect in this paragraph?

1. The paragraph will describe modern methods of birth control. YES NO

2. Some birth control programs are successful. YES NO

3. Some birth control programs are not successful. YES NO

Now read the first sentence of Paragraph 6. What ideas do you expect in this paragraph?

1. The paragraph will talk about successful birth control programs. YES NO

2. The paragraph will try to answer the following question: Why do some birth control programs fail? YES NO

3. The paragraph will describe another possible solution to the problem of overpopulation. YES NO

Let's think about Paragraph 3 again. From Paragraph 3, we don't expect just one solution to the problem of overpopulation. We expect more.
   Read the first sentences of Paragraphs 7–9, and answer this question:

1. What paragraph(s) talk about a different solution to the problem of overpopulation? _____

Often an article like this will *summarize* its ideas in the final paragraph. Read Paragraph 9. What ideas does this paragraph give you about the article?

1. The article examines many different solutions to the problem of overpopulation. YES NO

2. The article suggests two different solutions to the problem of overpopulation. YES NO

3. The article looks at the causes and the effects of overpopulation, but it does not suggest any answers to the problem. YES NO

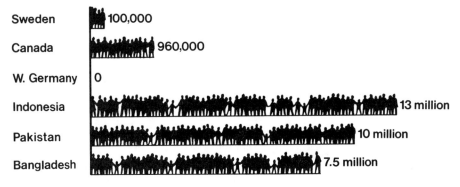

Sweden	100,000
Canada	960,000
W. Germany	0
Indonesia	13 million
Pakistan	10 million
Bangladesh	7.5 million

Population Growth 1975–79

Our Exploding Population: Problems and Solutions

1   Almost everyone thinks about the future. We try to imagine   1
2   life in thirty, forty, or fifty years. What will life on the earth be
3   like? According to many people, it will not be very pleasant. These
4   people are very worried about the future. One of the main problems
5   which worries them is overpopulation. In 1975 there were about
6   four billion people in the world, and the population is increasing by
7   about 2% every year. At the end of the twentieth century, the
8   population of the world will reach six billion people.
9   Why is this increase in population a problem? First, a large   2
10   part of the growth is taking place in countries that do not always
11   have enough food for their present population. Without a great
12   deal of money, food, and medical assistance from other nations,
13   these countries will not be able to support their growing popula-
14   tions. Many of their people, perhaps millions of them, will die of
15   starvation or disease. But overpopulation is not only a problem for
16   developing countries. It is also a serious problem for the countries
17   of the world which do not usually have food problems. In wealthy,
18   industrial nations large increases in the population will have nega-
19   tive effects on life. We will have to heat and cool more houses,
20   apartment buildings, schools, and hospitals. We will have to trans-
21   port more people to and from work. For all this, we will have to use
22   more of the world's natural resources. Perhaps the world will not
23   have enough oil, water, coal, and wood for all our needs.
24   What can we do to solve the problems of overpopulation? Dif-   3

Sweden	$$$$$$$$$$$$$$$$$$$$$$$$$$$$$ $7820
Canada	$$$$$$$$$$$$$$$$$$$$$$$$$$$ $6321
W. Germany	$$$$$$$$$$$$$$$$$$$$$$$$$ $6035
Indonesia	$$$$201
Pakistan	$$$183
Bangladesh	$110

Per Capita National Income 1975

25 ferent groups of people have different answers to this question, and
26 there is disagreement about the solutions that they suggest.
27   One solution which many people suggest is to limit the num-   4
28 ber of children who are born. There are now a number of safe,
29 modern methods of birth control. A married couple who uses birth
30 control can choose the size of their family. A number of countries
31 with large populations have government programs for birth con-
32 trol. India, for example, advertises birth control on the radio and
33 television. Teams of workers go out into the countryside and teach
34 the people about the benefits of family planning. In China, couples
35 who only have one child or no children get apartments before
36 couples with three children or more. In many other countries, birth
37 control is a subject that school students study in special classes.
38   But how successful are these birth control programs? Some are   5
39 very successful. In countries like Sweden, West Germany, Denmark,
40 Switzerland, and Great Britain, families are quite small, and the
41 population is increasing very slowly; in some of these countries, it is
42 not growing at all. But these are wealthy, developed countries,
43 which can feed their people without difficulty. In developing coun-
44 tries many of the birth control programs are not successful.
45   There are a number of possible reasons for the failure of birth   6
46 control programs in developing countries. One reason is religion.
47 Many people belong to religions which do not accept modern meth-
48 ods of birth control. For them, birth control is wrong, and they nat-
49 urally refuse to listen to family-planning workers. Another reason
50 for the failure of birth control programs is economics. Often a large
51 number of children are necessary for very poor families in develop-

52 ing countries. Children can work and help support the family. Also,
53 without a welfare system, people have to depend on their children
54 for food, clothing, and shelter in their old age. In these countries,
55 people just cannot see any reason for small families.

56   Some years ago many family-planning programs did not real-   7
57 ize the real connection between poverty and the need for large
58 families. But now family-planning workers agree about one thing:
59 We have to improve the lives of people in developing countries
60 first. Then perhaps they will see benefits in small families, and
61 they will accept birth control as something which makes sense for
62 them.

63   For other people, birth control is definitely not the solution the   8
64 world needs for the problem of overpopulation. In their opinion,
65 governments should not decide family size. It is not right. The
66 solution which these people suggest is to increase world food pro-
67 duction. They draw our attention to the progress that agricultural
68 scientists are making. With irrigation, for example, we can now
69 produce food in many parts of the world which did not produce
70 anything fifteen or twenty years ago. We can even grow plants in
71 water without soil. Scientists are also doing research into plants
72 which grow quickly and into new farming techniques. But this type
73 of progress costs money: money for the modern equipment that is
74 often necessary; money for irrigation programs; money for new
75 types of plants; money to teach farmers new techniques. The gov-
76 ernments of rich countries will have to help the poor countries.
77 Without economic assistance from the wealthy nations, poor coun-
78 tries will not be able to use the new products and farming tech-
79 niques that scientists are developing.

80   Birth control and an increase in food production are two possi-   9
81 ble solutions to the problem of overpopulation. Perhaps there are
82 other solutions. Almost certainly there is no one easy answer to the
83 problem; we will have to use a number of solutions. Then perhaps
84 we will be able to solve the problem of the population explosion.

MAIN IDEAS CHECK

Here are the main ideas of the paragraphs in this article. Write the correct paragraph
number opposite each main idea.

PARAGRAPH   IDEA

_____   An increase in food production is another possible answer to the
             problem of overpopulation.

_____ We must first fight poverty. Then we can introduce birth control programs.

_____ Birth control programs are successful in developed countries, but they often fail in developing countries.

_____ The population of the world is increasing very quickly.

_____ Different people suggest different solutions to the problem of over-population.

_____ One solution will not be enough to solve the problem of overpopulation.

_____ Religion and poverty are two reasons for the failure of birth control programs in developing countries.

_____ Birth control is one possible solution to the problem of overpopulation.

_____ Overpopulation is a problem for developing countries and wealthy industrial nations.

COMPREHENSION CHECK

1. In the year 2000, the population of the world will be   Line(s) _____
   a. about four billion.
   b. six billion.
   c. two billion.

2. T F   In countries which often cannot feed their present   Line(s) _____
           number of people, the population is not increasing.

3. T F   Overpopulation is only a problem for countries that   Line(s) _____
           already have food problems.

4. Why is overpopulation a problem for industrial countries?   Line(s) _____
   a. They do not have enough water, wood, coal, and oil at present.
   b. Perhaps they will not have enough natural resources in the future.
   c. They will not be able to produce enough goods for six billion people.

5. T F   An increase in population will mean a pleasant life   Line(s) _____
           for everyone in the industrial countries of the world.

6. T F   The writer is not worried about overpopulation.   Line(s) _____

7. T F   Not everyone likes the same solutions for the prob-   Line(s) _____
           lem of overpopulation.

8. Birth control programs   Line(s) _____
   a. are always successful.
   b. are sometimes successful.
   c. are always a failure.

9. Family planning is not very successful   Line(s) _____
   a. in countries which do not have welfare.
   b. in countries which do not have any food problems.
   c. in countries which give people money in their old age.

10. T F   Modern techniques of birth control are acceptable to   Line(s) _____
            all religions.

11. T F   Family planning is only one possible solution. There   Line(s) _____
            are other solutions.

12. According to the writer,   Line(s) _____
   a. we will not be able to produce more food in the future.
   b. we will probably be able to produce more food in the fu-
      ture.
   c. the amount of food which we can produce is not increasing.

13. T F   Developing countries will soon be able to improve   Line(s) _____
            their agriculture. The writer is certain about this.

14. What is the writer's solution for the problems of overpopula- Line(s) _____
    tion?
   a. We have to have birth control.
   b. We have to produce more food.
   c. We have to improve the lives of people.
   d. We have to do all these things.

Now do the paragraph reading exercise on the next page.

PARAGRAPH READING

These sentences form a paragraph, but they are not in the correct order. Put the sentences into their correct order. The first sentence is already in its correct place.

__1__ Overpopulation is a serious problem for the world.

_____ In these countries, people need children who will support them in their old age.

_____ But not all of these programs are successful.

_____ So perhaps we will have to improve life in these countries, and then we can expect success for birth control programs.

_____ Many countries are trying to solve this problem with birth control programs.

_____ They fail very often in developing countries that have no welfare for poor, old, and sick people.

_____ Some countries, for example, give information about family-planning methods on radio and television or in their schools.

Education in the United States

Grammar for this unit: Sentence connectors
Clauses with missing words
You will find information and practice on these grammar points in
Appendix 1, Unit 3.

Vocabulary Study and Preparatory Reading ───────────

PART A

elementary (adjective)

DEFINITION   elementary: 1. easy
2. beginning

EXAMPLES   1. I'm not happy with my math course. It's too *elementary* for
me. I studied the same things in high school.
2. Children start *elementary school* at the age of six. They go
to *elementary school* for five or six years.

to **educate** (verb)
education (noun)

DEFINITION   to educate: to teach people the things that they need for life
and work

EXAMPLES   1. *Education* is free in many countries. You don't have to pay
for your children's classes.
2. Countries which do not *educate* their people will have
problems in the future. They will not be able to compete
with countries which have good schools.

system (noun)

DEFINITION   a system: a number of things that work together

EXAMPLES   1. The postal *system* here is improving. This letter from New York reached me in two days.
2. The U.S. has a very large welfare *system*. It takes care of people who have no money or no work.

private (adjective)

DEFINITION   private: something which belongs to one person or a number of people (It does not belong to everyone.)

EXAMPLES   1. There are *private* elementary and high schools in the U.S. Parents have to pay for their children's education in these schools.
2. This parking place is *private*. It is only for the people who live in this apartment building.

public (adjective)

DEFINITION   public: something which belongs to everyone (Everyone can use it. It is *not private*.)

EXAMPLES   1. Many years ago there was no *public* education here. Parents had to send their children to private schools or to church schools.
2. Many towns have *public* libraries. Anyone can go there and borrow books or records.

similar (adjective)
similarity (noun)

DEFINITION   to be similar to something: to be like something, but *not* to be 100% the same

EXAMPLES   1. The two friends do not disagree often. They have very *similar* ideas about many subjects.
2. Look at these two paintings. Can you see any *similarities* between them? The same person painted the two pictures.

tuition (noun)

DEFINITION   tuition: the money that students pay for their classes

EXAMPLES   1. *Tuition* is going up at many universities. Some students will not be able to continue their studies.
2. People who work for this university can take one class free. They don't need to pay any *tuition* for that class.

Now read this paragraph and answer the questions about it.

1   The education system of the United States is similar to the
2 education systems in many other countries of the world. For ex-
3 ample, people in the U.S. and in other countries do not have to pay
4 for education in the public elementary schools and high schools.
5 Also children *have* to go to school; their parents cannot keep them
6 at home or send them to work. However, there are also many
7 important differences between the U.S. system and the systems of
8 other countries. Many of these differences exist in the universities.
9 In many countries, the government controls the universities, and
10 the people who work in the universities get their money from the
11 government. In the U.S., however, there are many private univer-
12 sities, as well as public, or state, universities. There is another
13 important difference between universities in the U.S. and universi-
14 ties in other countries. In many other countries, students often do
15 not have to pay for their studies. But in both state and private
16 universities in the U.S., students have to pay tuition for the classes
17 which they take.

1. T F   The paragraph shows only the similarities between   Line(s) _____
        the education system of the U.S. and the systems of
        other countries.

2. T F   There is no tuition in U.S. public elementary schools   Line(s) _____
        and high schools.

3. T F   The writer does not write about any differences be-   Line(s) _____
        tween the public high schools of the U.S. and the pub-
        lic high schools of other countries.

4. T F   Students in the U.S. have to pay tuition at private   Line(s) _____
        universities but not at state universities.

5. T F   The writer gives two examples of the things which   Line(s) _____
        make the U.S. university system different from the
        systems of other countries.

6. T F   The government pays all the people who work at   Line(s) _____
        American universities.

PART B

to **elect** (verb)
election (noun)

        DEFINITION to elect: to choose the people whom you want for the govern-
                ment or for any group of people who control something

EXAMPLES
1. In the U.S. there is a presidential *election* every four years. Then the country can *elect* a new president.
2. In many countries people can *elect* their government. They can choose the people whom they want in the government.

community (noun)

DEFINITION
a community: a number of people who live in a place (big or small)

EXAMPLES
1. In Chicago there is a very large Polish *community*. Many people from Poland came to live there early in this century.
2. This new factory will help our *community*. It will make new jobs for the people who live here.

board (noun)

DEFINITION
a board: a small number of people who control something

EXAMPLES
1. Big companies usually have a *board* of directors. These people make decisions about the actions of the company.
2. In the U.S. each community has a school *board*. The *board* makes decisions about the schools of the community.

to **train** (verb)
training (noun)

DEFINITION
to train people: to teach people or to practice for a job or for some other thing that you will do
training: education for a job

EXAMPLES
1. There are a number of universities in the U.S. which *train* people for jobs in English as a Second Language.
2. The *training* usually lasts one or two years.

center (noun)
central (adjective)

DEFINITION
the center of something: the part in the middle

EXAMPLES
1. The *central* government is the government of the whole country. The *central* government of the U.S. is in Washington, D.C.
2. The Seine River runs through the *center* of Paris.

local (adjective)

DEFINITION   local describes something that belongs to a small part of the country; it can also describe something that belongs to the small part of the country or city where you live.

EXAMPLES   1. I live in a nice part of the town. But there is one problem. You cannot buy all the things you need in the *local* stores. For some things, you have to drive three or four miles.

         2. In the U.S. the *local* government has to build the roads in its part of the country. It also has to keep them in good condition. The central government looks after the interstate highways.

to **influence** (verb)
influence (noun)

DEFINITION   to influence people: to have an effect on them

EXAMPLES   1. Why did I decide to come to the U.S.? A lot of things *influenced* my decision. First, I wanted to learn English. Second, I wanted to see a new country. Third, my friends told me good things about the U.S.

         2. People who have a lot of money can have a lot of *influence* in a community. Other people will listen to them and believe them.

Now read this paragraph and answer the questions about it.

1   In the U.S. and many other countries parents do not have to
2   pay for the education of their children in elementary school or in
3   high school. Like in many countries of the world, public education
4   here is free. However, there is one big difference between the U.S.
5   public school system and the systems of many other countries. In
6   many countries, the central government or the state government
7   controls the public schools and makes all the decisions about books,
8   programs, and the training of teachers. In the U.S. the people who
9   control the schools of a community are the local school board of
10   that community, not the central or state government. The people
11   who live in a community usually elect their school board; each
12   community has a different school board (there are over 30,000 in
13   the U.S.). The school board can make decisions about school sub-
14   jects, teachers' pay, and other important questions. Therefore, in
15   the U.S., the people who live in a community can have a lot of
16   influence on their local schools.

1. T F   In the U.S. elementary education is free, but high   Line(s) ____
           school education is not.

2. T F   In many other countries the central government con-   Line(s) ____
           trols the education system.

3. T F   In the U.S. the central government chooses the sub-   Line(s) ____
           jects which children study in school and the books
           which they use.

4. T F   In the U.S. parents can choose the men and women   Line(s) ____
           who work on the school boards.

5. T F   In the U.S. communities do not have any control of   Line(s) ____
           their public schools.

Exercises for Parts A and B

SAME OR DIFFERENT?

Read the two sentences in each example. Do they express the same ideas, or do they express different ideas? Write *S* for sentences with the same ideas; write *D* for sentences with different ideas.

    Remember: You can express the **same** ideas with **different** words and **different** grammar!

1. a. In the U.S. public education is free for students in elementary   ____
      school and high school.
   b. Parents do not have to pay tuition for their children's classes in
      U.S. public schools.

2. a. There are many similarities between the education system of the   ____
      U.S. and the education systems of other countries.
   b. The education system of the U.S. is quite different from the edu-
      cation systems of other countries.

3. a. In some countries local people can have a lot of influence on the   ____
      schools of their communities.
   b. In some countries local people cannot decide anything about the
      schools of their communities.

4. a. Next semester the university is going to increase tuition for all   ____
      classes.
   b. We're going to have to pay more for classes at the university
      next semester.

5. a. In some countries the central government controls the education   _____
system.
   b. The central government makes all the important decisions about
schools and universities in some countries.

6. a. In the U.S. the people who live in a community elect their local   _____
school board.
   b. In the U.S. the people who live in a community choose the men
and women who will work on the local school board.

7. a. In many countries there are only public, or state, universities.   _____
   b. Private universities do not exist in the university systems of
many countries.

8. a. The biology course which I am taking this semester is too ele-   _____
mentary. I'm not happy with it.
   b. I can't understand the biology course I am taking this semester.
It's too difficult for me.

EXPECTATIONS

Read the first sentence in each of these examples. Think about the ideas in it. Then choose the sentence or sentences that can follow it.

1. In public elementary schools and high schools, education is free.

   a. In the universities, however, students have to pay tuition for their classes.
   b. Parents have to pay tuition for all the classes which their children take.
   c. Even children who come from very poor families can get an education.

2. The training that some high school teachers get is not very good.

   a. Not many of them have problems in their first teaching jobs.
   b. They don't know a lot about the subjects they have to teach.
   c. They know a lot about modern research in education.

3. There are a number of similarities between universities in the U.S. and universities in Great Britain.

   a. In each country, students have to pay tuition for the classes they take.
   b. Not many universities in Great Britain have more than 10,000 students; U.S. universities often have between 25,000 and 40,000 students.
   c. In the U.S. there are private and state universities; in Great Britain private universities do not exist.

4. In many countries the central government makes all the important decisions about school subjects, teachers' pay, and other questions.

   a. Local communities have a lot of influence on the education that their children get in the local schools.

b. Local communities elect their own school boards, which control the schools of those communities.

c. In the U.S., however, local communities elect school boards that control the public schools of the community.

5. In the U.S. an education at a good private university can be very expensive.

a. Tuition can be very high, sometimes over $8,000 a year.

b. Students who go to state universities often get jobs during their vacations.

c. A lot of rich people find jobs at these universities.

VOCABULARY QUIZ

Choose the correct word for each empty space. Use each word only once.

public	community	system	center
influence	election	educate	elect
similarity	train	elementary	similar
central	tuition	local	private

1. Some words in French are very _____ to words in English (for example, the French word *assister,* and English verb *to assist*). But often the meanings of these words are very different.

2. In the U.S. education in the public schools is free; in _____ schools, however, you have to pay tuition.

3. Students who know very little English usually begin in the _____ class. After a semester, they can then go to another class.

4. The education _____s of France and the U.S. are very different. In France the government controls all the schools. In the U.S. each small community controls its own schools.

5. London has a good system of _____ transport. There are buses and subways which take you to all parts of the city. The city government controls the transport system.

6. My soccer season begins next month. I started to _____ for it three weeks ago. I run three miles every day.

7. Our parents have a great _____ on us. We learn a lot from them.

8. There is going to be a(n) _____ here next year. The people of the country will be able to choose a new government.

9. A large company wants to move into our part of the city. It wants to destroy a lot of houses and build a large factory. However, the people of the _____ are not in agreement with the plan. They don't want a dirty, noisy factory near their homes.

10. The movie houses downtown are very expensive, but our _____ theater gets good movies and only costs $2. You can walk there too!

PART C

quality (noun)

> DEFINITION   the quality of something: how good or how bad it is
>
> EXAMPLES   1. This television is very expensive, but a lot of people buy it. Its *quality* is very good. People don't have many problems with this type of television.
> 2. I like the *quality* of this furniture. The work and the materials are very good.

to **entertain** (verb)
entertaining (adjective)

> DEFINITION   to entertain people: to make them happy with songs, funny or exciting stories, and so on
>
> EXAMPLES   1. On long flights, airlines *entertain* their passengers with movies and stereo music.
> 2. The movie which we saw last night was very *entertaining*. It didn't examine any serious questions, but it was funny. I enjoyed it.

to **attract** (verb)
attractive (adjective)

> DEFINITION   to attract people: to cause people to like you; to cause people to come to a place

EXAMPLES
1. Colorado *attracts* large numbers of people every winter. They go there to ski and to enjoy other winter sports.
2. Maria is a very *attractive* girl. She's pleasant and pretty, and she wears nice clothes.

audience (noun)

DEFINITION the audience: the people who are listening to something (like a concert) or watching something (like a film)

EXAMPLES
1. The new *Star Journey* movie is attracting large *audiences* in many cities. It is very popular.
2. The *audience* really liked the concert. At the end, they stood and applauded for five minutes!

fault (noun)

DEFINITION a fault: a mistake (We often use the word in this way: X is the fault of Y. This means Y caused X [X is something bad].)

EXAMPLES
1. The car accident was my *fault*. I did not stop at a red light!
2. Our plane was late, but it was not the *fault* of the airline. The weather was very bad. No planes could leave for eight hours.

to lack (verb)
lack (noun)

DEFINITION to lack something: not to have something that you need or not to have enough of it

EXAMPLES
1. Japan *lacks* oil and other things. It depends on other countries for them.
2. The flowers died through *lack* of water.

to criticize (verb)
critic (noun)

DEFINITION to criticize people or things: to mention the faults that they have
a critic: a person who criticizes

EXAMPLES
1. The television program which I saw last night *criticized* the government. According to the program, the government is spending too much money.
2. This writer is a *critic* of the government. He does not agree with many of the things which the government does.

Now read this paragraph and answer the questions about it.

1	Television in the U.S. gives people the choice of many different
2	programs on many different channels. However, many people today
3	are criticizing the quality of the programs. According to these crit-
4	ics, there are too many programs that only entertain; there are not
5	enough interesting programs that give information about the world
6	around us. Perhaps the lack of serious programs is the fault of the
7	commercial television system, not the fault of the people who own
8	or who control the television stations. Television in the U.S. de-
9	pends on money from people who advertise their products on televi-
10	sion. Therefore, television stations need to attract advertisers. The
11	programs which attract advertisers are, of course, the programs
12	which have large audiences. And the programs which attract large
13	audiences are usually programs with lots of entertainment and
14	action. Programs about serious subjects, for example, medicine, sci-
15	ence, or history, are not very popular, so advertisers do not buy
16	commercial time during programs like these. The commercial sys-
17	tem, therefore, has a great influence on the kind of programs that
18	television stations decide to show.

1. T F Everyone is happy with the kind of programs on tele-   Line(s) _____
vision in the U.S.

2. T F For everyone, there are enough television programs   Line(s) _____
about science, history, medicine, and other serious
subjects.

3. T F The writer does not criticize the people who own or   Line(s) _____
control the television stations.

4. T F Television in the U.S. depends on money from the   Line(s) _____
government.

5. Why do television stations like to have popular programs?   Line(s) _____
  a. The stations can buy popular entertainment programs at
     low prices.
  b. The stations can make a lot of money from the commercial
     time that they sell to advertisers.
  c. Stations have to pay a lot of money to the people who make
     programs about medicine or science.

6. T F The commercial system has an effect on the quality of   Line(s) _____
the programs on television.

PART D

society (noun)
social (adjective)

DEFINITION society: a (large) group of people who live together in one country and who usually have their own language and rules for life

EXAMPLES 1. Sometimes different *societies* have different *social* rules. In the U.S., for example, you can go to a party late (30–45 minutes), but not too late (3 hours).
2. Some scientists study *society*. They want to discover the rules which influence the actions of people in *society*.

to **change** (verb)
change (noun)

DEFINITION to change: to become different
to change something: to make it different

EXAMPLES 1. The weather is going to *change*. The sun is shining, but I see a lot of dark clouds in the west. They are coming in this direction.
2. Carlos went back to his old university. He saw many *changes*. For example, there was a new gymnasium and swimming pool, and there were two new science buildings.

divorce (noun)
divorced (adjective)

DEFINITION to get a divorce or to get divorced: to end a marriage

EXAMPLES 1. Married people sometimes are very unhappy with each other, so they *get divorced.*
2. *Divorce* is not possible in some countries. The government does not allow it.

to **satisfy** (verb)
satisfied (adjective)
dissatisfied (adjective)

DEFINITION to satisfy people: to give them the things that they want

EXAMPLES 1. Ali is very *satisfied* with his new apartment. It is clean, very comfortable, and near the university.
2. This job does not really *satisfy* me. The work is too easy, and it's not interesting. I am really *dissatisfied* with it.

recent (adjective)
recently (adverb)

DEFINITION   recent: describes something which happened a short time ago, not long ago

EXAMPLES   1. For a new passport, you need a *recent* photograph. It cannot be a photograph of you four or five or more years ago.
         2. Mike: Hi, Bob. Do you have any news of Steve?
              Bob: Yes. I talked to him *recently* on the phone. I think it was last week. He's doing well. But he misses his friends here.

conservative (adjective)

DEFINITION   conservative people: people who do not like fast change

EXAMPLES   1. Old people often are *conservative*. They don't like to see big changes in the world around them.
         2. Young children are often very *conservative* with food. They don't like to try new food.

pressure (noun)

DEFINITION   pressure: how much something pushes against another thing
to put pressure on people: to use strong influence on people to make them do what you want

EXAMPLES   1. You need some air in the front right tire of your car. The *pressure* should be 27 not 20.
         2. A computer company called John yesterday and said, "We have a job for you and we want you in our company. We will double your present salary." They only gave him forty-eight hours to decide. They are putting a lot of *pressure* on him.

common (adjective)

DEFINITION   common: describes something that happens often or something that you see *often*

EXAMPLES   1. Many foreign students become homesick during their first months in the U.S. This is a *common* problem.
         2. In northern states of the U.S. it is very cold in winter. Temperatures of 0°F are quite *common*.

Now read this paragraph and answer the questions about it.

1   Society in the U.S. and Europe is changing a lot; things that
2 were unusual some years ago are now quite common. For example,
3 forty or fifty years ago not many people got divorced. Society put
4 pressure on people who were having marriage problems, and, as a
5 result, they stayed married. Often the problems that made them
6 unhappy and dissatisfied continued, but few people decided to get
7 divorced. Today, however, divorce is a solution which many people,
8 even conservative people, accept. According to recent studies in the
9 U.S., West Germany, and Switzerland, one out of every four mar-
10 riages will fail and end in divorce. What is causing this increase in
11 the number of divorces? Is the number of people who are having
12 marriage difficulties increasing? Or is the number of people who
13 accept divorce increasing?

1. T F   Forty or fifty years ago, divorce was not very common   Line(s) _____
in Europe and the U.S.

2. T F   The number of divorces in the U.S. and Europe is   Line(s) _____
increasing.

3. T F   In the U.S., Switzerland, and West Germany, 50% of   Line(s) _____
marriages will end in divorce.

4. Why were there not so many divorces in the past?   Line(s) _____
  a. People did not have problems in their marriages.
  b. There was social pressure to stay married.
  c. Many people were unhappy and dissatisfied.

5. T F   The writer gives us a clear answer to the question,   Line(s) _____
Why is the number of divorces increasing?

6. T F   The studies that show an increase in divorce are from   Line(s) _____
fifteen or twenty years ago.

PART E

free (adjective)
freedom (noun)

DEFINITION   free describes something that doesn't cost anything; it also
describes people who can do and think the things they want.
(No other person controls them.)

EXAMPLES   1. Blacks in the U.S. won their *freedom* in the 1860s. Before
that time they were slaves.

2. Elementary school is *free* in the U.S. You don't have to pay for it.

right (noun)

DEFINITION to have the right to do something: to be able to do it (the law allows you)

EXAMPLES
1. In the U.S. everyone has the *right* to follow the religion they choose.
2. Freedom of speech means the *right* to express opinions and ideas.

official (adjective)

DEFINITION official: describes something which comes from the person or people who have the right to control it

EXAMPLES
1. English and French are the two *official* languages of Canada. You can use French or English for all jobs in the government.
2. The news about the plane accident is now *official*. The airline informed the newspaper about it thirty minutes ago.

to **discuss** (verb)
discussion (noun)

DEFINITION to discuss something: to talk about it with other people who perhaps do not agree with your ideas

EXAMPLES
1. John teaches at the university here. A university in another part of the U.S. offered him a good job. He is going to *discuss* it with his wife. He wants to get her opinion. Then he will decide about the job.
2. In the U.S. there is a lot of *discussion* about the future of hospitals. Some people want to keep private hospitals. Many others want free public hospitals. Each side tries to win public support for its ideas.

excellent (adjective)

DEFINITION excellent: very good

EXAMPLES
1. I really enjoyed my vacation in Paris last summer. The hotel was *excellent:* The food was first class, and my room was very comfortable.
2. Jane is an *excellent* student. She receives A's in all her classes.

constitution (noun)

DEFINITION   a constitution: the laws which the government of a country must follow

EXAMPLES   1. According to the U.S. *Constitution,* there must be a presidential election every four years.
                 2. In a *constitution* a country describes the system of government it wants.

to **protect** (verb)

DEFINITION   to protect people or things: to keep them from danger, to keep them safe

EXAMPLES   1. The police *protect* us from people who break the law.
                 2. In West Germany and Belgium, people have to wear seat belts in cars. A seat belt can *protect* you in an accident.

Now read this passage and answer the questions about it.

1   In public schools in the U.S., students do not have classes in
2   religion. What is the reason for this? To answer this question we
3   have to look at the history of the people who first came to America
4   from Europe in the seventeenth and eighteenth centuries.
5   Many of these people who left Europe were hoping for free-
6   dom in their new country. Many of them had religious ideas
7   which the government or the official church of their native coun-
8   try did not accept. In their native lands they had no freedom. In
9   the eyes of the government and the official church, their religious
10   ideas were dangerous. The government took their money and
11   houses, put them in prison, and sometimes killed them. The law
12   gave them no protection.
13   The people who wrote the U.S. Constitution at the end of the
14   eighteenth century decided to protect the rights of every person
15   who lived in the country. One of the first rights they protected was
16   freedom of religion. They decided not to have an official religion for
17   the country. There had to be no connection between the govern-
18   ment of the country and any religion. As a result, public schools
19   could not teach religion.
20   Today, however, there is a lot of discussion about religion in
21   public schools. Many people want to change the system and have
22   Bible classes and prayers in schools. However for many other
23   people, the Bible is still not a suitable subject for the public schools
24   of a country which has a great number of very different religions.

1. T F   Public school students in the United States learn the   Line(s) _____
          rules of their own religions in school.

2. T F   Many of the people who came to America before 1800   Line(s) _____
          did not have religious freedom in their native lands.

3. T F   The U.S. Constitution made Christianity the official   Line(s) _____
          religion of the country.

4. T F   For the people who wrote the U.S. Constitution, free-   Line(s) _____
          dom of religion was an important right.

5. T F   The education in the public schools is excellent and   Line(s) _____
          needs no changes. Everyone is in agreement about
          this.

Exercises for Parts C, D, and E

SAME OR DIFFERENT?

Read the two sentences in each example. Do they express the same ideas, or do they express different ideas? Write *S* for sentences with the same ideas; write *D* for sentences with different ideas.

Remember: You can express the **same** idea with **different** words and **different** grammar!

1. a. My brother is dissatisfied with his job.   _____
   b. My brother really enjoys his job.

2. a. The quality of many teachers in U.S. public schools is excellent.   _____
   b. There are many bad public school teachers in the U.S.

3. a. The television program about Russia attracted a big audience   _____
      last week.
   b. A lot of people watched the television program about Russia
      last week.

4. a. In our English class yesterday we had an excellent discussion   _____
      about education in the U.S.
   b. In our English class yesterday we read a very interesting pas-
      sage about education in the U.S.

5. a. The red coat which Maria bought last week really suits her.   _____
   b. Maria looks very attractive in the red coat which she bought
      last week.

6. a. Recently I received news from home about a friend who just got   _____
   married.
   b. A recent letter from home gave me the news of a friend who
   just got married.

7. a. In some countries there is a great lack of food.   _____
   b. Some countries do not have enough food for their people.

8. a. The accident that happened to us on the way home last night   _____
   was not my fault.
   b. I caused the accident that happened to us on the way home last
   night.

9. a. John visited his old university, and he saw a lot of changes   _____
   there.
   b. On a visit to his old university, John saw many differences between the university which he knew and the university now.

10. a. In winter a hat and gloves will protect you from the cold.   _____
    b. A hat and gloves will help to keep you warm in winter.

11. a. In the 1960s, many African countries won their freedom from   _____
    Great Britain and France.
    b. In the 1960s, Great Britain and France controlled the govern-
    ment of many African countries.

12. a. In a free country a person who is not satisfied with the gov-   _____
    ernment has the right to criticize that government.
    b. In a free country a person who is dissatisfied with the govern-
    ment cannot criticize that government.

EXPECTATIONS

Read the first sentence in each of these examples. Think about the ideas in it. Then
choose the sentence or sentences that can follow it.

1. Many people in the U.S. are worried about the quality of new teachers in the
   public schools.
   a. According to these people, education courses in the universities are excellent, and they attract very intelligent students.
   b. They criticize the university programs that train the teachers.
   c. According to them, teachers often lack suitable training for the classes
   they will teach.

2. The number of people who get divorced is increasing in many countries.

   a. People are satisfied with their marriages.
   b. According to recent research, modern life puts a lot of pressure on marriages.
   c. Twenty years ago, one out of five marriages ended in divorce; today, one out of ten marriages ends in divorce.

3. My brother is a very conservative person.

   a. He likes new ideas, and he criticizes people who cannot accept changes in society.
   b. He is not happy with the changes that he sees in U.S. public education today.
   c. My sister is similar. She loves to travel to new places and meet new people.

4. Commercial television stations do not show many programs about serious subjects.

   a. Entertainment programs are not very popular.
   b. Programs about science, history, or social problems do not attract the large audiences that advertisers like.
   c. The stations depend on money from advertisers, who like to buy time for commercials on serious programs.

5. In some countries people do not have real freedom.

   a. They do not have the right to criticize the government of their country.
   b. There are laws which protect them from the police and from the government.
   c. Sometimes they cannot even receive letters and newspapers from other countries.

6. Today many people in the U.S. are not satisfied with the government.

   a. They are criticizing some new laws which the government is making.
   b. According to these critics, the government is trying to solve many serious problems.
   c. According to them, the new laws which the government is planning will limit our freedom.

7. Today in the U.S. there is a lot of discussion about television; according to some people, the poor quality of television programs is the fault of the advertisers.

   a. They are only interested in the size of the audience which the program will attract.
   b. They only advertise their products on excellent programs.
   c. According to these people, television companies have little influence on the quality of the programs.

8. This apartment does not really suit us.
   a. It is too far away from the university.
   b. The rent is very high.
   c. We do not have enough room to entertain people.

VOCABULARY QUIZ

Choose the correct word for each empty space. Use each word only once.

excellent	common	satisfied	change
official	protect	criticize	society
similar	right	recently	fault
entertaining	attractive	conservative	lack
quality	audience	discussion	pressure

1. I am reading a very _____ book at the moment. It's about a student who travels around the world. I am really enjoying the book.

2. Many people are dissatisfied with the _____ of teachers in the public schools. According to these people, the teachers do not get good training and do not know enough about their subjects.

3. That is a very _____ dress that Maria is wearing. She looks really good in it.

4. There was a very large _____ at the new film last night. The big theater was full, and I could not see one empty seat.

5. We arrived at the airport too late for our plane. It was my _____. I did not get up early enough that morning. My friends were angry with me.

6. I am very _____ with my new car. It's very comfortable, and it does not use a lot of gasoline.

7. _____ is changing. Twenty years ago, divorce was not common; today, 40% of new marriages end in divorce.

8. John looks very tired. He is under a lot of _____ at his job. He has to finish an important piece of work this week; a lot of money depends on this. But the work is difficult and is going very slowly.

9. *Get* is a very _____ word in English. People use it in almost every conversation.

10. Twenty years ago, there was no sex education in schools. Now there are classes in sex education in many schools. Some _____ people are against these new classes. They criticize the classes, the teachers, and the schools.

11. In our history class, there is usually a lot of _____. The professor is not the only person who talks. Many of the students talk about the things that we are studying.

12. That Chinese restaurant is very good. We had a really _____ meal there last week.

13. People who play American football have to wear special clothes which _____ them. Without these clothes, the game can be very dangerous.

14. Who decides the subjects that children study in schools? According to some people, only parents have the _____ to decide this. The school must not decide this.

15. Unlike some other countries, the United States has no _____ religion for the country. The Constitution does not allow this.

Main Reading

Pre-Reading Exercises

VOCABULARY IN CONTEXT

Read each example to the end. Pay attention to the words in italics. Think about them. They are words that you already know. Then try to guess the meaning of the new word (in boldface type). The words in italics will help you.

1. In the U.S., 70% of people who **graduate** *from* high school *go to a college or university. But* in Great Britain, only 20% of *eighteen-year-old* students in high school go on to university.

    To graduate means _____.
    a. to like
    b. to finish
    c. to study

2. Many *conservative* people *disagree* with some of the things that their children study in school. *For example, they* **object to** the classes in sex education that some schools give. They *also* **object to** schoolbooks which criticize past governments of the United States. *And they don't like* books which mention divorce or mothers who have jobs outside the home.

   To object to means _____.
   a. to go to
   b. to accept
   c. to be against

3. Many people in the U.S. are *worried* about education. *Some* are *worried* about the quality of education. In their opinion, their children are not learning enough. *Others* are **concerned** about the things that their children learn. They do not like many of these new things.

   To be concerned about means to be _____.
   a. worried
   b. happy
   c. satisfied

4. Sometimes teachers *cannot control* students who are not interested in class and who *do not want* to learn. These students **disturb** the classes. *As a result, other students* who are serious about their studies *cannot learn.*

   To disturb means _____.
   a. not to attend classes every day
   b. to improve the quality of classes a great deal
   c. to stop classes from doing what they have to do

5. Schools are *failing* to teach students even the very *elementary* things that a person has to know. *As a result,* some students are leaving school who have *problems* with **basic** things in math and reading.

   Basic things mean _____.
   a. things that are very difficult
   b. things that are connected with science
   c. things that you have to learn first

6. Abdullah is very happy. He **received** a *letter* from his family yesterday. It contained a check. *Now* he *has* enough money for the last six weeks of the semester.

   To receive means _____.
   a. to write
   b. to get
   c. to send

7. Ten years ago the government began to *spend* a *lot* of *money* for *education,* *but* the number of high school graduates who cannot read is *increasing,* not **decreasing.**

> To decrease means ____.
>
> a. to fall
> b. to improve
> c. to become more

8. I had a car accident last night. According to the police it was clearly *my fault.* I drove into the back of a car which stopped. In my opinion, however, the other driver also **was to blame.** He *stopped* at a *green* traffic light.

> To be to blame for something means ____.
>
> a. to cause something bad
> b. to criticize something
> c. to agree with something

9. Some students **behave** very *badly* in class. They *make* a lot of *noise.* They *pay no attention* to their teachers. They *don't want to work,* and they *make life difficult* for other students.

> To behave means ____.
>
> a. to work
> b. to listen
> c. to act

10. There was an important *meeting* for all foreign students yesterday. Almost all the students **attended** the *meeting.* Only one or two *were not there.*

> To attend means ____.
>
> a. to be present
> b. to forget
> c. to talk about

EXPECTATIONS

Let's try to get ideas of the passage which we are going to read. Read the title carefully and think about it. Now read the ideas below. We can expect some of them in our passage. Others are ideas we do not expect. Choose the ideas that you expect and mark them YES. Choose the ideas which you don't expect and mark them NO. Here's an example:

1. U.S. public schools are very successful.   YES NO

Well, the title asks, "What's *wrong* with them," so we expect to hear bad things, *not* good things, about U.S. schools. So you mark NO!

Now do the following exercises yourself:

2. There are both differences and similarities between U.S. schools and the schools of other countries.   YES   NO

3. There are a number of problems in U.S. public education.   YES   NO

4. There are many things which you cannot get from an education in a private school.   YES   NO

5. The passage will give us the opinions of critics of the U.S. public education system.   YES   NO

6. The passage will examine some of the failures of the U.S. public schools.   YES   NO

7. Parents are quite happy with the education that their children are receiving in the public schools.   YES   NO

8. Most people are very satisfied with the public schools.   YES   NO

9. The passage will show us the excellent results that the public schools produce.   YES   NO

10. Parents are worried about some things in the public schools.   YES   NO

Now let's do something which is a little different. Let's read some sentences of the passage, and then let's stop and think. We are still trying to develop *Expectations*.

Read the first paragraph of the passage, the *introduction*. In a passage like this, a good introduction can help the reader a lot. Now choose the ideas which you expect in the rest of the passage, and choose the ideas which you don't expect.

1. There is one main problem in the U.S. public schools.   YES   NO

2. The passage will examine the ideas of the people who criticize the public schools. These ideas will be very different.   YES   NO

3. The critics of the public schools have very different opinions and will not agree with each other.   YES   NO

4. In the passage we will read the opinions of parents who are satisfied with U.S. public schools.   YES   NO

Sometimes the beginning of a paragraph will give you an idea of the things which the paragraph will say. Let's try to develop expectations for the ideas in paragraphs.

Look at Paragraph 2. Read the first sentence (lines 9–10). Now choose the ideas that you expect and the ideas that you don't expect in this paragraph.

1. Some parents do not help their children with their school work.   YES NO

2. Students are having difficulty with basic math and reading.   YES NO

3. Students who leave school do not know enough.   YES NO

Look at Paragraph 3. Read the first sentence (lines 21–22). Now choose the ideas that you expect and the ideas that you don't expect in this paragraph.

1. The government spends a lot of money for good school buildings and teachers.   YES NO

2. Teachers are not good, and classes are sometimes very large.   YES NO

3. Many schoolchildren don't even know the name of the U.S. president.   YES NO

Look at Paragraph 5. Read the first sentence (lines 54–55). Think about your ideas for Paragraph 2. Now choose the ideas which you can expect and the ideas which you don't expect in this paragraph.

1. According to this group of people, their children are not learning enough.   YES NO

2. Schoolchildren are not learning to read well.   YES NO

The introduction talks about *disagreement* between people who are dissatisfied with the public schools. Read only the first sentence of each paragraph. Look for the section of the passage that talks about one group of critics. Then look for the section that talks about the other group.

1. The first group of people who are dissatisfied with the public schools   Paragraph(s) _____

2. The other group of people who are dissatisfied with the public schools   Paragraph(s) _____

Leave this exercise now. Don't try to correct it now. Wait. Begin to read the complete passage and answer the questions about it on pages 97–100.

U.S. Public Schools: What's Wrong with Them?

1　　　　There are many people in the U.S. today who are not satisfied
2　　with the education that their children are receiving in the public
3　　schools. They are very worried about a number of developments
4　　that are taking place in the schools. However, not all of these
5　　people are worried about the same things. In fact, they often do not
6　　agree about the problems in public education. So what is attracting
7　　the attention of these people? Are they correct? Is public education
8　　in the U.S. in serious trouble?

2

9　　　　One group of people is concerned about the quality of the edu-
10　　cation which young people are receiving. According to these par-
11　　ents, their children are not learning enough in school, and some
12　　researchers agree with them. For example, according to recent
13　　studies, the number of high school students who cannot read is
14　　increasing not decreasing. Also the number of students who have
15　　difficulty with simple mathematics is increasing. Even students
16　　who graduate from high school and go to college show a depressing
17　　lack of knowledge. In a geography class at a large university, 40%
18　　of the students could not find London on a map, 41% could not find
19　　Los Angeles, and almost 9% could not find the city where they
20　　were attending college.

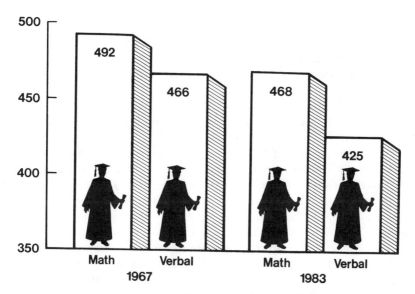

SAT Score Averages: College-Bound Seniors

3

There are a number of possible reasons for the increase in the number of students who are not receiving a good basic education. First, classes are sometimes too large. In some city schools, for example, there are often between forty and fifty students in a class. Second, there are many teachers who do not know enough about the subjects that they are teaching. The college programs which train future teachers are not always good and do not always attract the top students. But the problems are not always the fault of the teachers or the education system. Often students who do not want to learn behave badly and disturb the classes. As a result, the students who are really interested in their school subjects cannot learn much in these classes. Finally, according to some people, television is also to blame for the lack of success of the public schools. Young people often watch six or more hours of television a day. They do not take time for their homework. They grow to depend on television for entertainment and information, and, therefore, they cannot see any reason for reading in this modern world. All the entertainment and information they want comes from the television, not from books.

4

Clearly there are a number of different reasons for the poor quality of education that some students are receiving in U.S. public schools. Any solutions to this problem will have to answer at least four questions. How can we bring down the number of students in a class? How can we improve the quality of teachers and teacher training? How can we solve the problem of students who disturb classes? How can we fight against the negative influence of television? However, we do not have a great deal of time to find the answers to these questions. Already, as a result of their dissatisfaction with the schools, some concerned parents are taking their children out of public schools and are sending them to private schools. The number of students who are attending private schools is increasing, and the public schools are losing many excellent students.

5

A second group of people is dissatisfied with the public schools for very different reasons. These people usually have very conservative beliefs about life. They do not like the changes which they see every day in American society, and they disagree with many of the ideas which their children hear and read about in school. For example, they object to the sex education classes that some schools give. For them, sex education is not a suitable subject for schools. They also object to schoolbooks that describe the lives of mothers who work outside the home or of parents who are divorced. They do not like history books which criticize the U.S. for mistakes which

64 the U.S. made in the past. They even object to dictionaries that
65 define one or two dirty words.
66 These people have a solution to the problems of unsuitable 6
67 books and classes. Their solution is not to take their children out of
68 the public schools. They put pressure on the people on the local
69 school boards. They also elect to the school boards people who share
70 their ideas. Then the school boards will stop sex education and the
71 use of schoolbooks that do not agree with their ideas about life.
72 There are, however, many other people who completely dis- 7
73 agree with the actions of these conservatives. "They are trying to
74 limit our freedom. We must protect our children's right to learn
75 about many different ideas," these parents say. Thus, in the U.S.
76 today there is a lot of discussion about very important questions in
77 education. Who will decide school programs and books? Does the
78 government have the right to decide? Do the school boards have
79 the right to decide? Can teachers decide? Do only parents have the
80 right to decide the things that their children learn in school?
81 Watch the television and read news magazines; you will hear a lot
82 of different answers to these questions.

We can divide this passage into two sections and read it section by section.

Section I (Paragraphs 1–4)

MAIN IDEAS CHECK

Here are the main ideas for the paragraphs in this section. Write the correct paragraph number opposite each main idea.

PARAGRAPH   IDEA

_____   In the public schools there are a number of different problems
                 that we must solve soon.

_____   According to one group of critics, students are not learning
                 enough in the public schools.

_____   In the U.S. there is general dissatisfaction with public school
                 education.

_____   There are a number of reasons for the failure of students to learn
                 enough in school.

1. T F Only a small number of people are unhappy about the   Line(s) _____
quality of public school education.

2. T F Not everyone agrees about the problems which exist   Line(s) _____
in the public schools.

3. According to the passage, what does educational research   Line(s) _____
show?
   a. The number of high school students who cannot read is decreasing.
   b. The number of high school students is increasing.
   c. More high school students are having problems with reading and math.

4. Public school students are not learning enough. According to   Line(s) _____
the passage, the possible reasons are: (*Check all the answers
that are good!*)
   a. There are not enough schools.
   b. Students who are not interested disturb the class.
   c. Teachers are not always good.
   d. The reading and math programs are very difficult.
   e. At the university, top students often don't want to become
teachers.
   f. Students do not watch enough television.

5. T F For the writer, the problems in the public schools are   Line(s) _____
the fault of the education system only.

6. T F According to the passage, private schools are becom-   Line(s) _____
ing more popular with American parents.

Section II (Paragraphs 5–7)

MAIN IDEAS CHECK

Here are the main ideas for the paragraphs in this section. Write the correct paragraph
numbers opposite each main idea.

PARAGRAPH   IDEA

_____   In the U.S. today there is a lot of discussion and disagreement
about education in the public schools.

_____ People want to change school programs through the school boards.

_____ There is dissatisfaction among some conservative people with some of the ideas and subjects that schools teach.

COMPREHENSION CHECK

1. T F A second group of people is worried about the same   Line(s) _____
        problem—the poor quality of education which their
        children are receiving.

2. Why is the second group of critics dissatisfied with the public   Line(s) _____
   schools?
   a. Their children are not getting enough classes in sex educa-
      tion and social and political ideas.
   b. Their children have teachers who do not have good training.
   c. The schools are teaching ideas and using books that they do
      not like.

3. T F The second group of people is also beginning to take   Line(s) _____
        their children out of the public schools.

4. T F The conservative critics of schools can influence the   Line(s) _____
        choice of ideas which their children hear in school.

5. How do other people feel about the ideas and actions of this   Line(s) _____
   second group of people?
   a. Most people in America agree with them.
   b. A large number of people do not accept their ideas or
      actions.
   c. No one criticizes their ideas or actions.

6. T F Only the school boards and teachers have the right to   Line(s) _____
        decide about schoolbooks and programs. Everyone in
        the U.S. agrees with this.

Now go back and look at the answers to your Expectation exercises. How correct were your expectations?

Now do the paragraph reading exercise on the next page.

PARAGRAPH READING

These sentences form a paragraph, but they are not in the correct order. Put the sentences into their correct order. The first sentence is already in its correct place.

__1__   At present in the U.S. there is a lot of discussion and disagreement about public school education.

_____   They also want to stop the use of schoolbooks with political or social ideas they do not like.

_____   However, there are many other people who do not share the ideas of this group.

_____   They are, for example, against sex education in the schools, but they want religion as a subject.

_____   Most educators agree with the ideas of this second group of people.

_____   One group of conservative people in this discussion does not like many of the modern ideas that their children hear in school.

_____   According to these people, children have the right to learn about many different political, social, and religious ideas in school.

_____   These conservative people are using their influence to change school programs in some parts of the country.

Disaster at Sea

Grammar for this unit: Comparisons
Passive sentences

You will find information and practice on these grammar points in
Appendix 1, Unit 4.

Vocabulary Study and Preparatory Reading

PART A

to **warn** (verb)
warning (noun)

DEFINITION   to warn people: to tell them about something dangerous

EXAMPLES   1. The doctor *warned* the man about his health. "You smoke
too much," he said. "You get no exercise, and you eat too
much. You are going to have problems."
2. There was a weather *warning* on the radio this morning.
We are going to get 20 inches of snow in the next twenty-
four hours.

to **prevent** (verb)

DEFINITION   to prevent something: to stop it before it can happen

EXAMPLES   1. We planned to go to New York last weekend. But we did
not go. The weather *prevented* us. We got 15 inches of
snow, and we could not drive to the airport.
2. I wanted to go to a movie last night. But my work *prevented* me. I had to study for a test.

disaster (noun)

DEFINITION a disaster: a very bad thing that happens to someone

EXAMPLES
1. In 1981 a small plane hit a Boeing 727 over San Diego, California. More than 200 people died. It was one of the worst plane *disasters* in U.S. history.
2. After the accident, the government made new rules that will prevent other *disasters* like the one in San Diego.

to ignore (verb)

DEFINITION to ignore people or things: *not* to pay attention to them

EXAMPLES
1. The car driver had an accident. He *ignored* a stop sign, and he hit another car.
2. Maria was angry with Carlos yesterday. At the party last night she did not say a word to him. She *ignored* him all evening.

to inquire (verb)
inquiry (noun)

DEFINITION to inquire about people or things: to ask for information about them

to hold an inquiry into something: to have meetings that study the causes of something (usually something bad)

EXAMPLES
1. I want to fly to New York next month. I'm going to *inquire* about the price of a ticket. Then I will decide.
2. After the plane accident, the government held an *inquiry* into the causes of the disaster. The *inquiry* blamed the people who worked on the plane's engines. They made mistakes.

condition (noun)

DEFINITION the condition of people or things: how they are at a certain time

EXAMPLES
1. The *conditions* for driving are really bad tonight. There is a lot of ice and snow on the roads. The wind is blowing hard, and you cannot see well.
2. John is in the hospital, but his *condition* is not serious. He will be able to come home tomorrow.

department (noun)

DEFINITION   a department: a special part of a government, of a school or university, or of a store (Each department has its own special work.)

EXAMPLES   1. *Department* stores sell lots of different things. For example, they have a *department* for men's clothes, a *department* for women's clothes, a *department* for furniture, and so on.

    2. Many countries have a *Department* of Education. The people in this *department* control the schools of the country.

to report (verb)

DEFINITION   to report something: to give news of something which happened to people who are interested or to people who need to know

EXAMPLES   1. In the U.S. you have to *report* all the money that you earn to the government. Then you pay tax on the money.

    2. Someone stole Omar's car. He *reported* it to the police. They found his car yesterday, and he's going to get it back today.

Now read this passage and answer the questions about it.

1   Some years ago industries had more freedom than they have
2   now, and they did not need to be as careful as they must today.
3   They did not need to worry a lot about the safety of the new prod-
4   ucts that they developed. They did not have to pay much attention
5   to the health and safety of the people who worked for them. Often
6   new products were dangerous for the people who used them; often
7   conditions in the work place had very bad effects on the health of
8   the workers.
9   Of course sometimes there were real disasters which attracted
10 the attention of governments and which showed the need for
11 changes. Also scientists who were doing research into the health of
12 workers sometimes produced information which governments could
13 not ignore. At such times, there were inquiries into the causes of
14 the disaster or the problems. New safety rules were often intro-
15 duced as a result of these inquiries; however, the new rules came
16 too late to protect the people who died or who became seriously ill.
17   Today many governments have special departments which pro-

18 tect customers and workers. In the U.S., for example, there is a
19 department which tests new airplanes and gives warnings about
20 possible problems. It also makes the rules that aircraft producers
21 must follow. Another department controls the foods and drugs that
22 companies sell. A third department looks at the places where
23 people work, and then reports any companies that are breaking
24 laws which protect the health and safety of workers. Of course, new
25 government departments and new laws cannot prevent every acci-
26 dent or illness, but they are having some good results. Our work
27 places are safer and cleaner than before. The planes and cars which
28 we use for travel are better. Producers are thinking more about the
29 safety and health of the people who buy and use their products.

1. T F In the past companies were not as concerned as they   Line(s) _____
         are now about the safety of their products.

2. T F In the past cars and planes were not as safe as they   Line(s) _____
         are today.

3. T F Today there are not as many safety laws as in the   Line(s) _____
         past.

4. T F Today a drug company can sell any new drug that it   Line(s) _____
         develops.

5. T F In the past many governments and companies were   Line(s) _____
         less careful about customer protection than they are
         today.

6. T F In the U.S. the same department tests new drugs *and*   Line(s) _____
         new airplanes.

PART B

to **save** (verb)

DEFINITION to save people: to take them out of danger
            to save time or money: not to use it for one thing but to keep
                                   it for some other thing

EXAMPLES 1. After the accident, the driver lost a lot of blood. But the
             doctors in the hospital were able to *save* him.
          2. I go shopping once a week. It *saves* time. I buy all the food
             which I need for a week. Then I don't need to waste time
             with other trips to the supermarket.

to **sink** (irregular verb)
sank, sunk

> DEFINITION to sink: to go under the water, to fall to the bottom of the sea
>
> EXAMPLES 1. Wood does not *sink* in water. It stays on top of the water.
> 2. The car fell off the bridge into the river. It *sank* quickly, but the driver was able to get out.

to **survive** (verb)
survivor (noun)

> DEFINITION to survive: to continue to live after great danger
>
> EXAMPLES 1. The ship sank, but a lot of people *survived*. Another ship pulled them out of the water.
> 2. There was a very bad accident on the highway last night. A car went off a bridge into the river. Everyone in the car died. There were no *survivors*.

brave (adjective)

> DEFINITION a brave person: a person who goes into danger (usually for other people)
>
> EXAMPLES 1. This man is very *brave*. He saved a child from a house that was on fire.
> 2. Last year a man crossed the Atlantic alone in a small boat. In my opinion, you have to be very *brave* to do something like that.

wave (noun)

> DEFINITION a wave: a hill of water which moves on the sea
>
> EXAMPLES 1. I don't want to go swimming today. It's dangerous. The *waves* are too high.
> 2. A large *wave* hit the boat and filled it with water. The boat began to sink.

storm (noun)
stormy (adjective)

> DEFINITION a storm: bad weather with high winds and rain or snow, and with high waves on the sea
>
> EXAMPLES 1. There was a bad winter *storm* last week. Twenty inches of snow fell in a day. No one could use the roads, so the university closed for two days.
> 2. In a *storm* in the Atlantic the waves can be 50 or 60 feet high.

rough (adjective)
calm (adjective)

DEFINITION a rough sea: a stormy sea with high waves
a calm sea: the *opposite* of a rough sea

EXAMPLES 1. There was a storm yesterday. Today there is no wind, but the sea is still very *rough*.
2. I like to travel by boat, but only on a *calm* sea.

to **risk** (verb)
risk (noun)

DEFINITION to risk something: to put it in danger

EXAMPLES 1. People who drive fast on ice and snow *are risking* their own lives and the lives of other people on the road.
2. Mike is a very careful driver. He never takes *risks*.

Now read this passage and answer the questions about it.

1   Along the coast of the United States, the U.S. Coast Guard
2 helps ships that get into difficulty at sea. The Coast Guard, like the
3 Navy, is controlled by the U.S. government. It receives the money
4 that it needs from the government; therefore its ships, planes, and
5 helicopters are very modern.
6   In Great Britain the system is very different. There are a
7 small number of men, called lifeboatmen, who go out to help ships
8 in trouble. These brave men often risk their lives, but they receive
9 no money for their work. They live in small towns on the coast, and
10 most have other jobs. The special lifeboats that they need are pro-
11 vided by the Royal National Lifeboat Institution (R.N.L.I.), a pri-
12 vate group which depends completely on money from private
13 people. The R.N.L.I. does not accept any money from the govern-
14 ment. As a result, it cannot always buy the best and most modern
15 lifeboats. For example, about ten years ago, British researchers
16 began to criticize the lifeboats which were in use at that time.
17 According to their studies, the lifeboats never sank, but they
18 turned over in certain sea conditions and stayed upside down in the
19 water. However, there was a new kind of lifeboat that did not turn
20 over. The R.N.L.I. began to buy this safer kind of boat, but it could
21 only buy one or two every year.
22   Some years ago on the southwestern coast of England, a life-
23 boat station that did not have the new type of lifeboat received a

24   radio call from a small ship that was sinking. The call came in the
25   middle of the worst storm in forty years. The sea was very rough,
26   but the lifeboat went out to try to save the men on the sinking
27   ship. Two hours later, their radio stopped, and nothing more was
28   heard from them. One day later a helicopter found the lifeboat. It
29   was lying upside down in the sea. Probably a large wave hit it and
30   turned it over. There were no survivors.
31   The news of the disaster shocked the people of Great Britain. A
32   number of people began to criticize the lifeboat system. In their
33   opinion, the U.S. system is better. "We cannot send brave men out
34   in boats which aren't safe," they said. "They need the best boats
35   which money can buy. The government must control the lifeboat
36   system." Today, however, the system remains the same.

1. T F   The U.S. lifeboat system has more money than the   Line(s) _____
           British system.

2. T F   The British lifeboat system is controlled by the   Line(s) _____
           government.

3. What happened in the storm some years ago?   Line(s) _____
   a. The lifeboat saved the people of the small ship that was
      sinking.
   b. The lifeboat could not go out. The sea was too rough.
   c. The lifeboat sank, but some of the men survived.
   d. The lifeboat turned over, and all the men died.

4. T F   The lifeboats which are used in Great Britain are not   Line(s) _____
           always safe.

5. T F   The British system needs better lifeboats.   Line(s) _____

6. T F   Everyone is satisfied with the British lifeboat system. Line(s) _____

7. T F   No one expected the kind of disaster that happened   Line(s) _____
           some years ago.

Exercises for Parts A and B

SAME OR DIFFERENT?

Read the two sentences in each example. Do they express the same ideas, or do they express different ideas? Write *S* for sentences with the same ideas; write *D* for sentences with different ideas.

Remember: You can express the **same** *ideas* with **different** *words* and **different** *grammar!*

1. a. The government did not pay any attention to warnings about the   ——
   safety of the new plane.
   b. The government ignored warnings about the safety of the new
   plane.

2. a. The sea was very calm yesterday.   ——
   b. There were high waves on the sea yesterday.

3. a. The aircraft of forty years ago were not as safe as the aircraft of   ——
   today.
   b. Today's airplanes are safer than the airplanes of forty years ago.

4. a. Carlos is in the hospital; his condition is improving.   ——
   b. Carlos is in the hospital; he is getting better.

5. a. After the accident, the survivors were taken to the hospital by   ——
   ambulance.
   b. Ambulances took the people who died in the accident to the
   hospital.

6. a. The student is making inquiries about the kind of apartments   ——
   which can be rented near the university.
   b. The student is giving information about the kind of apartments
   which can be rented near the university.

7. a. The firemen were able to bring a number of survivors out of the   ——
   burning building.
   b. The firemen were able to save some people from the burning
   building.

8. a. We could not play our soccer game; the weather was really bad.   ——
   b. The bad weather did not prevent us from playing our soccer
   game.

EXPECTATIONS

Read the first sentence in each of these examples. Think about the ideas in it. Then choose the sentence or sentences that can follow it.

1. Last summer I traveled by boat from England to France in the middle of a
   bad storm.
   a. The sea was very rough, and I became very seasick.
   b. The water was very calm, and I enjoyed the journey.
   c. The waves were very large, of course, but I enjoyed the journey.

2. The apartment that Mayumi and Maria rented was in a really bad condition.

   a. There was a large living room, a bathroom, two bedrooms, and a modern kitchen.
   b. The floors were very dirty, the refrigerator and stove did not work, and some windows were broken.
   c. It was five miles from the university.

3. No one could be saved from the ship that sank in the storm last week.

   a. The bad weather prevented lifeboats and helicopters from reaching the ship.
   b. The survivors were pulled out of the water by a helicopter from the U.S. Coast Guard.
   c. The sea conditions were the worst in twenty years, and the ship sank very fast.

4. Two or three accidents happen every week at this corner, in front of the local elementary school.

   a. Many drivers ignore the school warning sign.
   b. The city government needs to do something to prevent a really bad accident.
   c. The local school board decides the programs at the school.

5. The government held an official inquiry into the cause of the plane disaster.

   a. According to its report, bad weather conditions were to blame for the crash.
   b. The pilot was able to land the plane safely and with no loss of life.
   c. They wanted to prevent similar accidents in the future.

VOCABULARY QUIZ

Choose the correct word for each sentence. Use each word only once.

survive	department	save	storm
ignore	disaster	sink	wave
inquire	condition	prevent	inquiry
warning	rough	calm	brave

1. My friend works for the _____ of the government that holds inquiries into plane accidents.

2. Driving _____s are very bad. There is a lot of ice and snow on the roads, and the wind is blowing very hard.

3. There is a _____ on cigarette packs in the U.S. It says, "Smoking can be dangerous to your health."

4. Medical science tries to do two things: It tries to cure people who are already ill; it also tries to _____ disease.

5. Two years ago scientists discovered a serious problem with a new plane which the government was building. They warned the government. But the government _____d the warnings and made no changes in the plane. Last week the plane fell into the sea.

6. That policeman is very _____. He jumped into the river and _____d a child who fell off the bridge.

7. The _____ is getting worse. The wind is stronger, and the _____s are higher than they were two hours ago. We are crossing by sea from England to France tonight. It is going to be a _____ journey.

PART C

to occur (verb)
occurrence (noun)

DEFINITION   to occur: to happen

EXAMPLES   1. Mike: I want to report an accident.
                   Police Officer: Okay, sir. Where did this accident *occur*?
                   Mike: At the corner of Main Street and Market.
               2. There are reports of many strange *occurrences* in the history of sea travel, things that happened but cannot be explained.

to prove (verb)
proof (noun)

DEFINITION   to prove something: to show the truth of something

EXAMPLES   1. This is the radio that was stolen from my apartment two weeks ago. I can *prove* it. My name is on the back, and I have the factory number of the radio.
               2. The police had no real *proof*. They had to free the man whom they arrested.

to **manage** (verb)

DEFINITION   to manage to do something: to succeed in it (after problems)

EXAMPLES   1. The test which I took last week was very difficult. But I *managed* to get a B on it. I was very pleased.
2. The road was icy, but the driver *managed* to stop his car in front of the red light. There was no accident.

to **damage** (verb)
damage (noun)
damaged (adjective)

DEFINITION   to damage something: to hurt something (but we only use *damage* with *things:* we damage some-*thing;* we hurt some*one* or we injure some*one*)

EXAMPLES   1. My car was *damaged* in the accident, but I was not hurt.
2. The *damage* was not serious. I just needed one new head-light.

to **disappear** (verb)
disappearance (noun)

DEFINITION   to disappear: not to be seen any more

EXAMPLES   1. The weather became warmer, and all the snow *disappeared.*
2. Sometimes ships at sea *disappear* without warning. They are never seen again, and no one can really explain their *disappearance.*

deliberate (adjective)
deliberately (adverb)

DEFINITION   Deliberate describes something that you plan and then do. You decide to do it, or you want to do it. It is not accidental. (Accidental is the *opposite* of deliberate.)

EXAMPLES   1. The soccer player *deliberately* kicked a player on the other team. The referee gave him a red card, and he had to leave the game.
2. "I didn't say hello to you. I'm sorry. It wasn't *deliberate.* I just didn't see you."

conclusion (noun)

DEFINITION conclusion: 1. the end
2. the belief which you accept after proof

EXAMPLES 1. At the *conclusion* of the meeting, everyone shook hands, said good-bye, and went home.
2. Mike (in history class): In my opinion, the U.S. did not want to support Great Britain and France in the war against Germany.
Professor: Okay. But how did you reach that *conclusion?*

Now read this passage and answer the questions about it.

1   Many strange things occur at sea. Every year, even nowadays,
2 ships disappear and are never seen again. One of the strangest
3 occurrences is the story of the *Mary Celeste,* a small sailing ship
4 which was carrying industrial alcohol from New York to Italy. The
5 *Mary Celeste* left New York in early November 1872. A month
6 later it was found in the eastern Atlantic 600 miles from Gibraltar.
7 The ship was not damaged and did not seem to be in any danger,
8 but the lifeboat and the ten people who left New York on the ship
9 were gone. They were never found.
10   Many explanations were suggested for the disappearance of
11 the people on the *Mary Celeste,* but no one managed to find proof
12 for any of the explanations. All the experts could come to only one
13 sure conclusion: The people deliberately left the ship in the life-
14 boat. Then perhaps the lifeboat sank in a sudden storm. But why
15 did the people leave the ship? We still do not have an answer to
16 that question.

1. T F The *Mary Celeste* disappeared in the eastern Atlantic. Line(s) _____

2. T F The *Mary Celeste* was on its way from the U.S. to Europe. Line(s) _____

3. T F The people on the *Mary Celeste* died of disease. Line(s) _____

4. T F We can now completely explain the story of the *Mary Celeste.* Line(s) _____

5. T F Probably a storm damaged the *Mary Celeste,* and it began to sink. Line(s) _____

PART D

in spite of (preposition)

DEFINITION   You do X in spite of Y: Y does not prevent you from doing X.

EXAMPLES 1. There was a lot of rain yesterday, and it was quite cold. But *in spite of* the bad weather, the students decided to play soccer.
2. For one week, Mike studied chemistry until two o'clock every morning. But *in spite of* all this work, he failed the chemistry test.

responsible (adjective)
responsibility (noun)

DEFINITION   to be responsible for people or things: to have to look after them
to be responsible for something bad: to be to blame for something

EXAMPLES 1. Governments have a *responsibility* to help people who have no work.
2. I was *responsible* for the accident. I was driving too close to the car in front of me.

to tear (irregular verb)
tore
torn

DEFINITION   to tear: to pull something, or to pull it into pieces

EXAMPLES 1. The storm *tore* the roof off our house. But our neighbor's house was not seriously damaged.
2. Be careful with that envelope! You don't want to *tear* the check that you are expecting from home, do you?

to prepare (verb)
prepared (adjective)

DEFINITION   to prepare: to get ready or to make something ready

EXAMPLES 1. Mike and his wife, Susan, are getting ready for their vacation. They are going to drive to the beach. Mike is packing the suitcases, and Susan is *preparing* sandwiches for the trip.
2. All the students in the class are *prepared* for the winter. Last week they went shopping. They bought warm coats, hats, gloves, and snow boots.

order (noun)

DEFINITION an order: words which tell people something that they have
to do; a command

EXAMPLES 1. A soldier who doesn't follow *orders* will get into bad
trouble.
2. Here are the doctor's *orders:* You have to stay in bed for
the next three or four days. You need a lot of rest. You
have to drink a lot and take your medicine every four
hours. Don't try to work!

to **obey** (verb)

DEFINITION to obey: to do the things that people tell you; to follow orders

EXAMPLES 1. Some people *obey* orders without question. Other people
often ask questions about the orders.
2. People who do not *obey* traffic rules will probably cause
accidents. Then they'll get into trouble with the police.

experience (noun)
experienced (adjective)
inexperienced (adjective)

DEFINITION experience: the knowledge or ability that you get from past
actions
an experienced person: a person with knowledge and ability
from past actions

EXAMPLES 1. My sister did not get the job she wanted. Her education
and training were good, but she did not have enough *experience.* She only graduated from the university two months
ago.
2. An *experienced* teacher is usually better than a teacher
who is just beginning his or her first job.

to **predict** (verb)

DEFINITION to predict something: to describe something which will happen in the future

EXAMPLES 1. People who follow soccer try to *predict* the results of important games. But often they are wrong.
2. Meteorologists, scientists who study the weather, are able
to *predict* the weather for the near future.

Now read this passage and answer the questions about it.

1   Hurricanes are storms that often begin in the Atlantic near
2 the equator and then move west. They often hit the islands of the
3 Caribbean, the countries of Central America, Mexico, and the
4 southern states of the U.S. between August and November each
5 year. In a hurricane the wind blows at more than seventy-five
6 miles an hour; it can tear trees out of the ground and the roofs off
7 houses. However, the greatest damage in a hurricane is caused by
8 water, by the heavy rain and high waves which come with the
9 hurricane.
10   The National Hurricane Center is located in Miami, Florida.
11 The responsibility of the scientists at the center is to follow hurri-
12 canes and to warn the places that are in danger. They are very
13 successful; the number of people who are killed in hurricanes is
14 now much lower than fifty or sixty years ago. In spite of all their
15 experience, however, the scientists of the National Hurricane
16 Center cannot always correctly predict the movements of a hurri-
17 cane. Sometimes a hurricane changes direction quickly and hits a
18 place that is not prepared. Problems can also be caused by people
19 who ignore hurricane warnings and who do not obey police orders
20 to move to safety. In 1969, in spite of many warnings, Hurricane
21 Camille caused more than 300 deaths along the coasts of Louisi-
22 ana, Mississippi, and Alabama.

1. T F   The hurricane season in the U.S. begins in November.   Line(s) _____

2. T F   In a hurricane, water causes more damage than high   Line(s) _____
   winds.

3. T F   The scientists at the National Hurricane Center know   Line(s) _____
   everything they need to know about hurricanes.

4. T F   The hurricane warnings which are given by the Na-   Line(s) _____
   tional Hurricane Center save a lot of lives.

5. T F   Some people do not pay attention to hurricane   Line(s) _____
   warnings.

PART E

shock (noun)
to **shock** (verb)

     DEFINITION   to shock people: to give them a bad or unpleasant surprise

EXAMPLES 1. I heard about my friend's accident from another friend. The news really *shocked* me.
2. I went to see my friend in the hospital. Her appearance really *shocked* me. She did not look well. She looked very different from the girl whom I knew.

immediate (adjective)
immediately (adverb)

DEFINITION immediately: without waiting; at once; just after something

EXAMPLES 1. Bob hurt his leg in the soccer game. It seemed to be serious, so his friends took him to the hospital *immediately*.
2. I received a letter from a friend today, but I won't be able to write an *immediate* answer. I have too much work to do this week. Maybe I'll have time to write next week.

terrible (adjective)

DEFINITION terrible: very bad

EXAMPLES 1. There was a *terrible* storm two nights ago. The wind blew down a lot of trees and caused a lot of damage to houses.
2. I went to see a movie last night. It was *terrible*. I left in the middle of it. I almost asked for my money back!

evidence (noun)

DEFINITION evidence: something which gives you a reason for a belief you have; something which supports your belief

EXAMPLES 1. According to this writer, public school education is getting worse, but he gives no *evidence* to support his ideas. He doesn't discuss the results of any studies or tests.
2. The police cannot arrest a person without *evidence*.

duty (noun)

DEFINITION duty: the thing(s) that you must do because of your job or because of your beliefs

EXAMPLES 1. The *duty* of the police is to protect people and to arrest people who break the law.
2. John is a police officer. He is *on duty* tonight. He works from twelve until seven o'clock in the morning.

in addition (sentence connector)

DEFINITION in addition: also (You are going to write something that is similar to the idea in the first sentence.)

EXAMPLES 1. The student came to the U.S. for a number of reasons. He wanted to learn English. He planned to study engineering at an American university. *In addition,* he had friends in the U.S., and he wanted to be with them.
2. For the history class the students will have to take two tests. *In addition,* they will write a research paper of fifteen pages.

message (noun)

DEFINITION message: a piece of information which one person sends to another

EXAMPLES 1. The ship sank very quickly. The Coast Guard heard only one radio *message* for help; then nothing more was heard.
2. The person whom I phoned was not in the office, so I left a *message* for her. She received it and called me back later.

instrument (noun)

DEFINITION an instrument: a piece of equipment or a tool which you use for a special job

EXAMPLES 1. A thermometer is an *instrument* that measures heat.
2. In bad weather the pilots of planes often cannot see the ground. For landings they have to depend on their *instruments.*

Now read this passage and answer the questions about it.

1   Around 1975 a number of books were written about strange
2   occurrences in the Bermuda Triangle, a part of the Atlantic Ocean
3   off the southeast coast of the U.S. They told the stories of planes
4   and ships that disappeared for no understandable reason and were
5   never found again. They told about ships which were found un-
6   damaged but with no one on them. According to the books, more
7   than 1,000 people disappeared in the Triangle from 1945 to 1975.
8   According to some writers, there were no natural explanations
9   for many of the disappearances, so they suggested other explana-
10 tions. For example, according to one writer, some strange and terri-
11 ble power exists in the Triangle. According to another writer,

12 people from space are living at the bottom of the Atlantic, and
13 sometimes they need human sailors and airmen for their research.
14 These ideas were not scientific, but they were good advertisements.
15 The books about the Bermuda Triangle were immediate successes.
16   However, the books give little evidence to support their unusual
17 ideas. In addition, they ignore at least three important facts that
18 suggest natural reasons for many of the occurrences. First, mes-
19 sages from some of the ships and aircraft which later disappeared
20 give us evidence of problems with navigational instruments. Simi-
21 lar stories are told by officers who were on duty on planes and ships
22 which finally managed to come through the Triangle without dis-
23 aster. Second, the weather in this part of the Atlantic Ocean is very
24 unpredictable. Dangerous storms that can cause problems even for
25 experienced pilots and sailors can begin suddenly and without warn-
26 ing. Finally, the Bermuda Triangle is very large, and many people,
27 both experienced and inexperienced, sail and fly through it. Perhaps
28 the figure of 1,000 deaths in thirty years shocks some people, but, in
29 fact, the figure is not unusual for an area of ocean that is so large
30 and that is crossed by so many ships.
31   The evidence which exists, therefore, supports one conclusion
32 about the Bermuda Triangle: We do not need stories about people
33 from space or strange unnatural powers to explain the disappear-
34 ances.

1. T F All the books about the Bermuda Triangle give nat-   Line(s) _____
         ural explanations for the things that happen there.

2. T F The books about the Bermuda Triangle were bought   Line(s) _____
         by a lot of people.

3. T F The writer of this passage agrees with the conclusions   Line(s) _____
         which were suggested in the books about the Ber-
         muda Triangle.

4. T F Perhaps some of the disappearances were caused by   Line(s) _____
         instruments that failed to work. There is some evi-
         dence for this.

5. T F The writer of this passage is shocked by the large   Line(s) _____
         number of deaths in the Bermuda Triangle between
         1945 and 1975.

6. T F According to the writer of the passage, perhaps the   Line(s) _____
         weather is connected with some of the disappearances.

7. T F None of the planes or ships which disappeared re-   Line(s) _____
         ported any problems before their disappearance.

Exercises for Parts C, D, and E

SAME OR DIFFERENT?

Read the two sentences in each example. Do they express the same ideas, or do they express different ideas? Write *S* for sentences with the same ideas; write *D* for sentences with different ideas.

Remember: You can express the **same** ideas with **different** words and **different** grammar!

1. a. Carlos was not well prepared for the history test he took yesterday. _____
   b. Carlos took a history test yesterday, but he did not study enough for it.

2. a. After an hour of work, I managed to fix the problem in my car. _____
   b. In spite of an hour of work, I failed to fix the problem in my car.

3. a. The storm was terrible, but it did not cause any serious damage. _____
   b. In spite of the terrible storm, nothing was damaged.

4. a. Road conditions were very bad, but many people still drove to work. _____
   b. Many people took their cars to work in spite of the terrible road conditions.

5. a. The people who survived the disaster received immediate medical help. _____
   b. Medical help was immediately given to the survivors of the disaster.

6. a. The police will arrest anyone who breaks the new traffic law. _____
   b. People who do not obey the new traffic rule will be arrested by the police.

7. a. Parents have a responsibility to give their children a good education. _____
   b. A duty of parents is to give their children a good education.

8. a. According to Ali, the accident last night was not his fault. _____
   b. According to Ali, he was responsible for the accident last night.

9. a. The students were not really surprised by the grades which they received on the chemistry test. _____
   b. The grades which the students got on the chemistry test did not shock them.

10. a. My friend Mike did not get the job which he wanted; he did not   _____
have enough experience in that kind of work.
    b. My friend Mike did not get the job which he wanted; he did not
have the necessary education for it.

11. a. The police did not believe the driver in spite of evidence that   _____
proved the truth of his story.
    b. According to the evidence, the driver was clearly telling the
truth; however, the police did not believe his story.

12. a. On September 10, 1952, a plane on its way from Miami to Lon-   _____
don disappeared.
    b. On September 10, 1952, a plane left Miami for London; it was
never seen again.

EXPECTATIONS

Read the first sentence in each of these examples. Think about the ideas in it. Then
choose the sentence or sentences that can follow it.

1. According to the inquiry, the plane accident was caused by the terrible
weather conditions.
    a. The inexperienced pilot made a number of bad mistakes.
    b. The pilot of the plane was not responsible for the crash.
    c. The storm on the night of the crash was the worst one in many years.

2. The teacher who got the job in the English language school has a lot of experience with foreign students.
    a. She taught in an American high school for ten years.
    b. She taught in West Germany, Venezuela, and Mexico before this job.
    c. In spite of this, she seemed to be the best person for the job.

3. A ship which was on its way from Miami to New York sank without warning;
no reason could be found for the ship's disappearance.
    a. The Coast Guard received a radio message that said: "We are without our
engine, and the sea is very rough. Please send help."
    b. Weather conditions were good for the trip; the officers and men of the ship
all had a lot of experience.
    c. On the day of the disappearance, there was a terrible storm that caused a
lot of damage at sea and along the east coast of the U.S.

4. In spite of her lack of experience in business or electronics,
    a. Jane managed to get a very good job with the phone company.
    b. Jane failed to find a job with the university.
    c. Jane was very successful in all her history classes.

5. There was a serious accident last night.

   a. It occurred at 11:45 P.M., at Exit 25 on the Interstate.
   b. There was little damage, and no one was hurt.
   c. A driver did not obey the stop sign at Market and Main. His car hit a truck at a speed of thirty miles an hour.

6. At the inquiry into the plane disaster, the final conclusion was: "The pilot was to blame. He made a bad mistake." But later, new evidence was found which did not support this conclusion.

   a. The pilot ignored a number of clear warnings about bad weather.
   b. The people who were responsible for the electrical systems of the plane were not trained for the job.
   c. The engines of the plane were not kept in good condition; perhaps they failed in the air.

7. In spite of all the winter storm warnings,

   a. most people stayed at home and did not try to use their cars.
   b. some drivers ignored police warnings and continued their journeys.
   c. a number of people were not prepared for the snow and high winds that hit the state.

8. The student failed to get any of the jobs which he wanted. There were a number of reasons for his lack of success. First, he had little experience in the type of work which he wanted to do.

   a. In addition, he lacked the necessary training.
   b. In addition, his university grades were all excellent.
   c. In addition, he could not give any evidence of an ability to learn quickly.

VOCABULARY QUIZ

Choose the correct word or expression for each empty space. Use each word or expression only once.

occur	evidence	terrible	message
prove	predict	immediately	prepared
tear	in spite of	shock	experience
damage	conclusion	manage	order
disappear	responsible	on duty	obey

1. The storm did not cause a lot of _____ to my apartment. It only broke one window.

2. A week ago, Bob's television _____ed from his room. Someone stole it.

3. Scientists discovered the remains of a Viking settlement in Newfoundland. The discovery _____d one thing: Columbus was not the first European to reach North America.

4. Yesterday, I could not find my dictionary. I looked for it for fifteen minutes. Finally, I _____d to find it. It was in the refrigerator!

5. The professor criticized my research paper. According to him, I gave no proof for the _____s that I reached at the end of my paper.

6. The company needs a person with good training and a lot of _____ for the job Mike wanted. However, Mike only finished school two months ago, so he didn't get the job _____ his excellent university grades.

7. All soldiers have to _____ the orders of their officers. Soldiers who do not do so will get into trouble.

8. There was an accident outside my apartment building yesterday. The person who was _____ for it did not stop. Now the police are looking for him.

9. Some students who come to the U.S. are not _____ for the problems which they have to solve here. They are shocked by many of the new things which they experience.

10. "Mike, your parents called an hour ago. They left a _____ for you. They are coming to town to see you this weekend."

11. The driver of one car was badly hurt in the accident, so he was taken to the hospital _____. The doctor who was _____ at the hospital that night saved the man's life.

12. According to some scientists, even the Vikings were not the first Europeans in North America. But they do not have any real _____ for this belief; they cannot find anything that was built or used by earlier people.

13. You can't really _____ the weather in this part of the ocean. It can change very quickly.

Main Reading

Pre-Reading Exercises

VOCABULARY IN CONTEXT

Use the context to guess the meaning of the new words (in boldface type). The words in italics in the first six examples will help you.

Remember: Read each example to the end. Do not stop after the new word!

1. On the *ship* there were 2,235 *people* in all, 1,320 *passengers* and 915 **crew.**

   A crew means _____.

   a. the people who buy tickets and travel on the ship
   b. the people who built the ship
   c. the people who work on the ship

2. In July last year, we left on our first **voyage** *across* the *Atlantic.* For the first part of the *journey,* the *sea* was very calm, but then we ran into a bad storm. I was happy at the end of the voyage. Next time, I'm going to fly!

   A voyage means _____.

   a. a long journey by ship
   b. a long summer vacation
   c. a large ship for passengers

3. Last *winter* I went to a football game. The *temperature* was only 15°F, and there was a strong wind. I had to leave the game after an hour. *In spite of* my *heavy* clothes, I was **freezing.** At home, I took a *hot bath* and drank three cups of coffee. Then I began to feel better. I was *warm again.*

   Freezing means _____.

   a. very tired
   b. very sick
   c. very cold

4. There was an *accident* outside my apartment building last night. A *truck* **collided with** a city *bus.* I heard the *noise* of the **collision** from my apartment. But luckily, no one was hurt.

   To collide with something means _____.

   a. to hit something
   b. to drive something
   c. to steal something

5. I had a car *accident* last month, but the car was not badly *damaged*. I was able to **repair** it myself. That saved me some money!

>   To repair means _____.

>   a. to damage something
>   b. to fix something
>   c. to change something

6. The crew *only* worked with the new ship for a week. Then the passengers arrived for the first trip. *As a result,* the crew did not really have time to **become familiar with** the new ship. There were still a lot of new things on the ship that they did *not know* well enough.

>   To become familiar with something means _____.

>   a. to get to know something
>   b. to reach something
>   c. to begin to enjoy something

7. Why did our soccer team lose the final game? We were too **confident.** For us, the other team was nothing. We did not prepare seriously for the game.

>   Confident means _____.

>   a. to be tired of something
>   b. to be very sure of success
>   c. to be successful in something

8. In hot weather, people with fair skin should **take precautions** against sunburn. Too much sun can be very dangerous. So they must not stay in the sun for more than a few minutes every day. They should put sun cream on their skin.

>   To take precautions means _____.

>   a. to take things with you on your vacation
>   b. to ask questions about something
>   c. to do things which will prevent problems

9. The ship hit an **iceberg.** It was badly damaged. It sank soon afterward.

>   An iceberg is _____.

>   a. a piece of land which runs out into the sea
>   b. a large piece of ice in the sea
>   c. water which is very cold

10. There was a bad fire in a department store downtown on Saturday afternoon. But no one was hurt. Everyone in the store managed to **escape** from the building in time.

>   To escape means _____.

>   a. to go shopping in a department store

b. to stay in a safe place
c. to find a way out of danger

11. The driver of the car was going very fast. He was going 75 miles an hour. Then he saw a police car. He **reduced** speed immediately, but it was too late. The police stopped him, and he had to pay $150.

    To reduce speed means _____.

    a. to drive on a highway
    b. to drive slower
    c. to drive faster

    Therefore, to reduce means _____.

    a. to drive
    b. to make bigger in size, in number, or in other ways
    c. the opposite of to increase

12. The ship was sinking fast. The captain ordered, "**Abandon** ship!" The passengers and crew got into the lifeboats.

    To abandon means _____.

    a. to stay
    b. to leave
    c. to remain

For the next example, use your knowledge of word families!

13. The warship was very large. It was bigger than the Empire State Building in New York, and it looked just as strong. To many people, it seemed **unsinkable.**

    Unsinkable means _____.

    a. nothing could destroy the ship
    b. the ship could not move
    c. the ship was sinking

PROPER NAMES AND TECHNICAL VOCABULARY

Look at this example sentence. Do you understand it?

Harland and Wolff is having economic problems.

Probably you are having difficulty with the words *Harland and Wolff*. Sometimes a writer has to use words which even American readers will not know. Often these words are

a. the proper names of people, places, etc.
b. technical words that are used by scientists
c. the initials for something (e.g., U.S.A., U.A.E.)

Writers who have to use these kinds of words will often help their readers. They will write more information in the sentence. Look at the next example.

Harland and Wolff, *the company which built many of the famous Atlantic passenger ships of the 1920s and 1930s,* is having economic problems.

With the noun and relative clause (in italics), the writer tells us: Harland and Wolff is the name of a company which builds ships. Now we can understand the sentence completely.

Now work with some more sentences that contain words which you don't know. Read these sentences. Each sentence has a word or expression which you cannot understand without more help. In some sentences, you get the help you need. After these sentences, write OK. In other sentences, you don't get the help you need. After these sentences, write a question mark (?).

1. The E.P.A. is being criticized by a lot of people. According to them, _____
   it is not doing its job properly.

2. Medical researchers are becoming very interested in the hippocampus, the part of the brain which is the center for feelings. _____

3. Right now I'm reading a book by Roy Medvedev. _____

4. Amniocentesis, a method to discover medical problems in babies who are not yet born, is used a lot by doctors. _____

5. O.S.H.A., the U.S. government department which is responsible for workers' safety and health at work, is very unpopular with the owners of some factories. _____

6. Scientists are looking for a way to prevent multiple sclerosis. _____

7. According to some research, serotonin has an important effect on the quality of sleep which people get. _____

8. The Food and Drug Administration made a terrible mistake last year. _____

Now go back to the sentences which you could not understand completely. Read them again. Then read these explanations, which the writer wants to put into the sentences. Where does each explanation belong? For each explanation, write the word(s) it explains.

1. A disease which slowly reduces control of the arms and legs _____

2. A chemical which is found in the brain _____

3. A Russian professor of history who criticizes the Russian government   _____

4. The U.S. government department that has the responsibility to keep our air and water clean   _____

5. The government department which controls the kinds of food and drugs that can be sold in the U.S.   _____

EXPECTATIONS

Read the title carefully and think about it. Also look at the picture on page 129. Then read the ideas below. Choose the ideas you expect in the article (YES). Also choose the ideas you don't expect (NO).

1. The article will examine the history of air travel across the Atlantic.   YES NO

2. The article will tell us about all the successful journeys of the *Titanic;* it will not mention any problems.   YES NO

3. The article will tell us about a bad accident that happened to the *Titanic.*   YES NO

4. The *Titanic* sank, but everyone on the ship was saved.   YES NO

5. The article will discuss the causes of the things which happened to the *Titanic.*   YES NO

6. The *Titanic* sank, and a great number of people died.   YES NO

7. The *Titanic* is still being used today.   YES NO

8. The article will give us a description of the *Titanic,* but it will not discuss anything else.   YES NO

9. The article will criticize some people who were connected with the *Titanic.*   YES NO

10. The article will examine the development of ships throughout history.   YES NO

Think about the title. It has *two* ideas:

1. the *Titanic* disaster
2. who was responsible

So perhaps the article will have *two* parts. Now read the first sentence of each paragraph of the article. Try to find the two main parts of the article. Write the numbers of the paragraphs which are in each part.

Part I: Perhaps this part describes the *Titanic* and the dis-   Paragraph(s) _____
aster.

Part II: Perhaps this part discusses the causes of the dis-   Paragraph(s) _____
aster.

Now read all of Paragraph 4. It gives you ideas for the later part of the article. What do you expect in the paragraphs after Paragraph 4?

1. We will read about problems with the ship but not about the   YES   NO
   actions of the ship's officers.

2. The writer will criticize the actions of the ship's officers, but he   YES   NO
   will not mention any problems with the ship itself.

3. The writer will examine possible safety problems in the ship.   YES   NO
   The writer will also discuss things the ship's officers perhaps
   did wrong.

4. The disaster was caused by a mistake which one person made.   YES   NO

Now read Paragraph 4 again quickly. Then read only the first sentences of Paragraphs 5–11. Pay attention to words like *in addition* (line 71), *however* (line 83), and *in conclusion* (line 109).
      Here are the two main subjects of this section of the article:

1. the actions of the Titanic's owners
2. the actions of the Titanic's officers

Which of these two subjects do you expect to find in each paragraph of this section?

Paragraph 5 _____   Paragraph 9 _____
Paragraph 6 _____   Paragraph 10 _____
Paragraph 7 _____   Paragraph 11 _____
Paragraph 8 _____

The Titanic Disaster: Who Was Responsible?

1   On April 10, 1912, the *Titanic,* the largest and most modern   1
2   passenger ship in the world, left England on its first journey across
3   the Atlantic to New York. The *Titanic* was already famous. At
4   46,328 tons and 882 feet long, it was bigger than any other transat-

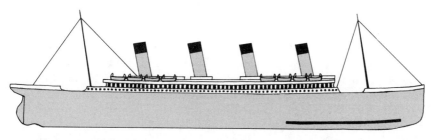

A View of the Titanic. The black line on the side shows the damage which was caused by the iceberg.

5   lantic liner of that time. Its rooms were as comfortable as the
6   rooms of the best hotels of Europe. Inside, it did not seem like a
7   ship; it seemed as safe as a large building on land. To many people
8   who saw it, the *Titanic* seemed unsinkable.

9   For the first four days, the voyage went very well. The sea was   2
10   calm, and no storm was expected for the rest of the trip. The pas-
11   sengers were able to enjoy all the comforts of the wonderful new
12   ship. Then, at 11:40 P.M. on April 14th, disaster occurred. At a
13   speed of almost 26 miles an hour, the largest ship in the world hit
14   an iceberg. The right side of the ship was torn open for about 300
15   feet, and the front of the ship immediately began to fill with water.
16   The damage was clearly too serious and could not be repaired, so
17   the order was given to the passengers and crew to abandon ship. At
18   2:20 A.M. on April 15th, only two and a half hours after the colli-
19   sion, the unsinkable *Titanic* disappeared below the freezing waves
20   of the North Atlantic. Only 713 of the 2,235 passengers and crew
21   survived. They managed to get into the lifeboats and were saved by
22   a ship that answered the *Titanic's* radio call for help. The rest,
23   including many famous and wealthy people, went down with the
24   ship or died quickly in the icy water.

25   The news of the *Titanic* disaster shocked American and British   3
26   society. Immediately people began to ask questions like: How did
27   this disaster happen? Why were so few people saved? Who is to
28   blame? The American and British governments quickly held in-
29   quiries into the disaster. They wanted to discover its cause or
30   causes; they also wanted to prevent a similar disaster. The in-
31   quiries were not perfect, but from the information which was given
32   in them and from information which was discovered years later, we
33   now have a clearer understanding of the disaster. From this infor-
34   mation one conclusion is clear: The disaster was caused by a num-
35   ber of factors, not just by one thing or by one person.

36   Two general questions need to be answered by anyone who   4

wants to discover the truth about the *Titanic* disaster. The first
question is about the ship and its owners. Did the White Star Line,
the company which owned the *Titanic,* deliberately take risks with
the safety of the people on the *Titanic?* The second question is
about the actions of the officers who were responsible for the *Titanic*. Did they make any mistakes on that terrible night?

First and perhaps most important, the *Titanic* did not have   5
enough lifeboats for all the people it could carry. There were
2,235 passengers and crew on the first voyage, but the *Titanic*
had room in the lifeboats for only 1,178 people. There were only
sixteen lifeboats and four other boats which could be used in an
emergency. Today, the company that owned the *Titanic* can be
criticized for this small number of lifeboats. However, the sixteen
lifeboats satisfied the British government's rules for the number
of lifeboats on a passenger ship. This number was decided by the
British Board of Trade, the government department that was responsible for safety at sea. However the rules of the Board of
Trade were almost twenty years old. Between 1895 and 1912
ships increased greatly in size, but the rules were not changed. In
1912 the rule was the same as in 1895: "Ships over 15,000 tons
must carry at least sixteen lifeboats."

At the inquiries in 1912, the White Star Line was able to say: 6
"We obeyed the law. The large number of deaths is not our fault."
However, according to Andrew Carlisle, the designer of the *Titanic,*
the large number of deaths was the fault of the ship's owners and
was completely predictable. According to him, in 1910 he suggested
a total of forty-eight lifeboats for the ship. The chairman of the
White Star Line, who survived the disaster, said at the inquiry, "I
do not remember any suggestion like this. The builders always
planned for sixteen lifeboats." Recently, however, evidence was discovered which proves the truth of Carlisle's words. He suggested
forty-eight lifeboats, but the White Star Line decided not to accept
his suggestion. They wanted to limit the costs of the *Titanic,* so
they reduced the number of expensive lifeboats.

In addition, the White Star Line wanted to make money from   7
the *Titanic* as soon as possible. As a result, they hurried the sea
tests that all new ships had to pass. The crew did not have enough
time to become familiar with the new ship; they were able to get
only very little experience with the ship, especially with its lifeboats. Their lack of experience and training became clear after the
collision with the iceberg. The crew behaved very bravely, but they
did not fill the lifeboats with the correct number of people. Each
lifeboat could hold sixty-four people, but no lifeboat was completely

80 filled. In fact, a few boats left the ship with only twelve people in
81 them. The lifeboats had room for 1,178 people, but only 713 man-
82 aged to escape from the sinking ship in them.

83 However, the British Board of Trade and the owners of the   8
84 *Titanic* were not the only people who had some responsibility for
85 the disaster. Before the collision, the officers of the ship received a
86 number of clear warnings about ice. In spite of these warnings,
87 they did not take any suitable precautions.

88 On April 14th, the *Titanic* received at least four radio mes-   9
89 sages that warned about ice in the ship's path. The last two warn-
90 ings, which were received at 1:00 P.M. and 7:30 P.M., were never
91 seen by the captain. The man who was working the radio was too
92 busy with private messages that he had to send out for wealthy
93 passengers. He forgot to send the two messages to the captain.
94 However, the captain received other warnings. There were two
95 earlier radio messages about ice; both of them were ignored. Fi-
96 nally, at about 10:30 P.M., the *Titanic* passed a ship which was
97 going in the other direction. With its lamp the ship sent a message
98 about heavy ice and large icebergs directly in the path of the *Ti-*
99 *tanic*. In spite of this clear warning, the officer who was on duty did
100 not reduce speed or change direction. He didn't even report the
101 message to the captain. About an hour later, an iceberg was seen
102 500 yards in front of the *Titanic*. But the ship was going too fast,
103 and the danger was seen too late. The *Titanic* collided with the
104 iceberg at almost full speed.

105 Why did the captain and other officers ignore all the warnings   10
106 about icebergs in their path? This question was never really
107 answered. Perhaps they had too much confidence in their new ship.
108 Perhaps the *Titanic* seemed unsinkable to them also.

109 In conclusion, then, the blame for the *Titanic* disaster is   11
110 shared by a number of people: by the owners of the *Titanic,* by the
111 people at the British Board of Trade, and by the officers who did
112 not take any precautions against the danger of icebergs. However
113 for many people today, the greatest share of the responsibility
114 must be given to the directors of the White Star Line. Money was
115 more important to them than the safety of their crew and pas-
116 sengers. They built a ship which did not have enough lifeboats for
117 even half of the people that the ship could carry. They rushed the
118 ship into use with an unprepared crew. The result was the worst
119 disaster in the history of sea travel, a disaster which will never be
120 forgotten.

We can read this passage in three sections.

Section I (Paragraphs 1–3)

MAIN IDEAS CHECK

Here are the main ideas of the paragraphs in this section. Write the correct paragraph number opposite each main idea.

PARAGRAPH   IDEA

_____   The effect of the disaster in Britain and the U.S.

_____   A description of the accident

_____   A description of the *Titanic*

COMPREHENSION CHECK

1. T F The *Titanic* was larger than any other passenger ship in the world in 1912.   Line(s) _____

2. T F Weather conditions were terrible for the *Titanic's* first transatlantic voyage.   Line(s) _____

3. Why did the *Titanic* sink?   Line(s) _____
   a. High waves turned the ship on its right side.
   b. The ship tore its side open in a collision with an iceberg.
   c. The ship hit another ship which was going in the other direction.

4. T F Half of the people on the *Titanic* died in the disaster.   Line(s) _____

5. Why were inquiries held into the *Titanic* disaster by the American and the British governments?   Line(s) _____
   a. They wanted to find the causes of the disaster.
   b. They did not want a similar disaster.
   c. Both (a) and (b)

Section II (Paragraphs 4–7)

MAIN IDEAS CHECK

Here are the main ideas of the paragraphs in this section. Write the correct paragraph number opposite each main idea.

_____   The owners of the *Titanic* decided to reduce to sixteen the number of lifeboats which were planned for the *Titanic*.

_____   The number of lifeboats on the *Titanic* was not enough for all the people on the ship.

_____   To save time and money, the owners of the *Titanic* gave the crew little time to get to know the ship.

_____   How can we answer the question, Why did the *Titanic* disaster occur?

COMPREHENSION CHECK

1. T F   The number of lifeboats on the *Titanic* was the number which was required by law.   Line(s) _____

2. T F   The owners of the *Titanic* did not break the law about the number of lifeboats. Therefore, according to the writer, the disaster was not their fault.   Line(s) _____

3. When was the truth finally discovered about the number of lifeboats that were planned for the *Titanic*?   Line(s) _____

   a. During the British inquiry
   b. Only a short time ago
   c. A few years after the disaster

4. Why did the directors of the White Star Line not accept Carlisle's plan for forty-eight lifeboats?   Line(s) _____

   a. They wanted to save money.
   b. There was no room on the *Titanic* for more lifeboats.
   c. Sixteen lifeboats were more than enough for all the people on the *Titanic*.

5. T F   The crew of the *Titanic* were well trained and had a good knowledge of the new ship.   Line(s) _____

Section III (Paragraphs 8–11)

MAIN IDEAS CHECK

Here are the main ideas for the paragraphs in this section. Write the correct paragraph number opposite each main idea.

PARAGRAPH	IDEA
_____	There are two possible explanations for the actions of the *Titanic's* officers before the disaster.
_____	Three groups of people can be criticized in the *Titanic* disaster, but the owners of the ship are more to blame than the others.
_____	The *Titanic's* officers ignored a number of ice warnings on the day before the accident.
_____	The officers of the *Titanic* also were partly to blame for the disaster.

COMPREHENSION CHECK

1. T F   The writer criticizes the officers of the *Titanic* for their actions on the night of the disaster.   Line(s) _____

2. What did the ship's officers do after the warnings about ice?   Line(s) _____
   a. They increased the speed of the ship and turned it in a different direction.
   b. They did nothing.
   c. They reduced the speed of the ship.

3. T F   The iceberg that the *Titanic* hit was not seen by anyone on the ship.   Line(s) _____

4. T F   The writer gives a clear and definite answer to the question, Why did the officers ignore the ice warnings?   Line(s) _____

5. According to the writer, who carries the greatest responsibility for the *Titanic* disaster?   Line(s) _____
   a. The officers who were on duty on the *Titanic*
   b. The British Board of Trade
   c. The company that owned the *Titanic*

Now do the paragraph reading exercise on the next page.

These sentences form a paragraph, but they are not in the correct order. Put the sentences into their correct order. The first sentence is already in its correct place.

__1__   Three groups of people share the responsibility for the *Titanic* disaster.

_____   For them, money clearly was more important than the safety of their passengers and crew.

_____   They failed to take any safety precautions in spite of a number of clear warnings about the danger of ice near them.

_____   They deliberately built a ship that did not have enough lifeboats for all the passengers it could carry, and they rushed it into use with an inexperienced and unprepared crew.

_____   One of these groups of people is the officers who were on duty on the *Titanic* on the night of the disaster.

_____   But the greatest share of the blame rests with the White Star Line, the owners of the *Titanic*.

_____   According to the rules of this department, the *Titanic* only needed to have sixteen lifeboats.

_____   In addition, the British Board of Trade, the government department which was responsible for safety at sea, must be criticized for its part in the disaster.

Freedom and Equality in the United States

Grammar for this unit: Object clauses with *that*

Future in the past

You will find information and practice on these grammar points in Appendix 1, Unit 5.

Vocabulary Study and Preparatory Reading

PART A

to **treat** (verb)
treatment (noun)

DEFINITION   to treat someone: 1. to behave with someone in a certain way
2. to give someone medical attention

EXAMPLES   1. This company *treats* its workers well. It pays them well, it gives them 50% more pay at Christmas, and it has very good health insurance for them.
2. Doctors are developing a new *treatment* for burns. With the new *treatment,* they hope that they will be able to save many more lives.

to **vote** (verb)

DEFINITION   to vote: to give your opinion in an election

EXAMPLES   1. In our last election I *voted* for Mr. Smith, but he did not win.

2. In Great Britain 100 years ago, women did not have the right to *vote*. Only men could choose the government of the country.

employment (noun)
unemployed (adjective)

DEFINITION employment: work, a job

EXAMPLES 1. After college, John was *unemployed* for six months. He couldn't find a job.
2. Many of John's friends could not find *employment* either.

to **demand** (verb)

DEFINITION to demand something: to ask for something strongly (Usually, in your opinion, you have the right to the things that you are demanding.)

EXAMPLES 1. The workers are *demanding* a 15% increase in their pay. Without the increase, they will stop work.
2. At the beginning of the twentieth century, women in England began to *demand* the right to vote.

equal (adjective)
equality (noun)

DEFINITION equal: the same (in size, in number, in value)

EXAMPLES 1. Let's have a game of soccer. There are sixteen of us, so we can have an *equal* number of players on each team.
2. Poor people in the U.S. want *equality* in education for their children. They want to send their children to schools which are as good as the schools in wealthier parts of the country.

to **deny** (verb)

DEFINITION to deny that: to say that something is not true
to deny someone something: to refuse to give people something they want

EXAMPLES 1. The driver whom the police stopped *denied* that he was drunk. But he could not speak clearly, and he could not walk straight.
2. Until 1920 the law *denied* women the right to vote in England. Men could vote, but women couldn't.

to **discriminate** (verb)
discrimination (noun)

DEFINITION to discriminate against someone: to treat a person differently (usually worse) than others

EXAMPLES 1. In the past, companies often *discriminated* against black people. They gave the best jobs only to whites.
2. In the U.S. there are now laws against *discrimination*. For example, an employer cannot say, "I will not give this job to a black person or to a woman." This would be *discrimination* on the basis of color or sex.

to **organize** (verb)
organization (noun)

DEFINITION to organize: to bring people or things together into a system

EXAMPLES 1. We're going to have a class party next Saturday evening. Carlos, Ali, and Panos are *organizing* it.
2. The National Organization of Women is an *organization* that wants to improve the lives of women in the U.S.

Now read this passage and answer the questions about it.

1	In many societies women are not treated as the equals of men.
2	In some societies women must always obey the men in their lives.
3	Other societies deny women basic equality in education, in employ-
4	ment, and in politics. For example, in Liechtenstein, a small coun-
5	try in Western Europe, women still do not have the right to vote.
6	In the U.S. discrimination against women perhaps is not as clear
7	as it is in some other parts of the world, but it exists. In 1971, for
8	example, 90% of elementary school teachers were women. How-
9	ever, 80% of elementary school principals were men. In the same
10	year only 7% of American doctors were women.
11	In the late 1960s, women's organizations began to demand an
12	end to sex discrimination. They were quite successful. Today there
13	are a number of laws that protect the rights of women. The women's
14	organizations are also trying to change people's ideas about women
15	and about their place in society. This is a very difficult goal. New
16	laws can perhaps change people's behavior, but they cannot always
17	change people's ideas. As a result, the changes in ideas are slower;
18	however, there is evidence that they are taking place.

1. T F   The writer believes that there is no equality for   Line(s)_____
            women in many countries of the world.

2. Why does the writer give the example of the number of women   Line(s)_____
   elementary school teachers and principals?
   a. He wants to show that there is discrimination in the U.S.
   b. He wants to demand the right to vote for women.
   c. He wants to show that women have equal rights in the U.S.

3. T F   Women's organizations in the U.S. failed to improve   Line(s)_____
            women's rights.

4. How can sex discrimination finally be ended? The writer sug-   Line(s)_____
   gests
   a. that we only need new laws against discrimination.
   b. that people's ideas about women, as well as their behavior,
      need to be changed.
   c. that we cannot change society.

5. T F   People's ideas about the place of women in U.S. soci-   Line(s)_____
            ety are the same as they were twenty years ago.

PART B

to **protest** (verb)
protest (noun)

DEFINITION   to protest something: to say that you don't agree with some-
             thing

EXAMPLES 1. The city government decided to increase bus fares by 40%.
             This made a lot of people angry. They *protested* the fare
             increase.
          2. In a free society people have the right to organize *protests*
             against the government.

violence (noun)
violent (adjective)

DEFINITION   violence: fighting; behavior which is planned to hurt other
             people

EXAMPLES 1. Some people say that there is too much *violence* on televi-
             sion. Some programs are full of fighting and killing.
          2. The people who were protesting the war did not want a
             violent protest. They just sat down in the road outside the
             government building.

peace (noun)
peaceful (adjective)

DEFINITION peace: no war; no violence

EXAMPLES 1. Europe had only twenty years of *peace* between World War I and World War II.
2. Many people believe that *peaceful* protests are the best way to show disagreement. They believe that violence does not do any good.

to **respect** (verb)
respect (noun)
respected (adjective)

DEFINITION to respect someone: to have a high opinion of someone; to think that someone or something is important

EXAMPLES 1. I'm going to vote for Martha Black in the next election. I *respect* her. She tells the truth, she is intelligent, and she wants to help other people. She doesn't want to get rich herself.
2. Dr. Smith is a very *respected* scientist. His students believe that his work is very good. They have a lot of *respect* for him.

race (noun)
racial (adjective)

DEFINITION race: one of a number of different types of people

EXAMPLES 1. There are people from a number of different *races* in the U.S. There are blacks; their ancestors originally came from Africa. There are white people of European origin. There are American Indians. There are people from Asia.
2. *Racial* discrimination in the U.S. means that blacks and other people of non-European origin are often treated worse than white people.

to **lead** (irregular verb)
led, led
leader (noun)

DEFINITION to lead: to direct people
to lead to something: to cause something

EXAMPLES
1. Hitler *led* the German people into a war that almost destroyed their country. They called him their *leader*.
2. High unemployment is *leading to* a lot of dissatisfaction with the government.

brutal (adjective)
brutality (noun)

DEFINITION   brutal person: a person who has no feelings for other people; a person who uses violence and hurts or kills others

EXAMPLES
1. The police beat a number of the leaders of the peaceful protest. Their *brutal* behavior caused a lot of problems for the government.
2. Many people who did not agree with the protesters saw television pictures of the violence. They were shocked by the *brutality* of the police.

extreme (noun)
extremely (adverb)

DEFINITION   an extreme: the furthest position that you can reach (in thoughts or in behavior)
extremely: very

EXAMPLES
1. Ali goes from one *extreme* to the other with his work. For weeks he doesn't study. Then he begins and works until three o'clock every morning.
2. Maria learned English *extremely* fast. She only needed one semester of English classes. Then she was able to begin her academic studies.

Now read this passage and answer the questions about it.

1   Mohandas Gandhi, the man who led India to independence
2 from Great Britain, is one of the most respected leaders in history.
3 He showed the world that people can win their freedom and other
4 basic rights without violence. As a young man in South Africa,
5 Gandhi had to live with racial discrimination. Indians did not have
6 the same rights as whites. To help the Indian population, he devel-
7 oped ideas for nonviolent protests. He believed that people could
8 refuse to obey laws which discriminated against them. Later he
9 became a leader of the movement for Indian independence. In India
10 he continued to use his nonviolent methods of disobedience against

11	the British, in spite of a number of years in prison and in spite of
12	the brutality of the British. (For example, at Amritsar in 1919 the
13	British shot and killed 400 peaceful Indian protesters.)
14	Gandhi, however, was not successful in reaching all his goals.
15	He failed to stop the hate between the Hindu and the Muslim
16	communities. This hate finally led to violence and to the division of
17	the country into the two independent nations of India and Paki-
18	stan. The same hate also led to Gandhi's own death a short time
19	later. On January 30, 1948, the man of peace was murdered by a
20	Hindu extremist who believed that Gandhi had no right to criticize
21	Hindu violence against Muslims.

1. T F   Gandhi believed that violence was the best way to get   Line(s)_____
social and political change.

2. T F   In South Africa, Indians and whites were treated as   Line(s)_____
equals by the law.

3. T F   The British did not treat Indian protesters well.   Line(s)_____

4. T F   The writer suggests that Gandhi criticized Hindus for   Line(s)_____
their violence against Muslims.

5. How did Gandhi die?   Line(s)_____
   a. He was shot by the British at Amritsar.
   b. He was killed by a Hindu after independence.
   c. He died in a British prison.

Exercises for Parts A and B

SAME OR DIFFERENT?

Read the two sentences in each example. Do they express the same ideas or do they express different ideas? Write *S* for sentences with the same ideas; write *D* for sentences with different ideas.

Remember: You can express the **same** ideas with **different** words and **different** grammar!

1. a. Many people in the nation can't find jobs.   _____
   b. There is a lot of unemployment in the country.

2. a. There is no racial discrimination in this country.   _____
   b. True racial equality does not yet exist in this country.

3. a. Yesterday there was a nonviolent protest against the government. _____
   b. The protest against the government which took place yesterday was peaceful.

4. a. The government denies that it is going to sell war planes to South Africa. _____
   b. The government says that it is going to sell war planes to South Africa.

5. a. The workers are demanding a 30% increase in their pay. _____
   b. The workers are getting a 30% increase in their pay.

6. a. In the U.S. there are laws against discrimination on the basis of a person's color. _____
   b. In the U.S. there are laws against racial discrimination.

7. a. A lot of people are protesting the government's decision to reduce welfare money. _____
   b. A great number of people are expressing their agreement with the government's decision to reduce welfare payments.

8. a. The people who organized the meeting made a lot of mistakes. _____
   b. A lot of mistakes were made by the people who planned the meeting.

EXPECTATIONS

Read the first sentence in each of these examples. Think about the ideas in it. Then choose the sentence or sentences that can follow it.

1. Today many women's organizations are demanding an end to sex discrimination in U.S. society.
   a. They want true equality for women.
   b. They are protesting the new law that will protect women's rights.
   c. Women enjoy the same rights as men in U.S. society.

2. There was no violence at yesterday's protest against the government's new laws.
   a. The leaders of the protest were beaten by the police.
   b. A small number of extremists threw gasoline bombs at the police.
   c. About 10,000 people walked peacefully to the White House and delivered a message to the president.

3. Before 1919 women in Great Britain were denied the right to vote.
   a. Not many people in the government supported discrimination.
   b. Many people had the belief that women could not understand politics and government.
   c. However, many women protested against this lack of equality.

4. Unemployment is increasing in this country.
   a. Last year seven million people were out of work. This year the number is eight million.
   b. New industries are leading to more jobs.
   c. A lot of people are saying that the government is to blame.

5. The constitutions of many countries give people the right to criticize their government, but many governments do not respect this right.
   a. From these countries, you often hear reports that critics of the government are brutally beaten by the police.
   b. Everyone in these countries can organize a peaceful protest.
   c. People who organize peaceful protests are arrested and sent to prison.

VOCABULARY QUIZ

Choose the correct word for each empty space. Use each word only once.

equal	extreme	respect	equality
vote	treatment	peaceful	demand
lead	employ	deny	violence
employment	brutal	discrimination	protest

1. Some years ago there was a lot of _____ in the U.S. For example, some people refused to rent apartments to black people.

2. The new company which is coming to the town will _____ 1,200 people. The community is very happy about these new jobs.

3. According to the U.S. Constitution, all men are _____. There is no difference between them. Their religion or race doesn't matter.

4. Everyone who is over eighteen years of age has the right to _____ in elections in the U.S.

5. After the accident, the driver was taken to a hospital fifty miles away. He needed special _____. It was available only at this hospital.

6. I don't always agree with Dr. Smith, but I _____ his ideas. I know that he has a lot of experience and knowledge.

7. The lack of jobs is _____ing to a lot of dissatisfaction with the government. People think that the government is not doing enough for people without work.

8. This film is not suitable for children. There is a lot of _____ in it.

9. It was a _____ protest. There was no violence.

10. The workers are _____ing the unhealthy working conditions in their factory. They are demanding improvements in conditions. They are going to stop work tomorrow. They want to show their employers that they are serious.

PART C

injustice (noun)
unjust (adjective)

DEFINITION an injustice: something which is wrong and which hurts a person or a group of people.

EXAMPLES 1. A great *injustice* was done to this man. He was put in prison for something that he did not do. Five years later the police discovered the real truth.
2. This is an *unjust* law. It gives a number of rights to one group of people. No one else has the same rights.

power (noun)
powerful (adjective)

DEFINITION power: strength; influence; the right to govern or to decide

EXAMPLES 1. In some countries, worker's organizations have a great deal of *power*. They can demand pay increases and get them.
2. The explosion was very *powerful*. It completely destroyed the large building.

federation (noun)
federal (adjective)

DEFINITION a federation: a group of states which has one central government for some questions but independent state
governments for other questions

EXAMPLES 1. The U.S. is really a *federation* of fifty states. The *federal*
government is in Washington, D.C. Each state has its own
government.
2. West Germany is also a *federation*. The official name of
West Germany is the *Federal* Republic of Germany.

to **attack** (verb)

DEFINITION to attack: to use violence against someone (first)

EXAMPLES 1. Germany *attacked* Poland in 1939. The German army
opened fire and moved into the country. This began World
War II.
2. The city was *attacked* by war planes. They caused a lot of
damage.

to **react** (verb)
reaction (noun)

DEFINITION to react: to give an answer (in words or in actions) to something

EXAMPLES 1. The workers demanded a 15% pay increase. The company
agreed. This *reaction* surprised many people. They expected that the company would say no to the workers'
demands.
2. Maria: I told my mother today that I was going to stay
in the U.S. for another three months.
Mayumi: How did she *react?*
Maria: She was surprised, but she understands my reasons for staying.

to **promise** (verb and noun)

DEFINITION to promise: to say to someone that you will do something
(Then the person can believe that you will do it.)

EXAMPLES 1. I can't go to the movie tonight. I *promised* to take Ali to
the airport. He's going to meet a friend from home.
2. Sometimes people *promise* that they will do something.
But later they don't do it. They break their *promises*.

area (noun)

> DEFINITION an area: 1. a part of the world, of a country, of a place
> 2. a special part of life, of work, etc.

> EXAMPLES 1. This *area* of the country has cold winters and warm summers.
> 2. There is discrimination against blacks in many *areas* of life—for example, in education, in employment, in housing.

to **struggle** (verb and noun)

> DEFINITION to struggle: to fight against people or difficulties

> EXAMPLES 1. Women and black people in the U.S. had to *struggle* for equal rights.
> 2. In the seventeenth century in England there was a *struggle* for power between the king and Parliament. Parliament finally won.

Now read this passage and answer the questions about it.

1   In 1789 the U.S. government passed a law which said that the
2 land of the American Indians could never be taken from them
3 without their agreement. One hundred years later, however, the
4 Indians only had a very small part of the land that originally
5 belonged to them. How did this great injustice occur?
6   After 1812 white settlers began to move west across North
7 America. At first, the settlers and the Indians lived in peace. How-
8 ever, the number of settlers increased greatly every year, and
9 slowly the Indians began to see the white settlers as a danger to
10 their survival. To feed themselves, the settlers killed more and
11 more wild animals. The Indians, who depended on these animals
12 for food, had to struggle against starvation. The settlers also
13 brought with them many diseases which were common in white
14 society, but which were new for the Indians. Great numbers of
15 Indians became sick and died. Between 1843 and 1854 the Indian
16 population in one area of the country went down from 100,000 to
17 30,000.
18   More land was needed for the increasing number of white set-
19 tlers. In Washington, the old respect for the rights of the Indians
20 disappeared. The old promises to the Indians were broken; the fed-
21 eral government began to move groups of Indians from their origi-
22 nal homelands to other, poorer parts of the country. Some Indians
23 reacted angrily and violently to this treatment. They began to at-
24 tack white settlers, and the Indian Wars began. For thirty years,

25	until the late 1880s, different groups of Indians fought against the
26	injustices of the white man. They had a few famous successes, but
27	the result of the struggle was never in doubt. There were too many
28	white soldiers, and they were too powerful. Many Indians were
29	killed; the survivors were moved from their homelands to different
30	areas of the country. It was a terrible chapter in the history of a
31	country that promised freedom and equality to everyone.

1. T F   In the U.S. there was never a law that protected the   Line(s) _____
           rights of American Indians.

2. Why did American Indians begin to see the white settlers as a   Line(s) _____
   danger to them?
   a. The settlers killed the animals which the Indians needed
      for food.
   b. The settlers brought new diseases which killed many Indians.
   c. Both (a) and (b)

3. Look at lines 19–20. What does the writer mean by "the old   Line(s) _____
   respect for the rights of the Indians disappeared"?
   a. The government had a new respect for the rights of the
      Indians.
   b. The government began to ignore the rights of the Indians.
   c. The government of the U.S. never had any respect for the
      rights of the Indians.

4. The U.S. government began to move Indians off their original   Line(s) _____
   land. How did the Indians react?
   a. They had to struggle against starvation.
   b. They began to fight the whites.
   c. They became sick and died.

5. T F   The Indians won the Indian Wars.   Line(s) _____

6. What is the writer's opinion about the treatment that the Indi- Line(s) _____
   ans received from the U.S. government?
   a. He believes that the government treated the Indians very
      unjustly.
   b. He believes that the government always respected the
      rights of the Indians.
   c. He believes that the government cannot be criticized for its
      treatment of the Indians.

PART D

opposition (noun)
opposed to (adjective)
opponent (noun)

DEFINITION to be opposed to something: not to agree with something; to be against something or to fight against it

opposition: the act of being against something

opponent: a person who struggles or fights against another person or idea

EXAMPLES
1. A lot of people in the U.S. were *opposed* to the war in Vietnam. They believed that the U.S. government was wrong.
2. The *opposition* to the war in Vietnam became stronger and stronger. The *opponents* came from all parts of U.S. society.

legal (adjective)
illegal (adjective)

DEFINITION legal: 1. describes something which is allowed by the law
2. connected with the law

EXAMPLES
1. Things which were *legal* some years ago are now *illegal*. For example, some years ago, a bar could refuse to serve a black person. Now this is against the law.
2. John begins his *legal* studies next year.

to **fear** (verb)
fear (noun)

DEFINITION to fear: to be afraid

EXAMPLES
1. In some parts of the city, people don't go out at night. They *fear* that they will be attacked.
2. *Fear* is a natural reaction to certain things. Most people are afraid at some time in their lives.

slave (noun)
slavery (noun)

DEFINITION a slave: a person without freedom who "belongs to" and works for another person

slavery: the system of having slaves

EXAMPLES 1. *Slaves* in the U.S. won their freedom in 1865.
2. In the seventeenth and eighteenth centuries many good people protested against *slavery*. They said that it was clearly against the laws of God.

to **punish** (verb)
punishment (noun)

DEFINITION to punish someone: to hurt a person who did something wrong

EXAMPLES 1. The boy did not tell the truth. He was *punished* by his father. The boy could not watch television for a week.
2. Sometimes *punishment* does not have the effect we want. Often the person who is *punished* does the same thing again.

severe (adjective)

DEFINITION severe: something which causes damage or hurt (Severe can be used to describe weather, heat, cold, pain, punishment, etc.)

EXAMPLES 1. The punishment for a person who helped a slave to escape was very *severe*. According to the law, the person who helped the slave could be killed.
2. Winters are very *severe* in this part of the country. The temperature often goes down to −30°F.

to **separate** (verb)
separate (adjective)

DEFINITION to separate: to divide

EXAMPLES 1. The Atlantic Ocean *separates* Europe and America.
2. I live in a one-room apartment at the moment. But I want to move. I want an apartment with a *separate* bedroom.

in theory (sentence connector)
in practice (sentence connector)

DEFINITION These connectors compare something that is only possible (**in theory**) with something different that really happens (**in practice**).

EXAMPLES 1. Plans which look good *in theory* sometimes do not work (succeed) *in practice*.

2. *In theory* black people can become doctors in the U.S.; there are no laws that stop them. *In practice,* however, it seems to be very difficult. Only about 3% of all doctors are black.

Now read this passage and answer the questions about it.

1　　　The African ancestors of today's black Americans were
2　brought to the U.S. as slaves in the seventeenth, eighteenth, and
3　nineteenth centuries. They worked on farms, especially the large
4　farms in the southern states. Slowly they became a necessary part
5　of the economic system of the South.
6　　　Slaves did not have the rights of people; according to the law,
7　they were "things" which belonged to the person who bought them.
8　They had to obey the orders of their owners without question. They
9　were not allowed to learn to read; their owners feared that edu-
10　cated slaves would begin to think about the injustice of the system
11　and would learn to struggle for their freedom. Slaves had to work
12　long hours in extremely unhealthy conditions. Their owners had
13　complete power over them. They could be bought and sold like
14　animals. At the slave markets, black children were separated from
15　their parents and never saw them again. Slave owners had the
16　right to punish severely any slave who broke rules or protested
17　against the system. Slaves were often beaten brutally by their
18　owners or killed. After the Civil War, one free slave reported that
19　his owner killed an older slave who was teaching him to read.
20　There was a law against brutality to slaves, so in theory an owner
21　who treated a slave badly could be punished. In practice, however,
22　the law meant nothing. Another law said that slaves could not give
23　evidence against white people, so very few owners were ever pun-
24　ished for their brutality.
25　　　Opposition to slavery began very early in the history of the
26　U.S.—in 1671—but little progress was made until the beginning of
27　the nineteenth century. By 1804 slavery was illegal in the north-
28　ern states. But it continued, it even grew, in the southern states,
29　which depended on cotton for their economic health. Slavery ended
30　in the South only after the Civil War. For blacks, however, the end
31　of slavery was only a beginning, the late beginning of a long and
32　difficult struggle for true justice and equality.

1. T　F　　Slavery in the United States began in the 1600s.　　Line(s) _____

2. According to the writer, why couldn't slaves learn to read?　　Line(s) _____
　 a. They did not have time for it.
　 b. Their owners were afraid that books would give them dan-
　　　 gerous ideas.

c. Reading was not something which they needed for their work.

3. T F   There were some laws that successfully protected the   Line(s) _____
            rights of slaves.

4. What happened to slaves who broke the rules of the system?   Line(s) _____
   a. They were punished.
   b. They were treated well.
   c. They were given different work.

5. T F   Nobody in the U.S. disagreed with slavery before   Line(s) _____
            1800.

6. Look at lines 26–27. Read the clause which begins "but little progress. . . ." What does it mean?
   a. The slave system did not become strong until the beginning of the nineteenth century.
   b. The slave system remained strong until 1800 and only began to disappear then.
   c. The slave system became weaker and weaker in the eighteenth century.

7. T F   The writer believes that after the Civil War, black   Line(s) _____
            people in the U.S. had true equality.

PART E

citizen (noun)

DEFINITION   a citizen: a person who belongs to a certain country

EXAMPLES   1. Many people from other countries become U.S. *citizens* every year.
           2. Carlos is living in the U.S. at the moment. But he's not an American *citizen*. He's a *citizen* of Mexico.

majority (noun)
major (adjective)
minority (noun)
minor (adjective)

DEFINITION   a majority: a greater number of people or things
             major: more important
             a minority: a smaller number of people or things
             minor: less important

EXAMPLES 1. Only 30% (a *minority*) of the population are satisfied with the government. A *majority* (55%) are unhappy with it. (Fifteen percent have no opinion.)
2. My car needs *major* repairs. The bill is going to be about $700!
3. The professor said that I had a few *minor* problems in my work. But in general it was very good.

crime (noun)
criminal (noun)

DEFINITION crime: a bad action that breaks the law (Use the verb *commit* with crime.)
to commit a crime: to do something bad; to break the law
criminal: a person who breaks the law

EXAMPLES 1. The police have two responsibilities: (1) to prevent *crimes* and (2) to catch *criminals*.
2. One hundred fifty years ago in England, a person who committed a minor *crime* was severely punished.

to judge (verb)
judge (noun)

DEFINITION to judge: to form an opinion about something or someone

EXAMPLES 1. Don't *judge* people too quickly. You need time to get to know them.
2. The *judge* sent the criminal to prison for two years.

to demonstrate (verb)
demonstration (noun)

DEFINITION to demonstrate: to show clearly
to demonstrate against something: to show that you are opposed to something

EXAMPLES 1. You are teaching people how to swim. But you don't just talk about it. You *demonstrate* it for them. You make the movements in the water, and the students watch.
2. There were many large *demonstrations* against the Vietnam War in the U.S. The war became very unpopular.

lawyer (noun)

DEFINITION a lawyer: a person who studied law and who now helps people who have problems with the laws

EXAMPLES 1. The criminal had a very good *lawyer*. He wasn't sent to prison. He only had to pay $5,000.
2. Mike had an accident. The police said that it was his fault. Mike thought that he wasn't responsible for the accident, so he went to a *lawyer* for help.

minister (noun)

DEFINITION a minister: a leader of a church (non-Catholic)

EXAMPLES 1. A number of *ministers* were in the peace demonstrations. Their religion said that wars were against God's law.
2. My *minister* came to visit me in the hospital. That was nice of him.

authority (noun)
authorities (noun)

DEFINITION authority: power or responsibility to control or give orders. authorities: people or (government) departments which have official power and responsibility

EXAMPLES 1. The army controls the country now. It has the *authority* to pass new laws, arrest its opponents, and so on.
2. The *authorities* in Washington are worried about the demonstration that is planned for this weekend.

Now read this passage and answer the questions about it.

1 According to the U.S. Constitution, the citizens of a free coun-
2 try have the right to protest against unjust actions by their govern-
3 ment. In fact, protests against injustice led to the American War of
4 Independence in 1776. This article, however, will examine protests
5 in more recent U.S. history.
6 In the early 1960s, the U.S. began to fight a war in Vietnam.
7 During the first few years, the war was ignored by the majority of
8 Americans. Then the American public began to learn more about
9 the war. They saw television and newspaper reports about the war;
10 they heard the numbers of U.S. soldiers who were fighting and
11 dying there; they read descriptions of the terrible effects of the war
12 on the people of Vietnam. Some American citizens began to believe
13 that their government was fighting a brutal and unjust war in
14 Vietnam. They decided to show their opposition to the war and
15 organized peaceful demonstrations against it. The peace movement
16 was born.
17 At first, only a small minority of Americans supported the peace

18	movement, but it grew quickly in size and influence. There were a
19	number of reasons for this. First, many U.S. soldiers were being
20	killed in the fighting. More and more Americans at home lost sons,
21	or husbands, or brothers, or friends. Second, Americans at home
22	were shocked by the television reports of the war. The reports
23	showed the terrible damage which U.S. planes and guns caused in
24	Vietnam. In addition, soldiers who returned from the war talked
25	about the brutal things they saw and did in Vietnam. People even
26	began to talk about war crimes. Third, the authorities reacted vio-
27	lently and often very brutally to the large, nonviolent demonstra-
28	tions of the peace movement. Protesters were attacked and beaten
29	by police in Chicago, San Francisco, and Washington, D.C. Six stu-
30	dents were shot and killed by the authorities in Ohio and Missis-
31	sippi during demonstrations on campuses. For many Americans, the
32	brutal reactions of the authorities painted a picture of a government
33	without feeling. The peace movement grew stronger.
34	In April 1971, 750,000 people demonstrated against the Viet-
35	nam War in Washington, D.C. On the same day, 300,000 protested
36	the war in San Francisco. Now the peace movement was *not* just a
37	group of students. It included judges, lawyers, church ministers,
38	soldiers, and factory and office workers. The movement seemed to
39	speak for a majority of Americans. In 1971, people were asked for
40	their opinion of the war. Fifty-eight percent of the people who
41	answered thought that the war was wrong. Finally, the govern-
42	ment realized that it could not win a war which its people did not
43	support. It began to plan to bring American soldiers home from the
44	war.

1. T F   According to the writer, the American War of Inde-   Line(s) _____
            pendence began with a protest against injustice.

2. T F   At the beginning of the Vietnam War, many Ameri-   Line(s) _____
            cans were worried about the war.

3. T F   The writer suggests that television reports of the   Line(s) _____
            Vietnam War led to changes in people's opinions
            about the war.

4. At the beginning, how many Americans agreed with the ideas   Line(s)_____
   of the peace movement?

   a. The majority of Americans
   b. All Americans
   c. No Americans
   d. A small number of Americans

5. T F   The authorities used violence to stop peace demon-   Line(s) _____
           strations.

6. What was the effect of the authorities' reactions?   Line(s) _____
   a. More American citizens supported the government.
   b. The war ended.
   c. More people accepted the ideas of the peace movement.
   d. The war became more popular.

7. T F   There were only students in the peace movement.   Line(s) _____

8. T F   In 1971 the number of people who supported the war   Line(s) _____
           was smaller than the number of people who were op-
           posed to it.

Exercises for Parts C, D, and E

SAME OR DIFFERENT?

Read the two sentences in each example. Do they express the same ideas, or do they express different ideas? Write *S* for sentences with the same ideas; write *D* for sentences with different ideas.

   Remember: You can express the **same** ideas with **different** words and **different** grammar!

1. a. The judge sent the criminal to prison for five years.   _____
   b. The person who committed the crime was sent to prison for five
      years by the judge.

2. a. The people in the demonstration were opposed to the govern-   _____
      ment's new law.
   b. The people in the demonstration supported the government's
      new law.

3. a. I had an accident last night in my car, but the damage was not   _____
      serious.
   b. Last night I had an accident in my car, but it only caused
      minor damage.

4. a. The young child was punished by his teacher.   _____
   b. The young child was attacked by his teacher.

5. a. In some countries boys and girls go to separate schools.   _____
   b. Boys and girls go to the same schools in some countries.

6. a. In the nineteenth century the U.S. government treated the American Indians very unjustly. _____
   b. In the nineteenth century great injustices were committed against the Indians by the U.S. government.

7. a. The slave system in the U.S. continued until 1865. _____
   b. Slavery did not end in the U.S. until 1865.

8. a. The people who organized the demonstration feared that extremists would cause problems with the police. _____
   b. The organizers of the demonstration feared that extremists would cause trouble with the police.

9. a. The majority of people in the country disagree with the president. _____
   b. Only a minority of people in the country are opposed to the president.

10. a. The teacher showed us how to use the equipment correctly. _____
    b. The teacher gave us a demonstration of the right way to use the equipment.

11. a. Our opponents in our next soccer game won the competition last year. _____
    b. The team that we meet in our next soccer game were the winners of last year's competition.

12. a. The protesters were severely punished for their actions. _____
    b. The punishment which the protesters received for their actions was unjust.

EXPECTATIONS

Read the first sentence in each of these examples. Think about the ideas in it. Then choose the sentence or sentences that can follow it.

1. The criminal was severely punished.
   a. The judge sent him to prison for fifteen years.
   b. The crime that he committed was a minor one.
   c. He parked his car illegally.

2. There was greater opposition to slavery in the northern states of the U.S. than in the southern states.
   a. The majority of white people in the South were opposed to slavery.
   b. The economy of the North did not depend on the work of slaves.
   c. In the North slavery was ended by 1804. In the South slaves did not win their freedom until 1865.

3. In theory, there is complete equality for every citizen of the U.S.
   a. But, in practice, a number of minorities are treated very unjustly.
   b. In practice, however, the white majority has much more economic power than the black minority.
   c. In practice, however, there are no injustices in American society.

4. Twenty years ago in the southern states of the U.S., black children and white children had to go to separate schools.
   a. According to local laws, schools for both races were illegal.
   b. Blacks and whites studied together, played sports together, and grew up together.
   c. This is an example of the racial discrimination which was everywhere in the society of that time.

5. Some peace demonstrations of the 1960s ended in violence.
   a. Sometimes it was started by small groups of extremists, but at other times the authorities were to blame.
   b. All the demonstrators were opposed to violence.
   c. The majority of them, however, were very peaceful.

6. Mike needs a lawyer.
   a. He is in the hospital and is extremely ill.
   b. The police say that he stole a car.
   c. He was arrested during a violent demonstration yesterday.

7. The government put 4,000 soldiers and policemen on duty for the day of the demonstration.
   a. They feared that government buildings would be attacked.
   b. They expected a small peaceful protest.
   c. This reaction showed that the authorities were worried about the possibility of violence.

8. The organizers wanted a peaceful demonstration, and everything went according to plan.
   a. A number of extremists attacked the police with stones and firebombs.
   b. There were some minor problems; a few people were arrested, but no one was hurt.
   c. Violent struggles between police and demonstrators started almost immediately.

VOCABULARY QUIZ

Choose the correct word for each empty space. Use each word only once.

demonstration	separate	power	federal
judge	struggle	legal	citizen
promise	opposition	opponent	major
illegally	severe	reaction	powerful
attack	authorities	crime	majority

1. The peace movement grew and became very _____. Finally the government had to pay attention to it.

2. The war planes _____ed the town and completely destroyed it. A large number of people were killed.

3. In the nineteenth century the U.S. government said that it would respect the rights of American Indians. But it broke this _____. It treated the Indians very unjustly.

4. Some people in the U.S. think that the _____ government in Washington has too much power. They want to give state government more responsibilities.

5. John damaged his father's car in an accident. He told his father about this. His father's _____ surprised John. He didn't get angry; he just said, "Don't worry about it. Accidents can happen to anyone."

6. We are expecting a _____ storm tonight. The radio is warning that we will get high winds and a foot of snow in the next twelve hours.

7. I have a _____ problem. Tomorrow I'm going to talk to a lawyer about it.

8. There is a lot of _____ to the government's new law. Many people are planning to disobey it deliberately.

9. Some people believe that _____ classes are better for boys and girls than classes where boys and girls are together. They say that girls learn better without boys in their classes.

10. I got a ticket from the police and had to pay $10. I parked my car

    _____.

11. This was a great injustice. This man was punished for a _____ which he did not commit.

12. Only people who are _____s of the U.S. can vote in elections here. Foreign visitors and foreign students can't vote.

13. In the U.S. people who are organizing a large meeting in a public place have to inform the _____ about it. The police and the city government need to know about the meeting.

14. A lot of people do not agree with the government's decision to increase taxes. They are organizing a number of _____s to show their disagreement on the streets of Washington, D.C.

15. The present government is very unpopular. A _____ of people do not agree with its ideas, so it will probably lose the next election.

Main Reading

Pre-Reading Exercises

VOCABULARY IN CONTEXT

Use the context to guess the meaning of the new words (in boldface type). The words in italics will help you in the first five examples.
Remember: Read each example to the end. Do not stop after the new word!

1. In South Africa there is **segregation** in many areas of life. *Black* people *can only* go to black schools, and there are *separate* schools for the other races— for the whites, for the Indians, and for the coloreds. People of different races *cannot* live together or get married. Even hotels are **segregated.** In South Africa this *system* is called apartheid.

   Segregation means _____.
   a. bad feelings between people who belong to different races
   b. a social system which separates different racial groups
   c. a special type of education system

2. The university is *improving* its **facilities.** It is *building* a *new swimming-pool* and a *new gymnasium*. The new *computer center* is almost finished. *These* new **facilities** will attract many more students to the university.

   Facilities means _____.

   a. people who go to the university
   b. subjects that students can study at the university
   c. things (places and equipment) that can be used for certain activities

3. The *audience listened to* the president's **speech.** He *spoke* for about thirty minutes. In the **speech** the president *explained* his new program against unemployment.

   Speech means _____.

   a. a meeting of people who are interested in politics
   b. a talk to a group of people
   c. an assistant of the president

4. Mike: *Who* will win the *election* for **mayor?**
   Kate: Tom Klein, I hope. This *city* needs a good, *honest* **mayor.**

   Mayor means _____.

   a. the leader of the city government
   b. a department of the city government
   c. an area of the city

5. The demonstration was peaceful. But then the police *attacked* the demonstrators without reason and beat them. *This* **incident** *took place* in front of television cameras. Soon the whole country was talking about it.

   Incident means _____.

   a. a person in a demonstration
   b. a policeman
   c. something that happens

6. Gandhi wanted independence for India. In 1947 he **achieved** his goal. India became fully independent from Great Britain in that year.

   To achieve means _____.

   a. to fail to do something
   b. to plan to do something
   c. to finish something successfully

7. This film is about **revenge.** It tells the story of a man who loses his wife and son. They are killed by criminals. The police have no evidence against the criminals. But the man knows them and plans his **revenge.** Finally, he kills them.

To take revenge means _____.

 a. to be extremely angry about something
 b. to deliberately hurt someone who hurt you
 c. to find the person who committed a violent crime

8. In a free country everyone has the same rights **regardless of** their race, religion, political ideas, native language, or economic power. The laws must be the same for everyone.

 Regardless of X means _____.

 a. according to X
 b. X has an influence on something
 c. X has no effect on something

9. Today's black Americans are the **descendants** of Africans who were brought to North America as slaves from the seventeenth to the nineteenth century.

 Descendants are _____.

 a. friends
 b. opposite of ancestors
 c. relatives

10. John's political ideas are quite **moderate.** He believes that there have to be some changes in our society, but he is opposed to violent changes.

 Moderate means _____.

 a. extremely conservative
 b. illegal
 c. not extreme

11. We went to a Chinese restaurant yesterday evening. We were **served** by Sue, a girl who was in our English class with us last semester. She works in the restaurant on weekends now.

 To serve someone means _____.

 a. to bring people the food and drink which they order
 b. to give people a lesson in something
 c. to help people with a problem which they are trying to solve

12. In ten minutes the temperature fell from 60°F to 32°F, the sun disappeared, and the wind started to blow strongly. This **sudden** change in the weather took a lot of people by surprise. They weren't expecting it, so they weren't wearing warm clothes.

 Sudden describes something _____.

 a. which happens quickly and which people don't expect
 b. which is very important for people
 c. which everyone can understand without difficulty

Read the title of this article carefully. Then choose the ideas that you expect in the article. For the moment, don't worry about the name Martin Luther King. Pay attention only to the words *The Black Struggle for Equality*.

1. The article will give a full description of the lives of American Indians.   YES   NO

2. The article will describe the lives of black people in the U.S.   YES   NO

3. The article will describe the lives of the first European settlers in North America.   YES   NO

4. The article will show that blacks in the U.S. were not treated fairly.   YES   NO

5. The article will talk about injustice and discrimination in the U.S.   YES   NO

6. The article will give a full description of slavery in the U.S.   YES   NO

7. The article will compare the U.S. system of government with the Russian system of government.   YES   NO

8. The article will contain examples of injustices against blacks in the U.S.   YES   NO

9. The article will show that blacks demanded equality.   YES   NO

10. The article will talk a great deal about demonstrations against the Vietnam War.   YES   NO

Some of you perhaps know the name Martin Luther King. The next three questions are for people who know something about this man.

1. The article will talk only about American blacks in the seventeenth, eighteenth, and nineteenth centuries.   YES   NO

2. The article will show that Martin Luther King was important for black people.   YES   NO

3. The article will examine recent American history (of the 1950s and the 1960s).   YES   NO

Now you can start to read the article. You will read it in sections. You will also get the chance to develop some expectations for each section. Turn to page 169.

Martin Luther King, Jr.

Martin Luther King and the
Black Struggle for Equality

The Lives of Black People: 1865–1955

1   The Declaration of Independence of the U.S. was written more
2 than 200 years ago, but its ideas are as important now as they
3 were in 1776. In it the leaders of the American Revolution ex-
4 pressed their belief that all men are born equal and that all men
5 have the right to live in freedom regardless of their race, the color
6 of their skin, their religion, or their social class. In spite of this
7 belief in equality, however, equal rights were not enjoyed by every-
8 one. The history of the U.S. to this day contains many examples of
9 different groups of people who had to struggle for the rights which
10 were promised to them. For some of these groups, the struggle is
11 still not finished. One of the largest of these groups is the black
12 Americans, the descendants of African slaves who were brought to
13 the U.S. before the middle of the nineteenth century.

The Civil Rights March on Washington, August 1963

14   After the Civil War, the law said that black people were free
15   and equal citizens of the U.S. In theory, they had the same rights
16   as everyone else. In practice, however, they did not enjoy the same
17   rights as the white majority of the country. In the southern states
18   of the U.S. the two races were segregated. Blacks could only attend
19   black schools. At bus stations there were separate seats and sepa-
20   rate waiting rooms, even separate drinking water, for blacks and
21   whites. Many bars and restaurants refused to serve black custom-
22   ers. A black who used a facility for whites could be arrested and
23   sent to prison. Most white people believed in segregation. Even
24   white ministers supported the system.

25   Blacks in the South had other problems in addition to segrega-
26   tion. According to federal law, they had the right to vote in elec-
27   tions. But local white authorities made it difficult for blacks to
28   register to vote. As a result, all of the political power remained in
29   the hands of whites, and life did not really improve for the black
30   population. Blacks usually went to the worst schools and lived in
31   the worst housing in these states. They had bad health care, and
32   their children were often sick and hungry. Unemployment was
33   very high in their communities, often higher than in even the

Freedom and Equality in the United States   **165**

34 poorest white communities. Those black people who had work often
35 had the most unpleasant jobs and earned less money than white
36 workers.

37   In the northern states there was no official segregation of the   4
38 races, but life for black people was not any easier. They had to live
39 with discrimination in all areas of life. Whites had better housing,
40 better schools, better jobs, and better health care. Many jobs were
41 not really open to black people. There were few or no black police-
42 men, judges, lawyers, or doctors. In both parts of the country blacks
43 could not expect fair treatment from the police or the legal system.
44 Often blacks who broke the law received punishment that was
45 more severe than the punishment which whites received for simi-
46 lar crimes. Even blacks who committed no crime could not depend
47 on the law for protection; sometimes blacks were killed by angry
48 white crowds who wanted revenge for a crime which was commit-
49 ted against a white person. For 100 years after the American Civil
50 War, blacks lived like second-class citizens in their own country.

The Beginnings of the Modern Black Protest Movement

51   On December 1, 1955, in Montgomery, Alabama, a black   5
52 woman named Rosa Parks refused to give up her bus seat to a white
53 man who did not have a seat. She was arrested. A law in Montgom-
54 ery said that black passengers had to give their seats to any white
55 passengers who were without seats! The incident seemed unimpor-
56 tant at first, but it was really the beginning of the black protest
57 movement of the 1960s. It gave blacks their first national leader, Dr.
58 Martin Luther King, the minister of a church in Montgomery.
59   After the arrest of Rosa Parks, Dr. King organized protests of   6
60 the black people of Montgomery against the city government and
61 the bus company. Like Gandhi, the Indian leader who won inde-
62 pendence for India from the British, Dr. King believed that people
63 did not have to use violence to change society. He believed that
64 nonviolent protests would finally change the minds of whites who
65 were opposed to equal rights for blacks. He therefore organized a
66 protest that would put pressure on the city government. For a year,
67 blacks refused to use the city public transport system. They walked
68 to and from work in good weather and in bad. They helped each
69 other: People who had cars gave rides to people without transport;
70 black taxi companies transported people for the same price as the
71 buses. The bus company and other white businesses in the city lost
72 a lot of money. Finally, after a year of protest, the city government
73 had to change the law.
74   The Montgomery protest showed blacks that they did have   7

75 enough power to change their own lives. In the years which fol-
76 lowed the Montgomery success, more and more blacks began to
77 demand the rights which federal laws gave them but which local
78 laws often denied them. In 1963, Dr. King led blacks in a number
79 of nonviolent demonstrations against segregation and discrimina-
80 tion in Birmingham, Alabama. However, the local white authori-
81 ties were afraid of change; they feared that they would lose their
82 power. They reacted violently. The demonstrators were attacked by
83 police with dogs. Men, women, and children were brutally beaten
84 by the police, and more than 2,000 blacks were arrested.

85 The television pictures of the police brutality in Birmingham 8
86 were seen all over the U.S. and in many other countries. Whites
87 who knew nothing about the problems of blacks were shocked; they
88 began to realize the injustices that existed in their society. The
89 federal government finally began to work on new laws which
90 would really protect the rights of black people.

The Struggle for Equality: Successes and Failures

91 The movement for black civil rights grew larger and more popu- 9
92 lar. In August 1963, 250,000 people attended a peaceful demonstra-
93 tion in Washington, D.C. It was the largest demonstration in the
94 history of the U.S. until then. At the demonstration, Martin Luther
95 King gave his famous "I Have a Dream" speech. In the speech, he
96 demanded justice for black people and described the United States of
97 his dream, a country where blacks and whites would be equal and
98 where one day blacks and whites would live in peace together. The
99 speech made Dr. King famous in the U.S. and all over the world.
100 Black people began to accept him as their national leader. Moderate
101 white people finally understood the need for change and began to
102 support his demands for equal rights for all citizens regardless of
103 their race. In 1964, Dr. King won the Nobel Peace Prize for his work
104 in the nonviolent struggle for equal rights.

105 In the next few years, Dr. King continued to protest against 10
106 the treatment of blacks in the U.S. The protests led to a number of
107 changes in the law, changes which showed that the government
108 finally was serious about equal rights for everyone. In 1963 the
109 federal government used soldiers to register black students at the
110 segregated University of Alabama. In 1964 the first Civil Rights
111 Act was passed. It gave the federal government the power to end
112 segregation everywhere. In 1965 the Voting Rights Act gave the
113 government the power to register black voters. In 1968 the second
114 Civil Rights Act made discrimination in housing and employment
115 illegal.

11

The story of Martin Luther King and the story of the struggle for black rights were not just stories of success. From the beginning the struggle was difficult, and the risks were great. Many whites could not accept the idea that blacks were their equals. Black demonstrators were attacked by the local white police and were often treated brutally by the local authorities. Dr. King was arrested and put in jail many times. White extremists, some of them police who were not on duty, attacked black demonstrators and beat them badly. In September 1963, whites put a bomb in a Birmingham church; it exploded and killed four young black girls. In June 1964, three young civil rights workers, two white and one black, were murdered by white extremists in Mississippi. In Alabama in 1965, extremists also killed a white woman who was telling black people that they had the right to vote in elections.

12

After 1965, Dr. King's popularity began to decrease with whites and blacks. Many young blacks were very dissatisfied with the slowness of the changes in American society. They began to disagree with Dr. King's idea of nonviolence. They began to think that it was not always the best way to achieve the goal of true equality. Some blacks even believed that they had to build their own separate society in the U.S. They believed that blacks could never be free and equal in a society with a white majority.

13

In spite of the opposition to him, Dr. King remained the most popular and most respected of black leaders. He did not forget his dream of a new America. He did not give up his belief in peaceful, nonviolent protest. In 1968 he began to work for the poor of the U.S., not only the blacks, but the whites, the Indians, and the Hispanics. On April 4, 1968, however, his work was ended brutally and suddenly. Dr. King, who was in Memphis, Tennessee, to support black city workers, was murdered by a white gunman. The news shocked the country and caused days and nights of violence in the black communities of major cities like Los Angeles, Chicago, and Philadelphia. Later, the gunman was arrested and sent to prison; even today no one really knows his reasons for the killing.

14

Today few people really believe that blacks have achieved full social and economic equality in the U.S. Many blacks still live on welfare; many still live in poor housing. Black children often still do not receive an education that will equip them for success in life. However, progress can be seen in many areas. Blacks now have political power. For example, in 1984 at least four of the largest cities in the U.S. had black mayors—Los Angeles, Chicago, Atlanta, and Philadelphia. There is no segregation in education, and an increasing number of blacks are graduating from college. The rights of blacks are protected by a number of new laws against

160   discrimination in housing, employment, and other areas of life. For
161   many people, Dr. Martin Luther King is the person who was most
162   responsible for all these changes. For this reason, he is respected
163   by Americans of every race and color today.

Section I: The Lives of Black People: 1865–1955

EXPECTATIONS

Read the title of Section I. Then choose the ideas that you expect in this section.

1. This section will show that blacks had complete equality with whites after 1865.   YES   NO

2. This section will describe the racial injustices which existed in the U.S. in the nineteenth and twentieth centuries.   YES   NO

3. Unemployment in black communities was higher than in white communities.   YES   NO

4. Health care in black communities was better than health care in white communities.   YES   NO

5. The majority of doctors, professors, lawyers, and judges were white.   YES   NO

6. Black people earned less money than white people.   YES   NO

Don't worry about your answers to these Expectation questions yet. Now read Section I of the article; do the Main Ideas Check and the Comprehension Check for this section. Then come back and look at your Expectation answers. How correct were they?

MAIN IDEAS CHECK

Here are the main ideas of the paragraphs in this section. Write the correct paragraph number opposite each main idea.

PARAGRAPH   IDEA

_____   In both North and South, there was discrimination against black people in all areas of life.

_____   The people who began the U.S. believed that all men were equal. But black people in the U.S. are still struggling for equality.

_____   In the southern states of the U.S. society was segregated.

_____   In the South blacks also had other problems.

1. T F Black people are the only group of people in U.S. history who had to struggle for equal rights. Line(s) _____

2. T F According to the writer, black people now have full equality. Line(s) _____

3. How was life for blacks after the Civil War? Line(s) _____
   a. In theory they had equal rights, but in practice they did not.
   b. They enjoyed complete freedom and full equality with all other citizens of the U.S.
   c. They were still slaves.

4. Why does the writer tell us that some bars and restaurants were only for white people? Line(s) _____
   a. The writer wants to give a clear example of segregation.
   b. The writer wants to show that blacks often were hungry.
   c. The writer wants to show that black people had the same rights as white people.

5. Why did blacks have little or no political power? Line(s) _____
   a. According to federal law, they could not vote in an election.
   b. Often black people could not register to vote.
   c. Black people did not want to vote for white people in elections.

6. T F Unemployment was a major problem in black communities. Line(s) _____

7. T F Life for black people in the North was much more pleasant than life in the South. Line(s) _____

8. What is the writer's opinion of the U.S. legal system up to 1955? Line(s) _____
   a. It protected the rights of black people fairly.
   b. It treated blacks and whites the same.
   c. It discriminated against blacks.

Section II: The Beginnings of the Modern Black Protest Movement

EXPECTATIONS

Read the title of Section II. Then choose the ideas that you expect in this section.

1. This section will show that the black protest movement achieved its goals. YES NO

2. This section will tell us that black people formed organizations that demanded equality for them. YES NO

3. This section will talk about recent history in the U.S. YES NO

Now read Section II of the article. Do the Main Ideas Check and the Comprehension Check. Then look back at the answers to the Expectations. How correct were they?

MAIN IDEAS CHECK

Here are the main ideas of the paragraphs in this section. Write the correct paragraph number opposite each main idea.

PARAGRAPH   IDEA

_____   The success of the Montgomery protest showed black people in Birmingham that they could demonstrate against injustice in their city.

_____   In 1955 a small racial incident in Montgomery began the black protest movement.

_____   The reactions of the white authorities in Birmingham helped to change people's ideas about the lives of black people.

_____   Martin Luther King organized the black people of Montgomery in a successful protest against the racial laws of the city government.

COMPREHENSION CHECK

1. What happened in Montgomery, Alabama, on December 1, 1955?   Line(s) _____
   a. A black woman got on a bus which was only for whites.
   b. A black woman did not give her seat to a white man who was standing.
   c. A black woman refused to get on a bus.

2. T F   Dr. Martin Luther King was a famous black leader before the Montgomery incident.   Line(s) _____

3. What were Dr. King's ideas about violence?   Line(s) _____
   a. He believed that blacks could achieve their goals by nonviolent protests.
   b. He believed that only violence could change the minds of whites who were opposed to equality for blacks.
   c. He believed that peaceful protests were useless.

4. How did black people in Montgomery achieve their goal?   Line(s) _____
   a. Yes, their protest was successful.
   b. They did not use the city buses.
   c. They did not go to work.

5. What effect did the Montgomery protest have on other black   Line(s) _____
   people in America?
   a. It made them more afraid of white people.
   b. It gave them more confidence to demand their rights.
   c. It satisfied them, and they stopped their protests.

6. Who started the violence at the demonstrations in Birming-   Line(s) _____
   ham, Alabama?
   a. The demonstrators
   b. The police
   c. The white population of the city

7. What effect did the television pictures of the Birmingham pro-   Line(s) _____
   tests have on American society?
   a. The pictures showed people that their society treated blacks
      unjustly.
   b. The pictures showed that black people enjoyed the same
      rights as whites.
   c. The pictures showed people that the federal government
      protected the rights of blacks.

Section III: The Struggle for Equality: Successes and Failures

EXPECTATIONS

Read the title of Section III. Then choose the ideas that you expect in this section.

1. This section will tell us that black people made no progress in   YES   NO
   their struggle for equality.

2. This section will give examples of the improvements that can   YES   NO
   be seen in the lives of black people today.

3. This section will show that the black protest movement   YES   NO
   achieved all its goals.

Read Section III. Now answer the Main Ideas Check and the Comprehension Check.
Afterward, come back to your answers to the Expectations. How correct were they?

MAIN IDEAS CHECK

Here are the main ideas of the paragraphs in this section. Write the correct paragraph number opposite each main idea.

PARAGRAPH   IDEA

_____   Martin Luther King was murdered in 1968 by a white gunman.

_____   There was violent opposition to black people's protests from the white authorities and from white extremists.

_____   The black protest movement led to a number of changes in the laws of the U.S.

_____   According to many people, Dr. King is responsible for the improvements which can be seen in black people's lives today.

_____   Dr. King became very famous, and his movement became powerful.

_____   In the black population there was opposition to Dr. King's ideas about nonviolent protest.

COMPREHENSION CHECK

1. What happened to the black protest movement between 1955 and 1963?   Line(s) _____
   a. It achieved its goals, and then it disappeared.
   b. It existed, but it remained extremely small.
   c. More and more people began to support it.

2. T F   In 1965, Martin Luther King was not known outside the U.S.   Line(s) _____

3. The new laws that the writer mentions in lines 110–115 show   Line(s) _____
   a. that the federal government was not interested in the problems of black people.
   b. that the federal government wanted equality for all races.
   c. that black people had equality in housing and employment in 1968.

4. T F   The people who worked for black equality were often in danger.   Line(s) _____

5. T F   The opposition to demands for equality only came from the local white authorities.   Line(s) _____

6. What did a large number of young black people think about Dr. King's ideas on nonviolent protests? Line(s) _____
   a. They agreed with his ideas.
   b. They thought that peaceful protests would not succeed.
   c. They believed that nonviolent protests were the best way to achieve true equality.

7. T F   Dr. King only demanded equal rights for the black minority of the U.S. Line(s) _____

8. What is the writer's final opinion about Dr. King and the black protest movement? Line(s) _____
   a. The writer believes that Dr. King won full equality for all blacks.
   b. The writer believes that progress was made and that Dr. King was responsible for it.
   c. The writer believes that Dr. King and the black protest movement failed to achieve any improvements in the treatment of black people.

Now do the paragraph reading exercise on the next page.

PARAGRAPH READING

These sentences form a paragraph, but they are not in the correct order. Put the sentences into their correct order. The first two sentences are already in their correct places.

___1___ In 1963 television brought pictures of the police violence against peaceful black demonstrators in Birmingham into almost every American home.

___2___ The television pictures caused a number of changes in American society.

_____ So it finally began to think seriously about introducing new laws which would really protect the rights of black people.

_____ This part of the white population then began to demand justice and equality for black people.

_____ In conclusion, therefore, you can say that television helped to change American society.

_____ First, blacks in other parts of the country who saw the pictures became angry that black people could still be treated by the white authorities in this way.

_____ Second, among moderate whites, the pictures of the violence led to the realization that their society was full of injustices.

_____ As a result, blacks everywhere began to demand justice, and the protest movement grew quickly from a small local movement into a powerful national movement.

_____ Third, the federal government was afraid that more television reports like the ones from Birmingham would damage people's ideas about the U.S., both in the U.S. and in other countries.

The Environment in Danger

Vocabulary Study and Preparatory Reading

PART A

to **pollute** (verb)
pollution (noun)

DEFINITION   to pollute something: to make something dirty and unhealthy

EXAMPLES   1. The heavy industries in this town *pollute* our air with their smoke.
    2. *Pollution* is now a major problem for the world. Our air and water are becoming very dangerous for living things.

reluctant (adjective)

DEFINITION   to be reluctant to do something: not to want to do something

EXAMPLES   1. The government is *reluctant* to punish this company for the pollution that it causes. The company is extremely important for the economy.
    2. We had a very enjoyable vacation in the Caribbean last summer. We were very *reluctant* to go home at the end of our vacation.

environment (noun)

DEFINITION   the environment: all the conditions (social and natural) that can influence the life and development of a person or of a thing.

EXAMPLES 1. A lot of people today are worried about the *environment*. They want to protect our air, water, and land from pollution.
2. Children need a good home *environment*. Without love and support, they will have problems as adults.

substance (noun)

DEFINITION   a substance: a general word for any material

EXAMPLES 1. This bottle contains a very dangerous *substance*. Only a little of it can kill a person.
2. Water, oil, and rubber are all *substances*.

acid (noun)

DEFINITION   an acid: a substance which contains hydrogen (An acid often destroys the things it touches.)

EXAMPLES 1. Be careful with that bottle. It contains *acid*—H_2SO_4. It'll burn you if it touches your skin.
2. Automobile batteries produce *acid*. So be careful with that battery you took out of your car!

amount (noun)

DEFINITION   an amount of X: some
a large amount of X: a great deal of
a small amount of X: not a lot of X, a little X

EXAMPLES 1. I spent a large *amount* of money for food last week. The bill came to more than $70.
2. This medicine is very strong. You only need to take a small *amount* of it.

plant (noun)

DEFINITION   a plant: a factory

EXAMPLES 1. The automobile *plant* here is closing. One thousand people are going to lose their jobs.
2. This new power *plant* will produce enough electricity for 25% of the state.

to **contaminate** (verb)
contaminated (adjective)

    DEFINITION   to contaminate: to make something dirty and unhealthy

    EXAMPLES   1. A large number of people who stayed at the hotel became sick. Scientists discovered that they ate some *contaminated* food.
               2. Some oil got into the town's water. It *contaminated* the drinking water.

Now read this passage and answer the questions about it.

1   According to some scientists, one of the most serious problems
2   for the environment is acid rain. Acid rain is caused mainly by
3   power plants that burn coal to produce electricity. The smoke from
4   these power plants contains acidic substances which later fall back
5   to earth in rain or snow. As a result, the amount of acids increases
6   in lakes and rivers, and fish die. Already many lakes in Canada,
7   the northeastern U.S., and Norway are contaminated by pollution
8   from power plants. Scientists are also warning that acid rain can
9   damage plants and trees and lead to the contamination of drinking
10   water. It is therefore a danger to human health.
11   Many governments are reluctant to pass laws that will reduce
12   the pollution which causes acid rain. They say that the causes of
13   acid rain are still not completely clear. However, it is clear to the
14   majority of environmentalists that economics is the real reason for
15   governmental reluctance. In most industrial countries the majority
16   of power plants use coal. It will be extremely expensive to develop
17   the special equipment that is needed to reduce the pollution from
18   these power plants.

1. T F   According to this passage, it is important to solve the   Line(s) _____
            problem of acid rain.

2. What is the cause of acid rain?   Line(s) _____
    a. Fish in rivers and lakes begin to die.
    b. The amount of acid in rivers and lakes begins to increase.
    c. Power plants burn coal.

3. T F   It is certain that governments will pass new laws to   Line(s) _____
            reduce acid rain.

4. T F   Acid rain is only a problem in the United States.   Line(s) _____

5. What is the real explanation for the reluctance of governments Line(s) ____
   to pass laws against acid rain pollution?
   a. It is not clear that acid rain causes problems.
   b. It will not be cheap to reduce pollution from power plants.
   c. It is not possible to produce electricity without coal.

PART B

to **conduct** (verb)

> DEFINITION   to conduct research: direct and do research (You can also *con-duct* meetings and experiments, investigations, or inquiries.)
>
> EXAMPLES   1. The scientist is *conducting* research into the causes of heart diseases.
> 2. Both the American and the British governments *conducted* inquiries into the causes of the *Titanic* disaster.

to **enforce** (verb)

> DEFINITION   to enforce a law: to make people obey the law and to punish them for breaking it
>
> EXAMPLES   1. There is a speed limit of 25 miles an hour in this town, and the police really *enforce* it. They'll stop you even if you're only driving at 30.
> 2. The responsibility of the police is to *enforce* the law.

to **forbid** (irregular verb)
forbade, forbidden

> DEFINITION   to forbid X: not to allow X
>
> EXAMPLES   1. Smoking is *forbidden* in movie theaters in the U.S.; it can cause dangerous fires.
> 2. Industries cannot build factories in this part of town. A local law *forbids* it. This part of town is only for homes and apartments.

chemical (noun and adjective)

> DEFINITION   a chemical: a general word for a substance that is used in chemistry; a substance which is produced in chemistry

EXAMPLES 1. An acid is a *chemical*.
2. I got some oil on my shirt. But I have a *chemical* which will take the oil off the shirt.

poison (noun)
poisonous (adjective)

DEFINITION poison: a substance that can harm or kill a living person or thing

EXAMPLES 1. During World War I, the German, French, and British armies used *poison* gas. Many soldiers died.
2. Be careful with that chemical. It's very *poisonous*.

to **waste** (verb)
waste (noun)

DEFINITION to waste something: to spend something but not get any benefit from it

EXAMPLES 1. I *wasted* a whole afternoon yesterday. I drove fifty miles to visit a friend. But he was not at home, and I didn't see him.
2. The chemical industry produces a lot of *waste*. Some of it is very poisonous.

dump (noun)

DEFINITION a dump: a place where people leave useless material

EXAMPLES 1. There is a *dump* for chemical waste near this town. People are worried about it. They think that it contains some dangerous substances.
2. Let's take this old furniture to the *dump*. We don't want it, and no one will use it.

to **claim** (verb)

DEFINITION to claim: to say that something is true (usually without evidence)

EXAMPLES 1. The police stopped a car. The driver *claimed* that the car belonged to him, but he had no papers; he didn't even know the license number of the car.
2. A student in my class *claims* to be a friend of the president. He likes to tell stories!

Now read the passage on the next page and answer the questions about it.

1	The Environmental Protection Agency (E.P.A.) is the U.S. gov-
2	ernment department that has the major responsibility for the envi-
3	ronment. It conducts research into the effects of chemicals on
4	people, plants, and animals, and it has the authority to forbid the
5	production or use of chemical substances which are dangerous to
6	health. The agency also enforces laws against pollution and is re-
7	sponsible for cleaning land which is contaminated by poisonous
8	chemicals from waste dumps.
9	Many environmentalists, however, are not satisfied with the
10	work of the E.P.A. The critics point out that the agency is con-
11	trolled by the government. They claim that there are people in the
12	government who once had close business connections with indus-
13	tries that cause a great deal of pollution. Therefore, according to
14	these critics, it is clear that the E.P.A. cannot really do a good job.

1. T F   The E.P.A. is the only U.S. government department   Line(s) _____
           that protects the environment.

2. According to the passage, what does the E.P.A. *not* do?   Line(s) _____
   a. It develops new chemicals.
   b. It examines the effects of new chemicals.
   c. It cleans contaminated land.

3. T F   Everyone believes that the E.P.A. is doing its job   Line(s) _____
           well.

4. T F   According to many environmentalists, it is impossible   Line(s) _____
           for the E.P.A. to really protect the environment.

5. According to the passage, why can't the E.P.A. protect the en-   Line(s) _____
   vironment successfully?
   a. It does not have the authority to enforce the laws against
      pollution.
   b. It does not satisfy environmentalists.
   c. It is not independent enough.

Exercises for Parts A and B

SAME OR DIFFERENT?

Read the two sentences in each example. Do they express the same idea, or do they express different ideas? Write *S* for sentences with the same ideas; write *D* for sentences with different ideas.

Remember: You can express the **same** idea with **different** words and **different** grammar!

1. a. Many governments do not want to pass laws against pollution.   _____
   b. Many governments are reluctant to pass laws against pollution.

2. a. That waste dump contains a large number of very useful chemicals.   _____
   b. There are many poisonous chemicals in that waste dump.

3. a. Some scientists claim that acid rain is caused mainly by power plants which use coal.   _____
   b. It is claimed by some scientists that power plants which burn coal are the main cause of acid rain.

4. a. The chemical company is going to build a new plant near this town.   _____
   b. The chemical company is going to build a new waste facility near this town.

5. a. It is important to conduct research into the effects of new chemicals on the environment.   _____
   b. Research which is being conducted shows that new chemicals are important for the environment.

6. a. This new law forbids the use of certain substances.   _____
   b. This new law makes the use of certain chemicals and materials illegal.

7. a. The new laws that protect the environment from industrial pollution are not being enforced by the government.   _____
   b. The government is not punishing industries that are breaking the new laws against environmental pollution.

8. a. It is clear that small amounts of this chemical can contaminate large areas of land.   _____
   b. It is clear that large areas of land can be treated with small amounts of this chemical.

EXPECTATIONS

Read the first sentence in each of these examples. Think about the ideas in it. Then choose the sentence or sentences that can follow it.

1. This new chemical is extremely poisonous.

   a. Only a small amount of it will contaminate a large area.
   b. It is not a danger to the environment.
   c. It can be used by humans without any risk.

2. The government is doing very little to protect the environment.
   a. It claims that pollution is not a serious problem in this country.
   b. It is not enforcing any of the laws against pollution.
   c. It is going to close some chemical waste dumps.

3. The water in this area of town is undrinkable.
   a. People blame the chemical plant that was built here ten years ago.
   b. It contains a number of extremely poisonous substances.
   c. Tests which were conducted on it last month show that it is contaminated.

4. It is clear that the government is not enforcing the laws against pollution.
   a. It is severely punishing companies which are causing pollution.
   b. Last month it arrested the manager of a company which illegally dumped chemicals into a lake.
   c. It seems that it is extremely reluctant to punish large companies which are breaking environmental laws.

5. It is possible that this new chemical will be very beneficial to agriculture, but we should not make it available yet.
   a. Not enough is known about its effects on the environment.
   b. The research that is being conducted into its effects on the environment is not yet complete.
   c. There is clear evidence that it is one of the most dangerous substances which the chemical industry produces.

VOCABULARY QUIZ

Choose the correct word for each empty space. Use each word only once.

claim	substance	plant	conduct
reluctant	forbid	environment	enforce
pollute	poisonous	dump	amount
waste	contaminate	pollution	acid

1. A large automobile company is opening a new _____ in this city. It will employ about 2,000 people.

2. "Be careful with that bottle. It contains _____. If you get it on your skin, it will burn you badly."

3. Ten years ago the _____ in this city was very bad. Then the city government passed a number of new laws. Now the city is much cleaner, and the air is much healthier.

4. This medicine is very strong. You can only take a small _____ of it every day. It is dangerous to take more.

5. Many people believe that it is important to reduce pollution. If we do not reduce it, we will cause a lot of damage to the _____.

6. "Don't drive at more than 55 miles an hour in this state. There is a speed limit, and the police _____ it. They will stop you even if you drive at 60."

7. This chemical is extremely poisonous. The government should _____ its use.

8. Yesterday I drove to the shopping mall at two o'clock. But I didn't find the things I wanted to buy. At five o'clock I came home with nothing! I was a little angry. I don't like to _____ whole afternoons like that!

9. Scientists who work for the chemical company _____ that this chemical is 100% safe. But they are ignoring other research which suggests that it causes health problems.

10. Scientists are _____ing a lot of research into how to protect the environment from the dangerous substances that industry produces.

PART C

brain (noun)

DEFINITION   the brain: the part of our body (in the head) which controls thoughts, feelings, and body movements

EXAMPLES   1. The human *brain* is very different from the *brain* of any animal.
        2. The driver hit his head in the accident. The doctors believe that there is some damage to his *brain*. He cannot move his right arm or leg.

lung (noun)

DEFINITION   the lungs: the part of our body that fills with air

EXAMPLES   1. Smoking can cause *lung* disease.
        2. This patient cannot breathe properly, so the doctor is going to examine his *lungs*.

to **suffer** (verb)

DEFINITION
: to suffer: to feel pain or to experience something difficult or unpleasant

EXAMPLES
: 1. Many people in this town *suffer* from lung problems. Doctors think that the problems are caused by the air pollution.
: 2. This part of the country is *suffering* from high unemployment. About 25% of the people can't find work.

fine (noun)

DEFINITION
: a fine: a punishment in money

EXAMPLES
: 1. I broke the speed limit. The police stopped me. I had to pay a $70 *fine*.
: 2. A certain chemical company contaminated many rivers in the state. It had to pay a $300 million *fine*. Some people thought that this punishment was not severe enough.

consequence (noun)

DEFINITION
: a consequence: something that happens as a result of something else

EXAMPLES
: 1. Pollution is often a *consequence* of the rapid growth of industries in an area.
: 2. One *consequence* of the *Titanic* disaster was that after it every ship had to carry enough lifeboats for all passengers and crew.

to **expose** to (verb)

DEFINITION
: to expose people or things to X: to leave them without protection from X

EXAMPLES
: 1. The sun is very strong. If you are not used to it, don't *expose* your skin to the sun for more than ten minutes. If you do, you'll be burned.
: 2. People who are *exposed* to this chemical at work often develop health problems.

strict (adjective)

DEFINITION
: Strict describes a person who is severe or a rule which demands complete obedience.

EXAMPLES
: 1. The police in this state do not enforce the 55-mph speed limit very *strictly*. You can drive at 60–64 mph without any problems.

2. There is a *strict* no smoking rule in our office. No one can smoke there, not even visitors.

defect (noun)
defective (adjective)

DEFINITION a defect: something wrong, something which does not work

EXAMPLES
1. Some children are born with serious birth *defects*. Medical science is still not able to correct many of these *defects*.
2. If you buy a product which is *defective,* you can bring it back to the store and get your money back.

Now read this passage and answer the questions about it.

1   Industrial pollution is not only a problem for the countries of
2   Europe and North America. It is an extremely serious problem in
3   some developing countries. For these countries, economic growth is
4   a very important goal. They want to attract new industries, and so
5   they put few controls on industries which cause pollution.
6   Cubatao, an industrial town of 85,000 people in Brazil, is an
7   example of the connection between industrial development and pol-
8   lution. In 1954, Cubatao had no industry. Today it has more than
9   twenty large factories, which produce many pollutants. The people
10 of the town are exposed to a large number of poisonous substances
11 in their environment, and the consequences of this exposure can be
12 clearly seen. Birth defects are extremely common. For example,
13 one out of every 200 babies suffers from anencephaly, a very un-
14 usual type of brain damage. Usually only one out of every 5,000
15 babies is born with this condition. And other serious health prob-
16 lems are caused by the pollution. Among children and adults,
17 asthma and other lung problems are sometimes twelve times more
18 common in Cubatao than in other places.
19   It is true that Brazil, like many other countries, has laws
20 against pollution, but these laws are not enforced strictly enough. It
21 is cheaper for companies to ignore the laws and pay the fines than to
22 buy the expensive equipment that will reduce the pollution. It is
23 clear, therefore, that economic growth is more important to the gov-
24 ernment than the health of the workers. However, the responsibility
25 does not completely lie with the Brazilian government. The example
26 of Cubatao shows that international companies are not acting in a
27 responsible way either. A number of the factories in the town are
28 owned by large companies from France, Italy, and the U.S. They are
29 doing things in Brazil that they would not be able to do at home. If
30 they caused the same amount of pollution at home, they would be
31 severely punished or even put out of business.

Vocabulary: Read the passage without a dictionary, and then answer questions 1 and 2. The context will help you.

1. Anencephaly is _____.   Line(s) _____
   a. a lung disease which attacks children
   b. a brain condition which babies have at birth
   c. a certain type of chemical which is produced in Cubatao

2. Asthma is _____.   Lines(s) _____
   a. a condition which affects people's lungs
   b. a type of poisonous substance in the environment
   c. a type of birth defect

3. Why don't developing countries have strict pollution controls?   Line(s) _____
   a. Pollution is not a serious problem for developing countries.
   b. If they put stricter controls on industry, fewer companies would build new plants in developing countries.
   c. The new industries they want to attract do not cause much pollution.

4. Why does the writer use the example of Cubatao?   Line(s) _____
   a. He wants to show that industrial growth can cause pollution problems for developing countries.
   b. He wants to show that the pollution problem in Brazil is extremely serious.
   c. He wants to show that industrial development can happen extremely quickly in developing countries.

5. How is the health of the population of Cubatao?   Line(s) _____
   a. Their health is better than the health of people who live in other places.
   b. Their health is worse than the health of people who live in other places.
   c. Their health is the same as the health of people who live in other places.

6. Why can the writer claim that anencephaly is probably   Line(s) _____
   caused by the pollution in Cubatao?
   a. Anencephaly is very common in many parts of the world.
   b. Anencephaly is a very serious birth defect which doctors cannot cure.
   c. Anencephaly occurs much more often in Cubatao than in other places.

7. T F   Brazil does not have any pollution laws.   Line(s) _____

8. T F   If a company causes pollution in Brazil, it is very   Line(s) _____
         severely punished.

9. Who does the writer blame for the problems in Cubatao?   Line(s) _____
   a. The Brazilian government
   b. International companies with factories in Cubatao
   c. Both (a) and (b)

10. T F International companies cause more pollution at   Line(s) _____
         home than they do in Brazil.

PART D

balance (noun)

DEFINITION a balance: the condition where all parts of a system are equal

EXAMPLES 1. I broke my arm yesterday. I was standing on a chair. I lost
             my *balance* and fell off!
          2. There is usually a natural *balance* in a given area. How-
             ever, man can disturb that *balance* if he introduces some-
             thing new into the environment.

situation (noun)

DEFINITION a situation: general conditions at a certain time

EXAMPLES 1. John is in a difficult *situation* right now. He wants to ac-
             cept a new job in Europe, but his wife doesn't want to give
             up her job.
          2. The economic *situation* in the country is improving: Unem-
             ployment is falling, and prices are not going up.

purpose (noun)

DEFINITION a purpose: an effect that is planned; a reason

EXAMPLES 1. What *purpose* does this double glass serve? It keeps cold
             air out of the apartment.
          2. Carlos came to the U.S. for one main *purpose*—to study
             engineering here.

especially (adverb)

DEFINITION especially: This word is used to introduce something which is
            even *truer* than the idea in the first part of the
            sentence.

1. I like a glass of cold lemonade—*especially* after a soccer game in hot weather.
2. I love this part of the country, *especially* in the fall. The leaves change color, and the countryside looks beautiful.

resident (noun)

DEFINITION a resident: a person who lives in a certain place

EXAMPLES 1. If you are a *resident* in this state, you have to get a state drivers' license. If you are a visitor, you can use a license from another state.
2. The *residents* of the area are objecting to plans for an automobile plant here. They don't want a noisy and dirty factory near their homes.

ecology (noun)
ecological (adjective)

DEFINITION ecology: 1. the connections between living things and their environment
2. the science which studies these connections

EXAMPLES 1. Pollution is damaging the *ecology* of this area.
2. It is disturbing the *ecological* balance.

to **threaten** (verb)

DEFINITION to threaten: 1. to say that you will cause damage to someone
2. to cause possible damage in the future

EXAMPLES 1. The police arrested the man. He was *threatening* some people with a knife.
2. The whole ecology of this area is *threatened* by pollution. If we don't reduce the pollution, trees, animals, and fish will disappear.

long-term (adjective)
short-term (adjective)

DEFINITION Long-term describes something that happens after a long time. Short-term describes something that happens after a short time.

EXAMPLES 1. The *long-term* effects of cigarettes are very serious. People who smoke for thirty years often suffer from heart disease and lung diseases.

2. The *short-term* effects of cigarettes are not serious. If a young person smokes a cigarette, he perhaps will feel ill after the cigarette.

Now read this passage and answer the questions about it.

1   Every year in many developing countries large areas of land
2   that once produced food become completely unproductive. The hun-
3   gry residents of these areas have to move or die. The problem is not
4   caused by pollution; it is not the result of poisonous chemicals
5   which contaminate the land. Pollution is not the only way to de-
6   stroy the environment. It can be destroyed by humans who disturb
7   the ecological balance of an area in other ways. In any area there is
8   a balance in nature. Each part of the natural system depends on
9   other parts. If one part is disturbed, then the balance of the system
10   is disturbed and other parts begin to suffer. This is the problem
11   that is now threatening the lives of many people in many coun-
12   tries, for example, in Nepal.
13   A number of years ago, the population of Nepal began to in-
14   crease, especially among the people who live in the small farms in
15   the mountains. More food and fuel were necessary for the larger
16   number of people, so the farmers in the mountains bought more
17   animals. For fuel and animal food, they cut down more and more of
18   the trees and plants which grew on the sides of the mountains. The
19   farmers did not know that these plants and trees served a very
20   important purpose. They protected the hills from the weather.
21   They held the top soil in place and prevented it from being pushed
22   down the mountain sides by wind and rain. Now without the pro-
23   tection of the trees and plants, the top soil is being washed away by
24   heavy rain. The farmers are losing their land. More and more have
25   to move to the lower areas of Nepal, which are already overpopu-
26   lated and cannot support a large increase in population.
27   To solve problems like this one, it is important that people un-
28   derstand the consequences of their actions. It was not clear to the
29   hill farmers of Nepal that they were to blame for the destruction of
30   their own land. Today environmental scientists are teaching the
31   farmers about ecology. They are also showing them ways to protect
32   their land with new trees and plants. Problems which are similar to
33   the problem in Nepal exist in many countries around the world, but
34   they can be solved. Ecologists are proving to us that actions which
35   give short-term solutions to problems can also have disastrous long-
36   term consequences. If governments and others pay more attention to
37   these scientists, then perhaps they will not make the same type of
38   mistakes that were made in Nepal and in many other countries.

1. T F   This passage is about the damage that pollution   Line(s) _____
           causes in the environment.

2. According to this passage, the environment will suffer   Line(s) _____
   a. if humans disturb the ecological balance of a certain area.
   b. if there is a balance in nature in a certain area.
   c. if large areas of land become completely unproductive.

3. T F   The amount of land in the world that can produce   Line(s) _____
           food is becoming smaller.

4. What did the hill farmers of Nepal *not* realize?   Line(s) _____
   a. They did not realize that their land was disappearing.
   b. They did not realize that they needed food for their animals
      and fuel for their homes.
   c. They did not realize that without the trees and plants, their
      land would be washed away by the rain.

5. T F   The problems in Nepal will be solved if more farmers   Line(s) _____
           move to the lower parts of the country.

6. The writer suggests that governments and people often ignore   Line(s) _____
   a. the short-term benefits of their actions.
   b. the possible long-term consequences of their actions.
   c. the need to grow enough food for people and their animals.

7. T F   According to the writer, the world can learn some-   Line(s) _____
           thing from the mistakes of the hill farmers of Nepal.

8. What does the example of the hill farmers of Nepal show us?   Line(s) _____
   a. It shows us that humans can destroy their own environ-
      ment if they disturb the balance of nature.
   b. It shows us that it is important to protect the environment
      from poisonous chemicals.
   c. It shows us that pollution is threatening the lives of many
      people and the whole economy of Nepal.

PART E

crops (noun)

> DEFINITION   a crop: 1. a plant which is grown for food or for other
>   purposes
>   2. the amount of a certain plant which is produced
>   in a year

1. The *crops* are in the fields. The farmers need rain soon.
2. This year's *crop* of oranges was quite poor. A number of weeks of really cold weather caused a lot of damage to the trees.

to **resist** (verb)
resistance (noun)

DEFINITION to resist something: to oppose something; not to be negatively affected by something

EXAMPLES 1. This material is very useful for aircraft. It can *resist* very high temperatures. It will not break or bend or become weak.
2. Many people have a natural *resistance* to certain illnesses. They do not suffer from these illnesses.

profit (noun)

DEFINITION a profit: the money you make in business; the opposite of *loss* (You buy X at a lower price and sell it at a higher price.)

EXAMPLES 1. John made a $300 *profit* on his old car. He bought it for $1,100 and then sold it for $1,400.
2. The company had a very successful year in 1982. Its *profits* were higher than in any year before.

insect (noun)

DEFINITION an insect: a type of small animal, usually with six legs (for example, a fly)

EXAMPLES 1. *Insects* usually need warm weather. They can't survive in cold temperatures, so in this part of the country, *insects* are only a problem during the summer.
2. Some diseases are carried from person to person by *insects* which bite them.

to **harm** (verb)
harmful (adjective)

DEFINITION to harm people or things: to hurt them or damage them

EXAMPLES 1. Some insects do not *harm* crops or people. In fact, they often control the *harmful* insects.
2. The car was completely destroyed in the accident, but the driver was not *harmed*. He was able to walk away from the accident. He didn't need any hospital treatment.

to **spray** (verb)

DEFINITION   to spray something: to throw out water, paint, etc., in very small amounts through the air (on to something)

EXAMPLES   1. Farmers often *spray* their crops with chemicals that kill harmful insects.
2. They often use aircraft to *spray* very large areas of crops.

to **permit** (verb)

DEFINITION   to permit: to allow

EXAMPLES   1. Smoking is *permitted* in the back part of this aircraft. Do not smoke in Seats 1–20 or in the rest rooms.
2. We will go to the beach tomorrow, weather *permitting* (if the weather is suitable).

to **encourage** (verb)

DEFINITION   to encourage: 1. to show someone that it is good or possible to do something
2. to give someone hope and support

EXAMPLES   1. Good teachers *encourage* their students. They try to give them confidence, to show them that they can learn.
2. I was having problems in a math course. I thought that I was going to fail it. I wanted to drop the course. Then I took the first test and got a B+. That *encouraged* me.

Now read this passage and answer the questions about it.

1 It is clear that some chemicals can damage the health of ani-
2 mals and humans. However, this is not the only problem that can
3 be caused by the careless use of chemicals. Chemicals can also
4 disturb the ecological balance of the environment. If the ecological
5 balance is disturbed, the consequences can be extremely serious.
6 The history of DDT illustrates the problem. DDT, a chemical
7 which kills insects, at first seemed to be a perfect answer to many
8 problems. It would control insects that caused dangerous diseases,
9 as well as insects that caused billions of dollars of damage to crops
10 every year. Governments permitted and even encouraged the use of
11 DDT. Farmers in many countries began to spray it on their crops.
12 The immediate results were good: Damage to crops went down, and
13 profits went up. However, the chemical had effects which the sci-
14 entists did not predict. First, it also killed insects which were the

15	natural enemies of the harmful insects and which were therefore
16	beneficial to farmers. Second, and perhaps worse, DDT did not kill
17	every harmful insect. A few insects had natural resistance to the
18	chemical. They survived and multiplied. In a few years there were
19	large numbers of insects which were not affected by DDT, and
20	there were fewer insects which could act as natural controls on
21	these new "super-insects." Finally, it became clear that DDT was
22	not solving the insect problem. In fact, it was making the problem
23	worse. It then became necessary to find a second cure for the effects
24	of the first!

1. Why are chemicals dangerous?   Line(s) _____

   a. They cause health problems for animals and people.

   b. They can disturb the ecological balance.

   c. Both (a) and (b)

2. T F At first, DDT seemed only to have benefits.   Line(s) _____

3. T F The long-term effects of DDT were not the effects that   Line(s) _____
          were expected.

4. According to the writer, what was the problem with DDT?   Line(s) _____
   (More than one answer may be correct.)

   a. It did not kill all the harmful insects.

   b. It caused an immediate decrease in damage to crops.

   c. It killed other insects that helped farmers.

5. T F At first, governments were reluctant to permit the   Line(s) _____
          use of DDT.

6. If a farmer used DDT today, in five years   Line(s) _____

   a. he would have no problems with harmful insects.

   b. insects would be an even greater problem for him.

   c. his situation would not be different.

Exercises for Parts C, D, and E

SAME OR DIFFERENT?

Read the two sentences in each example. Do they express the same ideas, or do they express different ideas? Write *S* for sentences with the same ideas; write *D* for sentences with different ideas.

   Remember: You can express the **same** idea with **different** words and **different** grammar!

1. a. Many residents of the town were opposed to the plan for a new chemical plant there. _____
   b. The people who lived in the town supported the plan for a new chemical factory there.

2. a. We cannot permit the use of this chemical. _____
   b. The use of this chemical must be forbidden.

3. a. Insects which attack crops cause billions of dollars of damage every year. _____
   b. Every year the harm that insects do to crops costs billions of dollars.

4. a. If you use that chemical, you may suffer from some health problems later. _____
   b. If you are exposed to that chemical, you may have some health problems later.

5. a. Often scientists do not know the long-term effects of chemicals on the environment. _____
   b. The long-term ecological consequences of chemicals are often not known by scientists.

6. a. It is easy for man to disturb the natural balance that exists in nature. _____
   b. The natural balance that exists in nature cannot be disturbed by man.

7. a. No one understood the purpose of Mike's trip to London. _____
   b. Mike went to London, but no one knew why.

8. a. In this state, the police enforce the 55-MPH speed limit strictly. _____
   b. In this state, the police will stop you even if you are driving at 58 MPH.

9. a. Farmers often spray their crops with chemicals to kill harmful insects. _____
   b. Farmers often contaminate their crops with the chemicals which they use against harmful insects.

10. a. Without chemicals it would be impossible to protect crops from insects. _____
    b. If farmers didn't use chemicals, they would not be able to prevent insect damage to crops.

11. a. If laws against pollution were stricter, our environment would be in less danger. _____
    b. We would be able to reduce the threat to the environment if we had stricter laws against pollution.

12. a. People think that the economic situation will get worse unless ———
the government encourages industrial growth.
   b. People believe that the economy will suffer if the government
does not control industrial development.

EXPECTATIONS

Read the first sentence in each of these examples. Think about the ideas in it. Then
choose the sentence or sentences that can follow it.

1. Often companies which produce chemicals seem to be only interested in the
short-term question of profits.
   a. They seem to ignore the possibility that the use of chemicals carries long-
term health risks.
   b. They conduct a great deal of research into the possible ecological effects of
their products.
   c. If they were really concerned about the environment, they would test their
products better.

2. The economic situation in this area will improve next year.
   a. A large local company is threatening to close its plant if the government
introduces new pollution laws.
   b. Many workers who now have jobs will suffer.
   c. This encouraging news came from an economist who is predicting that unemployment will fall.

3. There is a great deal of resistance to the government's strict new laws against
pollution.
   a. Everyone agrees that industries which pollute the environment should pay
heavy fines.
   b. The oil industry, especially, is claiming that the new laws are too severe.
   c. A large number of people, especially doctors, believe that certain chemicals
cause brain defects in unborn children.

4. This chemical is extremely dangerous.
   a. Exposure to even a small amount of it can cause serious harm.
   b. Last month the government wrote a report that encourages and supports
its use.
   c. Scientists agree that it is completely harmless.

5. There is evidence that certain chemicals which were widely used in agriculture are dangerous for humans.
   a. In areas which were sprayed with 2,4,5-T, for example, there was an increase in birth defects.

b. They seem to be especially harmful for small children and unborn babies.

c. However, the government still permits the production and sale of these chemicals.

6. Environmentalists are extremely concerned about the new law which the government is going to introduce.

   a. The government's purpose is to reduce the number of harmful chemicals that are now in use.

   b. It will encourage the use of cleaner fuel in the nation's power plants.

   c. They are especially worried about the part which permits more poisonous waste dumps.

7. Some chemicals that are used in agriculture serve very useful purposes.

   a. They are sprayed on crops to protect them from harmful insects.

   b. They cause a great deal of harm to agricultural crops.

   c. If farmers could not use them, the economic consequences would be extremely bad.

8. Medical researchers have evidence that some birth defects are connected with poisonous chemicals in the environment.

   a. For example, there is more heart disease among people who live near chemical plants than there is in the general population.

   b. For example, anencephaly, a very unusual type of brain damage, is more common in babies who are born near chemical plants.

   c. They also believe that such defects will increase unless exposure to these chemicals is reduced.

VOCABULARY QUIZ

Choose the correct word for each empty space. Use each word only once.

resist	crops	balance	consequence
situation	suffer	strict	lungs
resistance	ecology	exposed	fine
threatened	harmful	encouraged	purpose
permit	brain	defect	resident

1. I parked my car illegally and got a ticket from the police. I had to pay a

   _____ of $20.

2. There is a serious _____ in the car that I bought last month. All

   cars of the same type have the same problem. So the producer will have to

   correct the problem free.

3. This chemical is dangerous. Health problems are now appearing in people who are _____ to it every day, for example, the chemical workers who make it and the agricultural workers who use it.

4. Without experience very young children do not understand the possible _____s of their actions. For example, they do not realize that if they touch a hot range, they will be burned.

5. The air in this city is very dirty. A large number of people _____ from health problems which are clearly connected with the pollution.

6. The economic _____ is getting worse. Prices are increasing very quickly. Last year 3 million people were out of work. This year 4½ million are unemployed.

7. Mike had an extremely noisy party last night. There were twenty-five people in his apartment. They were laughing and shouting and dancing. At 1:30 A.M. his neighbors _____ to call the police if the noise didn't stop.

8. Last summer some friends and I went sailing in a small boat. I tried to stand up in the boat, but I lost my _____ and fell into the water.

9. Only the _____s of this apartment building can use the swimming pool. If you don't live in the building, you can't use the pool.

10. Why did the U.S. government introduce the 55-MPH speed limit? The original _____ of the law was to reduce the amount of gasoline the country used.

11. It is clear that cigarette smoking is _____. It can cause heart disease and other health problems.

12. Farmers are extremely worried. Their _____ are being attacked by insects.

13. At first, I did not want to study in the U.S., but my brother _____ me. He said that I would enjoy life here and that my studies would help me a lot later. That's why I am here now!

14. In some countries, it is illegal to drive a car without insurance. The law does not _____ it.

15. Scientists are trying to develop new types of plants that have a _____ to disease. If they succeed, we will not have to use so many chemicals to protect agricultural plants.

Main Reading

Pre-Reading Exercises

VOCABULARY IN CONTEXT

Use the context and the words in italics (in examples 1–5) to guess the meaning of the new words (in boldface type).

Remember: Read each example to the end. Do not stop after the new word.

1. *Scientists* are *conducting research* into the effects of this chemical on health. In one **experiment** they put the chemical into the drinking water of some animals. After five weeks, they compared the health of the animals that drank the contaminated water with the health of other animals that drank clean water. The *results* of the **experiment** showed that cancer was developing only in the animals which were exposed to the chemical.

   An experiment is _____.
   a. a type of scientist who works with animals
   b. a type of animal which is used in research
   c. a test which a scientist does to discover something

2. There are many *dangerous* waste dumps in the country. They are full of **toxic** *chemicals* and *other poisonous* substances.

   Toxic describes something _____.
   a. which can prevent pollution
   b. which cannot be used for any purpose
   c. which can kill you or make you very ill

In the example on the next page, also use your knowledge of word families to help you.

3. This bottle contains a **deadly** chemical. Just a *small amount* of it would *kill* thousands of people.

   Deadly describes something _____.
   a. that helps sick people
   b. that kills people
   c. that makes people sick

4. It is clear from a great deal of research that smoking is extremely *dangerous*. It can cause lung cancer and heart disease. Many people in government believe that government *must not encourage* smoking. In some states, the government is *even* going to **ban** smoking in public places and at work. Smokers *will only be able to smoke at home.*

   To ban something means _____.
   a. to need something
   b. to forbid something
   c. to make something possible

5. If you want to *dry* something, it's best to use a *cotton* cloth. Cotton is the best material for this job. It **absorbs** *water* better than other materials.

   To absorb something means _____.
   a. to take it in
   b. to produce it
   c. to improve it

6. The number of road accidents is increasing. The main reason for this increase is that people drink alcohol and then drive their cars. But drunk driving is not the only **factor** in the increase. There are two other **factors** that are connected with the growing number of accidents. First, there are more cars on the roads today than ten years ago. Second, the roads are in worse condition than they were ten years ago.

   A factor is _____.
   a. a dangerous automobile accident on a highway
   b. a person who drives an automobile dangerously
   c. something that helps to cause another thing

7. There is strong evidence that this chemical can cause birth defects. So **pregnant** women must not be exposed to it.

   A pregnant woman is _____.
   a. a woman who is expecting a baby
   b. a woman who has a job in a chemical factory
   c. a woman who works with children

In the next three examples, we will practice something different. Often we cannot guess the exact meaning of a word which we see for the first time. However, often it is not necessary to know the exact meaning. A more general meaning will be enough for us to understand the sentence. Try to guess the general meanings for these new words:

8. This chemical seems to be very dangerous to human health. It was sprayed on land in some areas of the country. In these areas 30% of women who were pregnant suffered **miscarriages.**

    A miscarriage is _____.
    a. a type of dangerous chemical
    b. a certain time during pregnancy
    c. a health problem during pregnancy

9. DDT was also used by the health authorities of warm countries. It killed insects, so it could be used to kill insects that caused disease. For example, in India and Africa, it was used to kill the **mosquitoes** which carried **malaria.**

    A mosquito is _____.
    a. a certain type of chemical
    b. a certain type of insect
    c. a certain type of person

    Malaria is _____.
    a. a certain type of poison
    b. a certain type of medicine
    c. a certain type of disease

10. People who live in areas that have a lot of chemical pollution often have serious health problems. For example, **cancer** is much more common in polluted areas of the country than in cleaner areas.

    Cancer is _____.
    a. a type of plant
    b. a type of disease
    c. a type of chemical

Now look up **miscarriage, mosquito, malaria,** and **cancer** in your dictionary. Did you guess the correct *general* meaning?

EXPECTATIONS

Read the title of this article carefully. Then choose the ideas that you expect in the article. If you don't know the meaning of the word *time bomb,* look it up in your dictionary.

1. The article will talk about war and peace.   YES   NO

2. The article will talk about chemical pollution.   YES   NO

3. The article will mainly describe the benefits of chemicals.   YES   NO

4. The article will mainly talk about the bad effects that animals can have on the environment.   YES   NO

5. The article will conclude that chemicals are not dangerous to the environment.   YES   NO

6. The article will show that the effects of chemicals often appear only slowly.   YES   NO

7. The article will discuss the problem of overpopulation.   YES   NO

8. The article will criticize the use of chemicals.   YES   NO

9. The article will show the ecological dangers of chemicals.   YES   NO

Like the article in Unit 5, this article also has a number of different sections. And the sections have titles. Read the section titles carefully. Then choose the ideas that you expect. Perhaps you will also want to change your mind about one or two of the ideas 1–9.

10. Chemicals are not a serious problem for the environment in the modern world.   YES   NO

11. The article will describe some of the effects of chemicals.   YES   NO

12. The article will show that the use of chemicals is increasing.   YES   NO

13. The article will suggest a solution to the problem.   YES   NO

14. The article will prove that it is easy to solve the problem.   YES   NO

15. The article will suggest that people don't know enough about the dangers of chemical pollution.   YES   NO

Now you can start to read the article. You will read it in sections. You will also try to develop some expectations before each section. Turn to page 207.

Chemicals: Time Bombs in Our Environment

Introduction

1 In 1976 planes began to spray a chemical on large areas of   1
2 land in Oregon. Almost immediately fish and other small animals

Pollution from a Modern Power Plant

3   began to die, and larger animals that were pregnant began to suf-
4   fer miscarriages. Humans also began to feel ill.

5   In the same year there was an explosion at a chemical plant in   2
6   Seveso, Italy. After the explosion, small amounts of dioxin, a very
7   dangerous chemical, escaped into the air. Animals began to die,
8   people became sick, and the population of Seveso had to abandon
9   their homes. In 1983, seven years after the accident, the land
10 around Seveso was still contaminated by dioxin.

11   In 1983 the U.S. government decided to close the small town of   3
12 Times Beach, Missouri, and to buy the homes of all the residents.
13 The reason? The land in Times Beach is contaminated with acids,
14 dioxin, and other dangerous chemicals which are escaping from a
15 toxic waste dump there.

16   These and many other similar incidents have one thing in   4
17 common. They show that chemicals are polluting our environment
18 and causing an extremely serious problem for a growing number of
19 countries. According to many ecologists, this type of pollution is a

20 problem that governments and other responsible authorities are
21 not taking seriously enough.

The Growing Problem

22   The chemical pollution of the environment is connected closely   5
23 with the growth of the chemical industry between 1940 and the
24 present. During this time, scientists who worked for chemical com-
25 panies produced a large number of new chemicals which at first
26 seemed very useful. People thought, for example, that DDT, a
27 chemical that kills insects, would bring many benefits. It would
28 save people's lives; it would also protect agricultural crops and
29 animals from harmful insects. Another substance, called 2,4,5-T,
30 also promised great economic benefits for agriculture. It was a
31 herbicide, a chemical which controls the growth of plants which are
32 not wanted. Farmers were told that 2,4,5-T would save them a
33 great deal of time and money if they sprayed it on their land.
34   Because of the clear benefits of chemicals like DDT and   6
35 2,4,5-T, people in many countries began to use them. At first, the
36 chemicals seemed to be great successes. In Sri Lanka, for example,
37 DDT was used against the mosquitoes which carried malaria. In
38 ten years the number of people who became ill with malaria was
39 reduced by more than 95%. In other countries, DDT and other
40 chemicals were used to control the insects that caused much dam-
41 age to agricultural crops, such as cotton and corn. In the 1970s,
42 2,4,5-T was used by farmers and industrial companies in the
43 United States. People quickly began to depend on these useful
44 chemicals; farmers could not imagine life without them. If they did
45 not have these chemicals, they believed, their crops would fail and
46 they would lose a great deal of money.
47   However, after a short time of use, it became clear that the   7
48 chemicals were disturbing the balance which exists in the environ-
49 ment. Scientists soon realized that chemicals like DDT killed use-
50 ful insects as well as the harmful ones. It also became clear that
51 some of the most harmful insects were quickly developing resis-
52 tance to DDT. As a result, farmers had to use even stronger and
53 more poisonous chemicals against the new "super-insects." Another
54 problem was that the chemicals did not disappear: They remained
55 in the ground; they found their way into rivers, lakes, and oceans.
56 They were absorbed into the bodies of fish and animals, and the
57 animals began to suffer from new types of diseases. The chemicals
58 were poisoning them. Humans also began to experience serious
59 health problems, especially in areas which were sprayed with
60 2,4,5-T. In these areas doctors reported an increase of heart disease

61	and an increase in the number of birth defects. In addition, the
62	number of pregnant women who suffered miscarriages was 200%
63	greater than in other areas of the country.
64	Chemical pollution is not only caused by chemicals which are
65	deliberately sprayed on land for some specific purpose. It is also
66	caused by chemical waste that is carelessly or illegally dumped.
67	Certain other substances are produced in the production of chemi-
68	cals. These substances are often useless, and some of them are
69	extremely dangerous. Dioxin, or TCDD, is such a by-product of the
70	chemical industry. For some years, there were few laws that gov-
71	erned the dumping of dangerous chemical wastes. As a result, they
72	now lie in dumps all over the industrial countries. Today the
73	deadly chemicals are in the water and the soil of many communi-
74	ties; governments do not know exactly how many dangerous dumps
75	exist. In fact, according to environmentalists, people today are con-
76	tinuing to dump dangerous chemical waste illegally in spite of
77	strict new laws against dumping.

No Easy Answers

78	The solution to the problem of chemical pollution seems very
79	clear: Governments must forbid the use of chemicals which damage
80	the environment and which threaten animal and human life. The
81	situation, however, is made more difficult by two factors. First,
82	scientists disagree about the effects on humans of many chemicals;
83	second, the chemical industry is extremely powerful and is a very
84	important part of the economy of many countries.
85	It is difficult to be completely sure that a certain chemical
86	leads to certain health problems. One reason for this uncertainty is
87	that some effects may appear only very slowly. Some types of
88	cancer, for example, may need twenty years to develop. Another
89	reason for the uncertainty is the methods which are used to test
90	the chemicals. It is impossible, of course, to test the chemicals on
91	human beings, so experiments are conducted with animals. How-
92	ever, some scientists, especially scientists who are working for in-
93	dustrial companies, criticize the animal experiments. They claim,
94	for example, that the animals are exposed to very large amounts of
95	the chemicals. These amounts are much greater than the amounts
96	which a human would absorb during one lifetime.
97	It is difficult, therefore, to find definite proof that a chemical
98	can cause illness or death. However, the majority of scientists who
99	conduct independent research into the effect of chemicals on the
100	environment believe that complete certainty is not needed. Accord-
101	ing to them, if a connection is found between a chemical and seri-

The numbers 8, 9, 10, and 11 appear in the right margin marking paragraphs.

102   ous health problems in test animals, we must stop the use of that
103   chemical. It is better to ban a chemical which may be safe than to
104   use a chemical which may cause serious illness or death.

105   Economics, however, may be a much greater problem than   12
106   scientific disagreement for people who want to protect the environ-
107   ment. It is clear that the chemical industry is an important busi-
108   ness in many countries. If the government reduces the number of
109   chemicals which are used today, the chemical industry will experi-
110   ence economic problems. Companies will reduce the number of
111   people they employ. If unemployment increases and if the industry
112   earns less money, the economy of the whole country will suffer. If a
113   country's economy is bad, people will blame the government. Con-
114   sequently, governments may be reluctant to pass laws that will
115   immediately damage their economy.

116   Thus, short-term economic interests may be more important to   13
117   some governments and companies than the possible long-term
118   dangers to the health of their people. There is some evidence to
119   support this belief. First, chemical producers often ignore research
120   which shows that their products may be dangerous. For example,
121   in 1970 the U.S. government stopped the use of 2,4,5-T, but only in
122   homes and on farms. According to the government, it was possible
123   that the chemical caused problems for pregnant women. The gov-
124   ernment, however, did not forbid the industrial use of the chemical.
125   In 1979 the company that produced 2,4,5-T claimed that it was as
126   safe as aspirin! In the same year, however, the U.S. government
127   banned it completely. Second, the strange behavior of governments
128   shows that profits are often more important for them than people.
129   For example, the Swiss government allows the manufacture of
130   chemicals, but does not permit toxic waste dumps in Switzerland.
131   Dioxin and other toxic wastes which are by-products of the Swiss
132   chemical industry have to be transported to dumps in other coun-
133   tries. In 1972, the American government banned the use of DDT in
134   the U.S., but American companies were able to continue to produce
135   DDT and sell it to other countries. Does this mean that DDT is
136   only dangerous for Americans? Are only Swiss people at risk from
137   toxic waste? No, of course not. It means that the governments want
138   the economic benefits of chemicals without the heavy responsibili-
139   ties that go with them.

Conclusion: A Program of Education for the Public and for
Governments

140   In spite of the strong opposition to new and stricter environ-   14
141   mental laws, however, it is still possible to attack the problem of

142   chemical pollution; but we must attack it from three directions.
143   First, we need more independent research into the effects of chemi-
144   cals by scientists who are not paid by the government or by large
145   industrial companies. Second, scientists need to educate the gen-
146   eral public and inform them about the dangers of chemicals in the
147   environment. If the public knows that a certain chemical threatens
148   the health of their children, then it will put pressure on politicians
149   in local and national governments. If the politicians want to re-
150   main in office, they will take action to correct the situation. Third,
151   economists need to educate governments about the long-term eco-
152   nomic costs of chemicals. It will be extremely expensive to clean
153   areas of land which are contaminated by chemicals; it will be even
154   more costly to give medical treatment to people who are suffering
155   from serious illnesses after exposure to dangerous chemicals. If
156   governments realize this, the short-term economic benefits of
157   chemicals will seem much less attractive to them.
158   If we can put pressure on governments in these three ways,   15
159   perhaps they will begin to behave more responsibly. They will per-
160   haps pass new laws against pollution and enforce them strictly.
161   Perhaps, then, the chemical producers will begin to behave more
162   responsibly.

Section I: Introduction

Sometimes an article in a magazine will have an introduction with examples. The writer of the article uses examples to increase the interest of the reader. The introduction of this article is written in this way. Read Paragraphs 1–4; do the Main Ideas Check and the Comprehension Check.

MAIN IDEAS CHECK

Here are the main ideas for the paragraphs in this section. Write the correct paragraph number opposite each main idea.

PARAGRAPH   IDEA

_____   An example of chemical pollution after an accident.

_____   Chemical pollution is an extremely serious problem worldwide.

_____   An example of chemical pollution from a toxic waste dump.

_____   An example of chemical pollution from crop spraying.

1. T F   Chemical pollution is only a problem in the United   Line(s) _____
           States.

2. T F   Some people think that governments are not doing   Line(s) _____
           enough to control chemical pollution.

3. What is dioxin?   Line(s) _____
   a. An area of Italy
   b. An extremely toxic substance
   c. A type of animal that scientists use in tests

4. T F   It is easy to clean an area of land that is contaminated. Line(s) _____

5. What do the three examples show?   Line(s) _____
   a. Chemicals are only dangerous for animals.
   b. Governments are doing a lot to control pollution.
   c. Chemicals can improve the health of animals and humans.
   d. Chemical pollution is already a bad problem.

Section II: The Growing Problem

EXPECTATIONS

Read the first sentences in Paragraphs 5–8. Read *only* the first sentences. Then choose the ideas that you expect.

1. The growth of the chemical industry is a factor in the problem   YES   NO
   of chemical pollution.

2. Chemicals can never help us.   YES   NO

3. Chemicals which were sprayed on the land had bad effects on   YES   NO
   the ecology of those areas.

4. This section will only discuss the pollution that is caused by   YES   NO
   chemicals which are sprayed on crops.

Don't worry about your answers to these Expectation questions yet. Now read Paragraphs 5–8; do the Main Ideas Check and the Comprehension Check for this section. Then come back and look at your expectations. Were they correct?

MAIN IDEAS CHECK

Here are the main ideas of the paragraphs in this section. Write the correct paragraph number opposite each main idea.

PARAGRAPH   IDEA

_____   A great deal of pollution comes from unsafe, and sometimes illegal, toxic waste dumps.

_____   It became clear that chemicals were damaging the environment and people's health.

_____   After World War II, the production of chemicals increased.

_____   After 1940, the growing chemical industry began to produce many chemicals which seemed very useful.

COMPREHENSION CHECK

1. T F   DDT was used only by farmers.   Line(s) _____

2. Why were chemicals so attractive to farmers? (Choose all the   Line(s) _____
   right answers.)
   a. They saved people's lives.
   b. They protected crops from insects.
   c. They increased farmers' profits.
   d. They saved time.

3. T F   Many farmers believe that they cannot do without   Line(s) _____
           chemicals in their work.

4. What happened to people who lived in areas which were   Line(s) _____
   sprayed with chemicals?
   a. They all began to suffer from heart disease.
   b. They experienced some minor illnesses.
   c. They began to have serious health problems.

5. If you lived in an area which was sprayed with 2,4,5-T and you   Line(s) _____
   or your wife were pregnant, what would you do?
   a. I would stay in the area.
   b. I would move away from the area immediately.
   c. I would wait until the birth of my child; then I would move
      away from the area.

6. T F   Health problems were the only negative effects of the   Line(s) _____
           use of chemicals.

7. T F   The controls on toxic waste dumps are not strict   Line(s) _____
           enough.

8. What does Paragraph 8 tell us about toxic waste dumps?   Line(s) _____
   a. They are always in areas of the country that have no
      people.
   b. New laws now mean that there is no problem with toxic
      waste dumps.
   c. Some of the dumps are near people's homes.

Now go back and look at your expectations for this section. Were they correct?

Section III: No Easy Answers

EXPECTATIONS

Read the *first* sentences in Paragraphs 9–13. Read *only* the first sentence of each paragraph. Then choose the ideas that you can expect in this section.

1. It is difficult to prove a connection between illness and the use   YES   NO
   of chemicals.

2. This section will continue to describe the effects of chemicals   YES   NO
   on people's health.

3. This section will discuss solutions to the problems which   YES   NO
   chemicals cause.

4. Scientific disagreement is the only thing that makes a solution   YES   NO
   difficult.

5. Governments always believe that the health of their people is   YES   NO
   the most important thing.

6. If a government stops the use of chemicals, there may be prob-   YES   NO
   lems for the economy of the country.

MAIN IDEAS CHECK

Here are the main ideas of the paragraphs of this section. Write the correct paragraph
number opposite each idea.

PARAGRAPH	IDEA
_____	There are economic reasons for people's reluctance to stop the use of chemicals.
_____	For a number of reasons, scientists cannot be 100% sure that a certain chemical causes a certain illness.
_____	There is clear evidence that the economy is more important to governments than people's health.
_____	We do not need to be 100% certain that a chemical is dangerous. We must ban it if we find evidence which only suggests that it is dangerous.
_____	There are two factors that prevent an easy solution to the problem of chemical pollution.

COMPREHENSION CHECK

1. T   F   According to the passage, there is only one reason   Line(s) _____
              why governments are reluctant to stop the production
              or use of certain chemicals.

2. Why does the writer mention cancer?   Line(s) _____
   a. The writer wants to show the serious health problems
      which chemicals can cause.
   b. The writer wants to show that the negative effects of chemi-
      cals often do not appear until many years later.
   c. The writer wants to prove without doubt that chemicals can
      have extremely serious effects on human health.

3. T   F   All scientists agree that we must first be 100% sure   Line(s) _____
              about the effects of a chemical. Then we can decide to
              ban it or not.

4. According to the passage, what will happen if the government   Line(s) _____
   bans the use of a number of popular chemicals? (There is more
   than one answer!)
   a. People will criticize the government.
   b. The economy of the country will suffer.
   c. Unemployment will grow.
   d. Scientists will protest.

5. T   F   In 1970 there was evidence which suggested that   Line(s) _____
              2,4,5-T was unsafe.

6. Why does the writer use the example of the company which claimed that 2,4,5-T was as safe as aspirin?   Line(s) _____
   a. To show that chemicals really can benefit us, as does aspirin
   b. To show that producers ignore studies which show problems with their chemicals
   c. To show that the government did not act correctly

7. Why does the writer use the examples of the U.S. government and the Swiss government?   Line(s) _____
   a. To show that chemicals like DDT, dioxin, and 2,4,5-T are extremely dangerous to human health
   b. To show that money is more important to these governments than people's health
   c. To show that a number of governments do not believe that chemicals are a real problem

Now go back to your expectations for this section. How correct were they?

Section IV: Conclusion: A Program of Education for the Public and for Governments

EXPECTATIONS

Read the title of the conclusion. Then read the first sentences of Paragraphs 14 and 15. Read *only* the first sentence of each paragraph. Then choose the ideas that you can expect in the conclusion.

1. The writer will conclude that it is not possible to solve the problem of chemical pollution.   YES NO

2. The writer will suggest that governments are reluctant to pass stricter laws against chemical pollution.   YES NO

3. The writer will suggest one solution to the problem of chemical pollution.   YES NO

4. The writer will suggest that we need to do three things to solve the problem of chemical pollution.   YES NO

5. The writer will suggest that people do not fully realize the dangers of chemical pollution.   YES NO

1. T F The writer does not believe that it is possible to solve the problem of chemical pollution.   Line(s) ____

2. T F According to the writer, the public does not know enough about the dangers of chemical pollution.   Line(s) ____

3. T F The writer believes that present laws against pollution are not strict enough.   Line(s) ____

4. What does the writer believe about governments?   Line(s) ____
   a. They will not ban the use of chemicals unless the public puts pressure on them.
   b. They fully realize the long-term economic costs of chemical pollution.
   c. They are already behaving in an extremely responsible way.

5. What is *not* part of the writer's solution to the problem of chemical pollution?   Line(s) ____
   a. We must teach people about the effects of chemical pollution.
   b. We must put pressure on governments.
   c. We must show the long-term costs of pollution.
   d. We must show the economic benefits of chemicals.

6. T F The writer is certain that the problem will be solved.   Line(s) ____

Now go back and look at your expectations for the conclusion. Were they correct?

Now do the paragraph reading exercise on the next page.

PARAGRAPH READING

These sentences form a paragraph, but they are not in the correct order. Put the sentences into their correct order. The first two sentences are already in the correct place.

__1__ Sometimes problems are caused by the use of chemicals which were not tested enough.

__2__ An example of this is the history of 2,4,5-T.

_____ In 1980 the government finally decided to ban the use of 2,4,5-T everywhere.

_____ However, it soon became clear that the chemical was having disastrous effects that scientists did not predict.

_____ At first, industry scientists claimed that 2,4,5-T would bring great benefits to agriculture.

_____ For example, in areas which were sprayed with the chemical, there were increases in the number of women who suffered miscarriages and in the number of men with heart disease.

_____ If farmers used it on their land, they would save billions of dollars a year.

_____ It also led to serious health problems in humans who were exposed to it.

_____ It caused disease and death in animals.

The Changing Role of Women in the United States

Grammar for this unit: Objects and infinitives after verbs
Subordinate clauses
Present perfect
You will find information and practice on these grammar points in Appendix 1, Unit 7.

Vocabulary Study and Preparatory Reading

PART A

housekeeper (noun)
to do the **housekeeping** (verb phrase)

> DEFINITION housekeeper: a person who looks after a house and the people who live in the house
>
> EXAMPLES 1. Some wealthy families employ a *housekeeper* who cooks, cleans the house, makes the beds, and does the laundry.
> 2. Many working wives have two jobs: They have their work outside the home, and they also are expected *to do the housekeeping* when they come home.

to **attempt** (verb)
attempt (noun)

> DEFINITION to attempt to do something: to try to do something
>
> EXAMPLES 1. Some years ago a team of scientists *attempted* to find the *Titanic* at the bottom of the Atlantic, but the *attempt* failed.

2. After three unsuccessful *attempts,* the student managed to pass his driving test.

career (noun)

DEFINITION   a career: a job which you plan to keep for your life

EXAMPLES   1. It is difficult to choose a *career* at age eighteen or twenty-one, when you have little experience.
2. My sister is planning a *career* in medicine. Next year she will finish college and go to medical school.

to **require** (verb)
requirement (noun)

DEFINITION   to require: to need; to order or demand

EXAMPLES   1. This new law *requires* industry to clean areas that they pollute.
2. The *requirements* for my history class aren't hard: I have to pass two tests and write a research paper.

to **raise** (verb)

DEFINITION   to raise something: to move something up
to raise children: to care for and educate children until they are grown

EXAMPLES   1. Jane heard yesterday that her employer is going to *raise* her salary. She is very happy, of course.
2. In many cultures women *raise* the children while men work to support the family.

role (noun)

DEFINITION   a role: the work that is done by a person or by a thing in a certain system

EXAMPLES   1. In many societies the *role* of the father is to earn money for the family.
2. In many societies the *role* of the mother is to raise the children and to do the housework.

subordinate (adjective)

DEFINITION   subordinate: less important

EXAMPLES   1. In many countries women are *subordinate* to men. Men have much more power.

2. Some sentences have a main clause and a *subordinate* clause. The *subordinate* clause contains ideas which are less important than the ideas in the main clause.

feminist (noun)
feminism (noun)

DEFINITION a feminist: a person who demands equal rights for women and men

feminism: the belief that women and men are equal

EXAMPLES 1. *Feminists* want to show people that women do not get equal treatment. They want to change this situation and win equality for women.

2. *Feminism* really began more than 100 years ago, but it became very powerful in the 1970s.

Now read this passage and answer the questions about it.

1   One hundred and fifty years ago, the position of women in U.S.
2   society was very different from their position today. At that time,
3   women were completely subordinate to men. Society did not en-
4   courage women to have a career outside the home. Although they
5   received an education at elementary school and high school, they
6   were not allowed to attend college or university. Even when a
7   married woman did work outside the home, she could not keep the
8   money that she earned. The law required her to give the money to
9   her husband! Society expected women to do the housekeeping, to
10 raise the children, and to obey their husbands. That was their role
11 in society. They did not have the right to vote. In many ways, they
12 were almost like slaves.
13   This situation began to change slowly after the first feminist
14 group was organized in 1848. After that year, small groups of
15 women began to protest the lack of equality and justice in U.S.
16 society. Progress was slow; for many years, their attempts to im-
17 prove women's position ended in failure. Slowly, however, more
18 and more people began to share their ideas and support their de-
19 mands until, in 1920, women were given the right to vote in a
20 national election.

1. How much freedom did women have in U.S. society 150 years ago?   Line(s) _____

   a. Women had more freedom than they have today.
   b. Women had much less freedom than they now have.
   c. Women had the same amount of freedom as they have today.

2. T F   Society did not permit women to work outside the   Line(s) _____
           home.

3. What was the traditional role of a married woman in Ameri-   Line(s) _____
   can society 150 years ago?
   a. She was expected to earn money for her family.
   b. She was expected to have a career outside the home.
   c. She was expected to keep house and raise the children.

4. What was *not* true about the position of women in the U.S. 150   Line(s) _____
   years ago?
   a. They could not vote in national elections.
   b. They received no education.
   c. They were expected to be subordinate to men.

5. T F   The first feminist groups which demanded equality   Line(s) _____
           and justice for women were immediately successful.

PART B

male (adjective)
female (adjective)

DEFINITION   male: describes men
             female: describes women

EXAMPLES   1. This factory employs 3,000 workers: There are 2,000 *fe-
              male* and 1,000 *male* workers.
           2. One hundred and fifty years ago American colleges did not
              allow *female* students. Women were expected to work in-
              side the home, so men felt that they did not need a college
              education.

to **bear** (irregular verb)
bore, borne

DEFINITION   to bear: to carry; to have
             to bear a child: to have a child, to give birth to a child

EXAMPLES   1. Three different groups of people *bear* responsibility for the
              Titanic disaster.
           2. An English king divorced his wife because she could not
              bear any children for him.

to **nurse** (verb)
nurse (noun)

DEFINITION to nurse a baby: to feed a baby natural milk from the female
body
a nurse: a person who has training to look after sick people

EXAMPLES 1. Doctors believe that it is better for mothers to *nurse* their
babies. Natural milk contains everything a new baby
needs.
2. My sister works as a *nurse* in a large hospital in Chicago.

tradition (noun)
traditional (adjective)

DEFINITION a tradition: an idea or a behavior that comes from the past to
the present

EXAMPLES 1. At Christmas it is *traditional* to give presents to your
family and friends.
2. This *tradition* began many hundreds of years ago.

to **argue** (verb)

DEFINITION to argue: 1. to give reasons in order to prove something in a
discussion
2. to fight or disagree

EXAMPLES 1. Some scientists *argue* that people from Europe or North
Africa reached America long before the Vikings or Columbus.
2. "Don't *argue*," said Kate to her daughter. "Just do what I
told you to do."

appliance (noun)

DEFINITION an appliance: an instrument or piece of equipment
appliances: the machines that help in housework (a washing
machine, a dryer, a dishwasher, a refrigerator)

EXAMPLES 1. I'm going to take this apartment. It's clean and comfortable and has all new *appliances* in the kitchen.
2. The only *appliances* which came with Kate's apartment
were a refrigerator and a range. But there's a big laundry
room in her building.

biology (noun)
biological (adjective)

DEFINITION biology: the scientific study of life

EXAMPLES 1. In our *biology* class we had to study the development of animals before they are born.
      2. The *biological* role of women is to bear children.

function (noun)
to **function** (verb)

DEFINITION a function: the purpose of a person or a thing
to function: to work (successfully)

EXAMPLES 1. One *function* of language is to pass information from one person to another.
      2. The telephone was not *functioning,* so I couldn't call for assistance.

When you read, it is important for you to understand the difference between **fact** and **opinion**. In this passage only the ideas in the first sentence are facts. In the rest of the passage the writer describes the opinions of a group of people—the feminist movement. While you read, look for words and phrases which tell you that the writer is giving the opinion of feminists. Now read the passage and answer the questions about it.

1   In many cultures the role of a married woman is to take care of
2 her home and her family while her husband earns money to sup-
3 port them. However, feminist groups in the U.S. and in other coun-
4 tries claim that these male and female roles have their origins in
5 traditions which are not important for a modern society.
6   Feminists agree that women's biological function (only women
7 can bear and nurse children) requires them to stay at home for
8 some time before and after a child is born. In the past, feminists
9 argue, this biological function also decided women's social role.
10 Because women had to stay at home for some time, it seemed
11 natural for them to remain there permanently to look after the
12 children and the home.
13   But today, according to feminists, we do not need to allow a
14 woman's biological function to limit her social role. Life is different
15 now. Housework does not take the long hours it took in the past;
16 washing machines and other modern appliances allow us to do it
17 quickly and easily. When women get a fair chance in education,
18 they can develop skills which our society needs. In addition, femi-
19 nists point out, there are scientific studies which suggest that chil-

20 dren benefit greatly when both the father and mother share re-
21 sponsibilities for raising them.
22   Feminists conclude, therefore, that our society must encourage
23 men and women to forget some traditions. It must allow people to
24 choose the career that best suits them—inside or outside the home.

1. T F   According to the passage, feminist groups only exist   Line(s) _____
           in the U.S.

2. What is the traditional social function of women?   Line(s) _____

   a. To raise children and to look after the home
   b. To earn money to support their families
   c. To choose the career which best suits them

3. How do feminists feel about the traditional social role of   Line(s) _____
   women?

   a. They feel that it is natural for women to stay home to look
      after the children.
   b. They argue that a woman's social role does not have to be
      decided by biology.
   c. They feel that society must not change the traditional roles
      of women. If we change them, society will not be able to
      function.

4. Why do feminists mention scientific studies about raising chil-   Line(s) _____
   dren?

   a. The studies support their demands that women must be re-
      sponsible for the children.
   b. The studies suggest that it is better for children to be raised
      by their fathers.
   c. The studies support the idea that child raising is not only
      women's work.

5. List five words or expressions which show you that the writer
   is reporting the ideas of feminists.

Look for words and expressions in the passage which show you that you are reading the
opinion of the writer. Then answer Question 6.

6. What does the writer think about the feminist ideas in the
   passage?

   a. The writer disagrees with these ideas.
   b. The writer agrees with these ideas.
   c. We don't really know the writer's opinion.

Exercises for Parts A and B

SAME OR DIFFERENT?

Read the two sentences in each example. Do they express the same ideas, or do they express different ideas? Write *S* for sentences with the same ideas; write *D* for sentences with different ideas.

Remember: You can express the **same** ideas with **different** words and **different** grammar!

1. a. One hundred and fifty years ago, U.S. law required women to give their husbands any money they earned outside the home. _____
   b. According to American law 150 years ago, women had to give their husbands any money they made outside the home.

2. a. Nineteenth-century society did not encourage women to have careers outside the home. _____
   b. In the nineteenth century, society did not permit women to have careers outside the home.

3. a. Society traditionally expected women to look after their families and their homes. _____
   b. The traditional role of women was to take care of their homes and families.

4. a. In nineteenth-century U.S. society, women were subordinate to men. _____
   b. Women enjoyed full equality with men in nineteenth-century American society.

5. a. It is a tradition in some cultures that parents must choose the person whom their son or daughter will marry. _____
   b. In some cultures, tradition does not permit people to choose their own future wife or husband; parents are required to do this.

6. a. In the nineteenth century, feminist groups in America made many unsuccessful attempts to win women the right to vote. _____
   b. Although nineteenth-century feminist groups tried many times to win women the right to vote, they failed in their attempts.

7. a. According to feminist groups, women and men must share the responsibilities for raising children. _____
   b. Feminist groups argue that it is better for children to be raised by women.

8. a. My record player is not functioning well. _____
   b. There is something wrong with my record player.

EXPECTATIONS

Read the first sentence in each of these examples. Think about the ideas in it. Then choose the sentence or sentences that can follow it.

1. This piece of equipment has an extremely important function.
   a. It gives a warning to nurses when the blood pressure of a patient falls.
   b. It was developed by scientists in California and costs $1 million.
   c. It enables a plane to land even when the crew can't see the airport.

2. Modern appliances make the job of housekeeping much easier and faster than it was fifty years ago.
   a. Color television and stereos, for example, can bring first-class entertainment into our living rooms.
   b. For example, people today cannot imagine life without a car.
   c. Washing machines and dryers, for example, reduce by many hours each week the amount of time we spend on laundry.

3. Some careers seem traditionally to attract more females than males.
   a. Teaching and nursing are examples of jobs where women are in the majority.
   b. In medicine, for example, 85% of all doctors are men.
   c. University education is one area where both men and women have made their careers.

4. In this state there is a law that requires drivers to have car insurance.
   a. Before you can register your car, you have to prove that you are insured to drive.
   b. It's legal to drive without insurance.
   c. It is hoped that the law will reduce the number of people who are hurt by drivers who cannot pay for medical expenses.

5. In some cultures, male and female roles are very different.
   a. For example, men are often expected to be the breadwinners, while women look after the home and family.
   b. For example, both men and women are expected to work outside the home to support the family.
   c. In other cultures, however, the traditional differences are disappearing.

VOCABULARY QUIZ

Choose the correct word for each sentence. Use each word only once.

tradition	feminist	function	requirement
role	male	biology	career
appliance	attempt	raise	argument
biological	subordinate	female	nurse

1. Nursing is a _____ which attracts a large number of women. But now men are beginning to see it as a good way to earn their living.

2. Experience is a _____ for this job. Although a person has a good education, without experience he or she will not get the job.

3. Mike is very happy. His employer told him that he is going to _____ Mike's salary by 15%.

4. After many unsuccessful _____s, the student managed to pass his driving test.

5. Society often believes that a working wife's career is _____ to her husband's career. His career comes first. If he wants to move to a new town for a better job, his wife is expected to give up her job and follow him.

6. In Scotland there is an unusual custom. After midnight on the first of January, people often go to visit family and friends. They carry a piece of coal in one hand and something to drink in the other. No one knows the origins of this _____.

7. When you rent an unfurnished apartment in the U.S. it usually has _____s. You don't usually need to buy a range or a refrigerator for the kitchen. Sometimes apartments even have dishwashers.

8. You can hear angry voices in the apartment above mine. I think the people who live there are having a(n) _____.

9. The equipment on the new plane _____ed perfectly. Everything was a complete success.

10. A number of years ago there were very few _____ doctors. More than 95% of doctors were men.

PART C

profession (noun)

> DEFINITION a profession: 1. a job which requires higher education and special training
> 2. all the people in a profession

1. Some *professions* have always been open for women, for example, teaching. But other *professions,* for example, medicine and law, discriminated against women for a long time.
2. The majority of the medical *profession* believes that the U.S. health system is good.

consumer (noun)

DEFINITION   a consumer: a person who uses the goods or work which others sell

EXAMPLES   1. There are many laws now that protect *consumers* from dangerous products.
2. Producers must always satisfy the people who buy their goods. If they don't, the *consumers* will choose another product.

to afford (verb)

DEFINITION   to afford (to do) something: to have enough money (or time) for something
cannot afford: not to be able to do something without serious problems afterward

EXAMPLES   1. I can't *afford* a long vacation this year because I've just bought a new car.
2. The student can't *afford* to fail this test. If he does, he will fail the whole course, and he will have to repeat it.

to promote (verb)
promotion (noun)

DEFINITION   to promote someone: to move someone to a better job

EXAMPLES   1. Kate is excited. At work she has been *promoted* from assistant director to director.
2. John left his job because there was no chance of *promotion* for him.

standard (noun)

DEFINITION   a standard: a way to measure something
standard of living: the comfort that people in a society enjoy

EXAMPLES   1. This teacher has very high *standards* in her classes. She expects students to work very hard. If students get below 70% on tests, they fail.

2. The general *standard of living* in the U.S. is quite high. It is higher than in many developing countries.

attitude (noun)

DEFINITION   a person's attitude towards X: how he thinks or feels about X, and, as a result, the way he behaves

EXAMPLES 1. The student has a really good *attitude* to her classes. She is interested, and she wants to learn. She makes mistakes, but she learns from them.
2. Men's *attitudes* to women are changing. Years ago, most men did not want their wives to work. Today, according to a study, the majority of male students expect that their wives will work after they get married.

figure (noun)

DEFINITION   a figure: a number

EXAMPLES 1. The unemployment *figures* for this month are better than for last month. Unemployment has decreased by 100,000.
2. In English, we usually write small numbers in words and large numbers in *figures,* for example, four people, but 14,528 people.

statistics (noun)

DEFINITION   statistics: 1. figures which show facts about the world
2. the science which studies statistics

EXAMPLES 1. This book contains important *statistics* about every country in the world. It shows the population, the number of children who are born, the number of people who die, etc.
2. Many scientists have to take classes in *statistics* so that they can use *statistics* in their own research.

Now read this passage and answer the questions about it.

1   Although women in the U.S. have worked outside the home for
2 many years, especially in nursing and teaching, statistics show
3 that the number of working women really began to increase in the
4 1950s and 1960s. In 1940, for example, only 15% of married women
5 had employment outside the home. In 1960 the figure was 30%,
6 and in 1982 it reached 68%.
7   However, the increase in the number of women with jobs out-

8   side the home has not been the only change in the area of female
9   employment. There has also been a clear change in the attitude of
10   women to their jobs. In the 1950s and 1960s many women accepted
11   jobs outside the home so that they could afford consumer goods that
12   would give their families a better standard of living. Only a minor-
13   ity of women were really interested in work as a career. In the last
14   fifteen years, however, the situation has changed. The attitude of
15   many women is now different. Their work means more to them
16   now than just money; they see it as a career which they can de-
17   velop and keep for life. Many more young women are going to law
18   school, or medical school, or business school because they want a
19   profession. For example, the number of women in medical school
20   has increased by 300% in the last twelve years.
21   As a result of this change in attitude, women are less reluctant
22   than before to demand true job equality with men. They want
23   equal opportunities to enter any profession, and after they have
24   entered a profession, they want equal pay for equal work and equal
25   opportunities for promotion.

1. T   F   Women did not begin to work outside the home until   Line(s) _____
               the late 1950s.

2. In the 1950s and 1960s, many women took jobs outside the   Line(s) _____
   home

   a. because they wanted to earn more money to buy goods.
   b. because work inside the home did not interest them.
   c. because they were interested in a career that they could
      keep for life.

3. Look at lines 19–20. Why does the writer use the statistic   Line(s) _____
   about the increase in the number of women who are attending
   medical school?

   a. It is evidence that more women want a career, not just a
      job.
   b. It is evidence that more women are planning to take em-
      ployment outside the home.
   c. It is evidence that women want to earn higher salaries than
      they earned in the past.

4. T   F   The writer suggests that in the past women often did   Line(s) _____
               not protest their lack of equality with men in the
               area of employment.

5. What does true job equality mean, according to this passage?   Line(s) _____

   a. People receive the same pay for the same work regardless of
      sex.

b. There are equal opportunities for men and women to enter any profession.

c. A person's sex does not influence his or her chances for promotion.

d. All of these

PART D

principal (adjective)
principal (noun)

DEFINITION   principal: main, most important
a principal: the head of a school

EXAMPLES   1. The *principal* goal of the new government is to improve the economy.

2. The school needs a new *principal*. Three of the most experienced teachers would like the job.

rapid (adjective)

DEFINITION   rapid: fast

EXAMPLES   1. There has been a *rapid* increase in the number of violent crimes in this city. Last year there were 1,000 crimes; this year there have been 1,500.

2. Prices of new cars are going up *rapidly*. My car cost $5,000 two years ago. Now it costs about $8,000.

to **rise** (irregular verb)
rose, risen

DEFINITION   to rise: to go up; to increase

EXAMPLES   1. The sun *rises* in the east every morning.

2. The price of food has *risen* a lot in the past year. For example, bread is now 30% more expensive than last year.

to **force** (verb)

DEFINITION   to force a person to do X: a person does X because he has to; he has no choice

EXAMPLES   1. The bad weather *forced* us to stop the game. We could not continue.

2. The workers *forced* the company to raise their pay. They threatened to stop work if the company did not agree.

stable (adjective)

DEFINITION   stable: describes something which will not move or change

EXAMPLES   1. Prices here are very *stable*. They haven't changed a lot in the last two years.
2. This table is extremely *unstable*. Don't stand on it.

to **tend** (verb)
tendency (noun)

DEFINITION   X tends to do Y, or X has a tendency to do Y: X usually does Y

EXAMPLES   1. Crime *tends* to increase when there is a lot of unemployment in a community.
2. I don't like John. He *has a tendency* to blame other people for mistakes that he makes.

to **provide** (verb)

DEFINITION   to provide something: to make something available
to provide someone with something: to give people something they need

EXAMPLES   1. Some people believe that the U.S. public schools are not *providing* a good education for their children.
2. The ski school will *provide* you with the equipment you need for this class. You don't need to have your own boots and skis.

to **combine** (verb)

DEFINITION   to combine: to come together
to combine X and Y: to bring a number of things together

EXAMPLES   1. The colors blue and yellow *combine* to make green.
2. For many sports you have to *combine* skill and strength. You need both in order to be good.

In this passage, like the passage in Part B, the writer also describes the opinions of other people. When you read, pay attention to the difference between fact and the opinions of the opponents of feminism. Now read the passage and answer the questions about it.

1   Although the feminist movement enjoys a great deal of support
2   in the U.S., it has also met a great deal of opposition since its
3   beginning. The critics of the movement tend to be very conserva-
4   tive men and women who are afraid of rapid social change. One of
5   their principal objections to feminism is that it threatens the tradi-

6 tional life and organization of the American family. A woman, they
7 argue, is the best person to raise children, and raising children is a
8 full-time career. No one can combine two full-time careers, one
9 outside the home and one inside the home. According to them,
10 when a woman has a full-time career outside the home, she cannot
11 provide the stable home life her family needs. To support their
12 argument, antifeminists use recent statistics which show that the
13 number of divorces is rising and that about 20% of children now
14 live in one-parent families.
15   The opponents of the feminist movement are organizing a pro-
16 gram of resistance to feminist ideas and demands. They have
17 formed groups which are putting pressure on the government and
18 on politicians. They are also attempting to prevent feminist ideas
19 from reaching their children in school. For example, one group has
20 forced schools in one state to stop using certain schoolbooks. The
21 group objects to the books because they contain descriptions of
22 family life where both parents are working or where the children
23 are living with only one parent after divorce.

1. T F   Very few people in the U.S. disagree with the ideas of   Line(s) _____
            the feminist movement.

2. T F   According to the passage, feminists tend to be very   Line(s) _____
            conservative people.

3. A woman's responsibility is to remain at home and look after   Line(s) _____
   her children. This is the opinion of
   a. the feminist movement.
   b. the opponents of feminism.
   c. the government.

4. T F   Feminist ideas are meeting some resistance in U.S.   Line(s) _____
            society today.

5. Why do some people object to schoolbooks which mention work-   Line(s) _____
   ing mothers and divorced parents?
   a. They believe that the books contain dangerous feminist
      ideas.
   b. They want their children to learn about modern U.S. society.
   c. The books give a traditional picture of the family.

6. T F   The group that the writer mentions in lines 19–23   Line(s) _____
            has failed in its attempt to ban certain schoolbooks.

7. List the words which show you that the writer is reporting the
   ideas of people who oppose feminism.

8. Now look at these ideas. Are they facts, or are they opinions of the opponents of the feminist movement?

   a. Feminism is a danger to the American family.   FACT   OPINION

   b. A lot of people do not agree with feminism.   FACT   OPINION

   c. If a woman has a full-time job outside the home, she   FACT   OPINION
   cannot provide a stable home life for her family.

   d. Antifeminists are putting pressure on politicians.   FACT   OPINION

   e. Children need to be protected from feminist ideas.   FACT   OPINION

   f. Opponents of feminism object to schoolbooks which de-   FACT   OPINION
   scribe the lives of divorced parents.

Now look for words or expressions that show the writer's opinion. Then answer Question 9.

9. What does the author think about the opponents of the femi-   Line(s) _____
   nist movement?
   a. The writer agrees with their ideas.
   b. The writer does not share their ideas.
   c. We do not know the writer's opinion.

PART E

feature (noun)

   DEFINITION   a feature: a part or a quality which you can see easily

   EXAMPLES   1. One of the *features* of this new car is a small computer. It
   controls the amount of fuel the car needs.
   2. My apartment has one *feature* that I really like. It has a
   fireplace in the living room.

occupation (noun)

   DEFINITION   an occupation: a job

   EXAMPLES   1. Nursing is an *occupation* which traditionally does not attract many men.
   2. You need to write your name, age, address, and *occupation*
   when you want to get a credit card.

qualification (noun)
qualified (adjective)

DEFINITION   a qualification: training that gives you the right to do some job

EXAMPLES   1. Kate has the right *qualifications* for this new research job. She has a degree in biology, and she has three years' experience in research.
2. John is teaching French? That's crazy. He's not *qualified*. He has never studied French in his life!

primary (adjective)

DEFINITION   primary: 1. earliest, first
2. main, most important

EXAMPLES   1. In England children start *primary* (or elementary) school at the age of five.
2. The student's *primary* purpose here is to learn English.

income (noun)

DEFINITION   income: general word for money that you receive (e.g., salary, pay, rent)

EXAMPLES   1. Every year you must report to the government all the *income* which you received during the year from your job and from any other place.
2. If a person writes a book, then the money which he receives for the book is *income*. He must report it each year to the government.

service (noun)

DEFINITION   service: work which you do for someone
service industry: an industry which provides a service but does not produce goods

EXAMPLES   1. The university helps students find suitable apartments. This is one *service* that the university provides for its students.
2. A garage which repairs your car belongs to the *service* side of the economy because it provides *service*. It doesn't make anything.

accurate (adjective)
inaccurate (adjective)

> DEFINITION   accurate: correct, free of mistakes, careful and correct
>
> EXAMPLES   1. In science we need to measure things very *accurately*. Even
>   a very small mistake will cause problems.
>   2. This report is *inaccurate*. It contains figures that are
>   wrong.

average (noun)
average (adjective)

> DEFINITION   average: a number which you calculate in this way: add some
>   quantities together and then divide that figure by
>   the number of quantities
>
> EXAMPLES   1. In this class the students' ages are 19, 18, 23, 21, 25, and
>   18. The *average* age of students in the class is 20.7 years.
>   2. The professor used the *average* of our test scores for our
>   final grade.

In this passage the writer also gives us facts and opinions. Pay attention to the difference.
Also pay attention to different opinions. How many opinions does the writer mention?
Does the writer discuss the opinions of one group of people more than the opinions of
others? Now read the passage and answer the questions about it.

1   According to figures from the U.S. Bureau of Labor Statistics,
2   the average weekly income for a woman in 1983 was $260. For the
3   same year, men had average weekly earnings of $393. For some
4   people, these figures are clear evidence that there is still sex dis-
5   crimination in the area of pay in the U.S. However, I would argue
6   that this explanation is too simple. In order to get an accurate
7   picture of the situation, we must examine the types of jobs which
8   are typically held by men and by women. When we do this, we find
9   that certain occupations seem to be primarily female while others
10   seem to be primarily male occupations. In the medical and legal
11   professions, for example, statistics show that 85% of all doctors and
12   lawyers are men (although this situation is changing). More than
13   90% of all engineers are men. Women, however, have been the
14   majority for a long time in other occupations. For example, 99 out
15   of every 100 secretaries are women, and 95% of all nurses are
16   female. From these statistics, it is clear that women tend to enter
17   certain occupations and not others. The occupations which they

18	enter are often in service industries and often have one common
19	feature: They do not pay well. It can be argued that this is the
20	principal reason for the difference in earnings between men and
21	women. In addition, we can expect the pay situation to change in
22	the future because more qualified women are beginning careers in
23	medicine, law, business, scientific research, and engineering.

1. T F Men tend to earn more than women in their jobs.   Line(s) _____

2. T F According to everyone, unequal earnings show that   Line(s) _____
there is still sex discrimination against women in the
area of pay.

3. T F The majority of people who work in the legal and   Line(s) _____
medical professions are female.

4. What jobs have typically been held by women?   Line(s) _____
   a. Jobs as doctors, lawyers, and engineers
   b. Low-paying jobs in service industries
   c. Jobs in areas that are primarily male

5. According to the passage, what can we expect in the medical   Line(s) _____
profession in the future?
   a. Eighty-five percent of doctors will be men.
   b. The number of female doctors will rise.
   c. The salaries of doctors will increase.

6. Now look at these sentences. According to the passage, are
they facts? Or are they only the opinions of a group of people?

   a. There is still a difference between the earnings of men   FACT   OPINION
   and women.

   b. The reason for this difference is that women tend to en-   FACT   OPINION
   ter low-paying jobs.

   c. There are more male doctors than female doctors.   FACT   OPINION

   d. On average, men still earn more than women.   FACT   OPINION

   e. There is still sex discrimination in the area of pay in the   FACT   OPINION
   U.S.

   f. The majority of nurses and secretaries are female.   FACT   OPINION

   g. The difference between men's pay and women's pay will   FACT   OPINION
   become smaller in the future.

Now look for words and expressions that show you the opinion of the writer. Do you see any? Now answer this question.

7. In the opinion of the writer, why do women still earn less   Line(s) _____
   money than men?
   a. We do not know the writer's opinion.
   b. There is discrimination—people pay women less because
      they are women.
   c. Women are often in the majority in low-paying jobs.

Exercises for Parts C, D, and E

SAME OR DIFFERENT?

Read the two sentences in each example. Do they express the same ideas, or do they express different ideas? Write *S* for sentences with the same ideas; write *D* for sentences with different ideas.

Remember: You can express the **same** idea with **different** words and **different** grammar!

1. a. Unemployment statistics show that the country is still having   _____
      economic difficulties.
   b. The country's economic problems are still not over, according to
      figures which show the number of people out of work.

2. a. Consumers cannot afford to buy new cars because prices have   _____
      risen more quickly than incomes.
   b. Incomes are not going up as rapidly as the prices of new cars;
      as a result, consumers don't have the money to buy new cars.

3. a. It is difficult for women to enter certain professions.   _____
   b. It is difficult for women to win promotions in certain professions.

4. a. The prices of new cars are forcing people to keep their old cars   _____
      longer than usual.
   b. People are having to drive their old cars longer because the
      prices of new cars are so high.

5. a. In the U.S. there is still a tendency for women to take jobs that   _____
      do not pay well.
   b. In the U.S. women still tend to enter low-paying occupations.

6. a. Ninety percent of people who work in elementary schools are   _____
      women.
   b. Ninety percent of elementary school principals are women.

7. a. Although the woman had better qualifications for the job, the _____
   company decided to hire the man.
   b. The company gave the job to the man because he had more
   experience and a better education than the woman.

8. a. Saudi Arabia provides about 25% of the world's oil. _____
   b. The world gets 25% of the oil which it needs from Saudi Arabia.

9. a. Carlos's primary reason for coming to the U.S. was to learn _____
   English.
   b. Carlos came to the U.S. mainly because he wanted to learn
   English.

10. a. A feature of many traditional female occupations is that they _____
    tend to be poorly paid.
    b. Typically, jobs that are traditionally held by women tend to
    have low pay.

11. a. People's attitudes to the roles of men and women are changing _____
    in the U.S. today.
    b. In the U.S. traditional ideas about the roles of men and women
    continue today.

12. a. If this company wants to be successful, it will have to provide _____
    better service to its customers.
    b. If this company does not improve the quality of its service, it
    will not be successful.

EXPECTATIONS

Read the first sentence in each of these examples. Think about the ideas in it. Then
choose the sentence or sentences that can follow it.

1. For two years, oil prices have been quite stable.
   a. They rose 25% last year and have already increased 17% this year.
   b. There has only been a small increase during the last twenty-four months.
   c. Last year they fell 21%, but in the last few months they have risen rapidly
   again.

2. An elementary school in this area of town is looking for a new principal; I
   think that Kate is well-qualified for the job.
   a. She has been a teacher of English for a year.
   b. She has an M.A. and has a great deal of experience in primary education.
   c. The principal's pay is much higher than the pay Kate is earning now.

3. It is clear that in U.S. society there are occupations which are typically male and occupations which are typically female.
    a. For example, a large number of both men and women are training to become lawyers.
    b. Statistics show, for example, that 99% of secretaries are women, while 90% of engineers are men.
    c. An increasing number of women are entering the legal and medical professions.

4. My sister started in a new job a year ago and has been very successful in it.
    a. The company has denied her promotion three times already.
    b. Her income has risen 30% in the past six months.
    c. She has received three promotions and three raises in the past eight months.

5. My parents' standard of living has improved a great deal in the past ten years.
    a. Now they can't afford to buy a new washing machine or other household appliances they need.
    b. Their income has risen more rapidly than consumer prices.
    c. My mother is now the principal of her school, and my father has also been promoted.

6. Society's attitude toward working women has changed greatly in the past fifteen years.
    a. People still tend to feel that it is more important for a man to have a career than for a woman.
    b. Today many more parents are encouraging their daughters to think seriously about a profession.
    c. This can be seen from statistics which show that more females are studying for professional qualifications today than fifteen years ago.

7. The driver claimed that the accident was not his fault.
    a. A car which was coming in the opposite direction forced him to drive off the road.
    b. The car in front of him stopped suddenly without warning and for no clear reason.
    c. There was no sign to warn drivers to reduce speed on that dangerous part of the road.

8. According to the opposition, these new unemployment figures from the government do not give an accurate picture of the situation.
    a. They do not show the number of discouraged workers, the people who have given up looking for work.
    b. The economic situation is much worse than the statistics show.
    c. The figures are correct and show that the economy is getting stronger.

Choose the correct word for each empty space. Use each word only once.

force	service	unstable	principal
provide	combine	rapidly	attitude
standard	accurate	tend	consumer
qualified	statistics	profession	feature
promotion	income	primary	afford

1. An increasing number of women want to enter the legal and medical
   _____s. We know that because the number of female students is
   rising in law schools and medical schools.

2. According to _____ which appeared recently, the number of women
   doctors has increased 300% in the last ten years.

3. Different people have different _____s to their jobs. Some work
   only because they need the money. For others, the satisfaction which they
   get from their work is almost as important as the money they earn.

4. In the U.S. there are laws that protect _____s. Companies must
   test products carefully before they sell them to the public.

5. Kate is very excited. She has just received a _____ at work. In her
   new position she has much more responsibility, and, of course, she is earning
   more money.

6. This country is very _____. The government has changed fifteen
   times in the past ten years, sometimes after violence has occurred.

7. The teachers decided to _____ the two classes and work together in
   one group because there were only four students in each class.

8. Traditionally, society expects the husband to _____ the food, clothing, and shelter his family needs.

9. Some women don't really want to work outside the home, but they have to.
   Their economic situation _____s them to look for work outside the
   home. Without a job, they would not be able to pay all the monthly bills.

10. In this part of the country, the weather can change quite _____.

Yesterday afternoon, for example, the temperature fell from 75° to 55° in one hour when a sudden storm hit the area.

11. John seems to be well _____ for the job. It requires a degree in engineering and two years' experience in industry. John has both.

12. Although the average _____ of a working woman has risen in the past five years, women on average still earn far less than men.

13. The _____ purpose of classes in the English Language Institute is to teach foreign students English. A secondary goal is to help students get used to American culture.

14. The economist's predictions were _____. She said that unemployment would rise to 10 million this year. The most recent figures show that a total of 9.9 million are now out of work.

15. Some large hotels provide a number of extra _____s for their guests. For example, often they have a special bus which takes guests to and from the nearest airport.

Main Reading

Pre-Reading Exercises

VOCABULARY IN CONTEXT

Use the context (and the words in italics in the first four examples) to guess the meaning of the new words (in boldface type).
Remember: Read each example to the end. Do not stop after the new word.

1. Mike is *not* very **realistic.** He has had difficulty with every French class he has taken. He knows that there are few or no jobs available for French teachers, but, *in spite of all this,* he still wants to train to be a French teacher.

    Realistic describes a person _____.
    a. who is intelligent and works hard
    b. who bases decisions on facts not on feeling
    c. who always tells the truth even when it is unpleasant.

2. The workers are *not* going to *accept* the company's *wage increase of 3%*. They say that it is completely **inadequate.** The *cost of living,* they point out, has *risen* by *12%* since their last wage increase.

> Inadequate describes something _____.
>
> a. that does not exist in the world
> b. that is impossible to do
> c. that does not satisfy your needs

3. Bill *cannot change* his ideas or his behavior when a situation changes. He also tends to have *very strict rules* for his children. His wife, *however,* is *more* **flexible,** so the children always ask her if they want permission to do something unusual.

> Flexible can describe people _____.
>
> a. who never change their minds because they are sure that they are right
> b. who understand the need to change when the situation requires it
> c. who are very conservative

4. Our *class* is going to have a party. We are going to *ask* each **member** *of the class* to bring some food from *his* or *her* country to the party.

   We have to pay the officials who control our soccer games. Each **member** *of the team* pays $5 every season.

> A member is _____.
>
> a. a person who plays on a team
> b. a person who belongs to a group
> c. a person who is a student in a class

5. It has not rained in this area of the country for two months. The lack of rain is **creating** serious problems for farmers. Their crops are not growing well because the ground is too dry.

> To create means _____.
>
> a. to make
> b. to solve
> c. to follow

6. In the U.S. women still earn less than men. In 1983 the average **wage** for a woman was $260 a week, while the average male worker earned $392.

> Wage or wages means _____.
>
> a. a certain type of employment or occupation

b. the pay you receive for work

c. the promotions you can receive in your job

7. Three months ago, unemployment was 10.2 million. This month it is 9.1 million. These figures **indicate** that the economy is improving.

To indicate means _____.

a. to cause

b. to decrease

c. to show

8. Feminists believe that men should share the **domestic** responsibilities with their wives. They want men to do the shopping, the cooking, and the laundry as often as their wives.

Domestic describes something _____.

a. which is connected with the home

b. which is connected with food

c. which is connected with our jobs

9. The students in the English Language Institute come from a wide **variety** of countries. There are students from Japan, from China, from Korea, from almost all the countries of the Middle East, and from Latin America. There are even students from Europe and Africa. Last semester there were students from thirty-five different countries.

A variety means _____.

a. a number of different things

b. a language which many people speak

c. a country which doesn't speak English

10. The state government has introduced **legislation** to try to solve the problem of drunk driving. The new laws will allow police to stop any motorist for an alcohol test. They will also require judges to send drunk drivers to prison.

Legislation means _____.

a. police

b. education

c. laws

So, a legislator is _____.

a. a member of the police

b. a judge or a lawyer

c. a person who makes new laws

Read the title of this article carefully. Then choose the ideas that you expect in the article.

1. This article will describe the social role of women in many different cultures.   YES   NO

2. This article will describe the historical development of women's rights in the nineteenth century.   YES   NO

3. This article will show that the role of women in the U.S. is different today from their role some years ago.   YES   NO

4. This article will show that there are people who do not agree with changes in the role of women.   YES   NO

5. This article will discuss the feminist movement in the U.S.   YES   NO

Now read the Introduction (Paragraph 1) and the *titles* of the remaining sections of the article. Choose the ideas that you expect.

6. The article will primarily discuss the role of women in nineteenth-century U.S. society.   YES   NO

7. Since the 1960s there has been a great increase in the number of women who work outside the home. The article will discuss the reasons for this increase.   YES   NO

8. The article will show that this increase has not really changed American society.   YES   NO

9. The article will show that feminism appeared recently for the first time in U.S. society.   YES   NO

10. The article will examine the connection between feminism and the increase in the number of working women.   YES   NO

Now go back to Expectations 1–5. Do you want to change any of these expectations?
    Now read the article section by section. Before you read each section, you will get a chance to develop some expectations for the ideas in it. Turn to page 248.

Women in Modern U.S. Society:
Resistance and Change

Introduction

1   There have been great changes in U.S. society since the end of
2   World War II, especially since the 1960s. One of the areas of great-
3   est change is the role of women in society. Statistics show this
4   clearly: In 1940, only 15% of all married women had employment
5   outside the home; in 1960, the figure was 30%, and in 1980, 50% of
6   all married women had jobs outside the home. What has caused
7   this rapid increase in the number of women who are working out-
8   side the home? What effects has the increase had on American
9   society? This article will attempt to answer these two questions.

1

Working Women and the Rebirth of the Feminist Movement

10   There is a popular belief that the feminist movement, which
11   became very popular and powerful in the early 1970s, caused
12   women to be dissatisfied with their traditional roles as wives,
13   mothers, and homemakers. These women then began to find more
14   satisfying work outside the home. This, however, is not an accurate
15   picture of the connection between working women and the feminist
16   movement. Although feminism, or women's liberation, has been an
17   important factor in the changes which have occurred in the role of
18   women since 1970, it did not begin these changes.

2

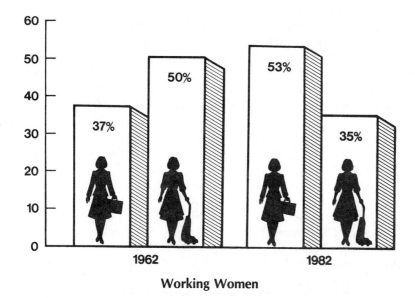

Working Women

3   There are two primary causes for the increase in the number of American women who work outside the home. First, between the end of World War II and the early 1960s, a large number of jobs became available in the service side of the U.S. economy. The population of the country was growing rapidly, and this growth created a need for more teachers, more medical assistants and nurses, more social workers, more secretaries, and more store assistants. These types of occupations had two important features in common: (1) they were jobs which were already traditionally held by women, and (2) in comparison with jobs which were traditionally held by men, they were poorly paid. They were, therefore, jobs that did not usually attract men.

4   The availability of new jobs that men did not want, however, is not by itself an adequate explanation for the rise in the number of working women. It does not answer the question of why women wanted to work. The second cause of the increase in the number of working women is the economic pressures which forced married women, especially young married women, to look for work outside the home. In the 1960s, people in the U.S. began to expect a higher standard of living; they wanted the expensive consumer goods that U.S. industry was producing. However, often the husband's earnings did not permit the family to buy the new kitchen appliances, the color television, the new clothes, the furniture, and the second automobile which seemed so necessary. It became necessary for wives to increase the family's income, and so women began to take the service jobs that were becoming available.

5   It is clear, therefore, that the increase in the number of working women began before the feminist movement was reborn in the late 1960s. In fact, many experts argue that the increase created the modern feminist movement. Working women were the cause not the result of women's liberation. According to these experts, economic conditions and the experiences of these working women were the main factors in the development of the feminist movement in the 1970s. The working women of the 1960s, they argue, soon realized that they could not afford to stop working. The costs of food, education, health care, housing, and consumer goods were rising much more quickly than the wages and salaries of their husbands. At the same time, however, women also realized that they were being treated unfairly: At work, they often had the jobs with the lowest wages and with little chance of promotion; at home, after they came home from work, their husbands still expected them to play the traditional role of housewife and mother. They realized that their situation would not improve unless they began to demand changes. These realizations led to the reappear-

63	ance of the feminist movement and to the creation of a number of
64	organizations that demanded an end to discrimination against
65	women.

Feminism and the Changing Role of Women

66	Feminist organizations showed people that discrimination ex-	6
67	isted everywhere. They showed that it was very difficult for women
68	to enter various professions. In 1972, for example, only 9.3% of
69	doctors and dentists were women, only 4% of all lawyers and judges
70	were female, and only 13% of all medical students were women. It
71	was also shown that society preferred to promote men to the posi-
72	tions of highest responsibility—even in traditionally female profes-
73	sions. For example, although more than 90% of elementary school
74	teachers in 1970 were women, more than 80% of the principals
75	were men. In addition, in many areas of employment, women re-
76	ceived lower wages than men for the same work.

77	According to feminists, this discrimination was made possible	7
78	by the attitude of society to women. U.S. society traditionally sees
79	women primarily as childraisers and homemakers. Men have tradi-
80	tionally been the breadwinners, who support their families with
81	their incomes. Therefore, when women began to work outside the
82	home, their income did not seem to be as important as the income
83	of their husbands. There was a belief that a man's wages needed to
84	be enough to support his family. This idea was then used to justify
85	higher wages for men than for women. Women's real responsibili-
86	ties were still in the home even when they had outside jobs.

87	Feminists argued that these attitudes were based only on tra-	8
88	dition and not on any law of nature. It is true, of course, that a
89	woman's biological function requires her to remain at home for
90	some time before and after a child is born. This is a fact of life.
91	Only women can bear children. However, this does not necessarily
92	mean that the woman has to raise the child and manage the house
93	while the husband works outside the home. No law of nature forces
94	people to accept these roles. A woman has the right to choose be-
95	tween a career as a full-time mother and housewife and a career
96	outside the home. Or she can combine the two careers if her hus-
97	band is prepared to assist her. Only tradition, not nature, prevents
98	this.

99	Therefore, feminists argue, attitudes toward women and their	9
100	roles in society must change. If society needs women workers, it
101	must permit them to have the same opportunities as men. If men
102	want the economic benefits of working wives, they will have to
103	accept changes in the traditional system of male and female re-

104 sponsibilities. Since the early 1970s, feminist organizations have
105 protested the lack of equality for women and have demanded an
106 end to sex discrimination. They have tried to educate both men and
107 women; they have attempted to show people that attitudes toward
108 the roles of men and women can be more flexible. It is possible,
109 they argue, for women and men to share the responsibilities of
110 supporting and raising a family. How successful has this program
111 of education been? Have feminists achieved their goals?

112   Statistics indicate that there has been some progress for   10
113 women in many professions. In 1972, for example, only 10% of all
114 students in law school were women; in 1982 the percentage of
115 women was 34%. A similar development can be seen in medical
116 schools. Here the percentage of female students rose from 13% to
117 29% between 1972 and 1982. In the same ten years the percentage
118 of female lawyers and judges increased from 4% to 15%. In addi-
119 tion, since 1970 the government has introduced legislation which
120 has encouraged employers to hire qualified women, and there are
121 now laws that forbid discrimination on the basis of a person's sex.

122   In spite of some clear improvements, however, women continue   11
123 to be the majority in occupations that traditionally have low
124 wages. In 1982 women held 99% of all the secretarial jobs and 95%
125 of all the nursing jobs in the U.S. Consequently, the average fe-
126 male worker still only earns about 60% of what an average male
127 worker earns. In other professions, women are either not accepted
128 or not promoted. For example, the number of women in state and

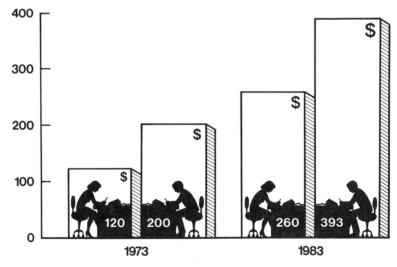

Average Weekly Earnings: Men and Women

129 federal government is still very low. In 1982 only 3% of all mem-
130 bers of Congress were women; only 5% of all mayors were women,
131 and only 12% of state legislators were women. In the banking
132 industry, although 70% of the workers are women, only 2% of the
133 top positions are held by women. From these figures one conclusion
134 is clear: Although the position of women in the U.S. is improving,
135 true equality of the sexes still has not been achieved.

Reactions to the Changing Role of Women

136 There has been, of course, a great deal of opposition to the   12
137 social changes that the feminist movement is demanding. Opposi-
138 tion is to be expected because the changes which women want are
139 changes in a part of the social system. If changes are made in one
140 part of a system, it becomes necessary to make changes in other
141 parts of the system. If other parts of the system do not change, then
142 the system cannot continue to function successfully. Changes in
143 women's lives mean, therefore, that there have to be changes in
144 other areas of society. However, often other members of society are
145 not prepared to make the necessary changes.

146 The goals of the feminist movement are opposed by men and   13
147 women who tend to be conservative, successful members of tradi-
148 tional society. They are clearly afraid that they will lose some of
149 their power and influence if the feminist movement achieves its
150 goals. For example, some men feel threatened by women who are
151 now competing with them for jobs. Some women are opposed to
152 feminism because it places so much importance on careers for
153 women outside the home. They have made successful marriages
154 and have been good wives and mothers. Now they feel threatened
155 because they believe that feminism places little importance on
156 their work as wives and mothers.

157 One of the major objections to women's liberation is that it   14
158 disturbs and perhaps even destroys family life. Critics can point to
159 statistics which show that divorce is increasing and that about 20%
160 of children today are living in single-parent families, usually with
161 their mothers. Statistics like these show, the opponents of femi-
162 nism argue, that women cannot successfully combine a career in
163 the home with a career outside the home. If they try to do so,
164 family life will suffer. If women cannot provide a stable home life
165 for their children, they argue, more and more children will experi-
166 ence difficulties in school; more and more will turn to drugs and
167 alcohol; and more and more will get into trouble with the police
168 and other authorities.

169 There is no doubt that the changes in women's roles are creat-   15

170 ing problems for U.S. society, especially in the area of family life.
171 Are there any solutions to these problems? The solution that the
172 opponents of feminism have chosen is to resist demands for change
173 and for sex equality. These people seem to suggest that the prob-
174 lems can be solved if women return to their traditional subordinate
175 role in society. However, this is not a realistic solution. It is based
176 on the mistaken belief that we can turn back the clock of history.
177 We cannot expect women to be satisfied with a subordinate role
178 after they have experienced something different.

179 A more realistic solution is to accept that society is changing. It   16
180 is useless to attack feminists and to attempt to bring back the "good
181 old days." It would be much better to teach people to be more flexible
182 in their attitudes toward male and female roles. The government
183 can do more than it has done up until now; it can encourage people
184 to change their attitudes. For example, in some European countries,
185 fathers can take leave from work for a few months in order to help
186 raise their new babies while their wives go out to work. In the U.S.
187 there is no legislation that enables men to help with child raising.
188 Most importantly, however, we must begin to teach our children to
189 be flexible in their attitudes toward the role of men and women. We
190 must show them that both men and women can have careers inside
191 or outside the home; we must teach them that men and women can
192 share the domestic responsibilities. They must learn that men and
193 women have the freedom to choose the career—inside or outside the
194 home—which suits them best. If we can teach our children to accept
195 a variety of possible roles for men and women, they will be better
196 able to live in the society of the future.

Section I: Working Women and the Rebirth of the Feminist Movement

EXPECTATIONS

Read the first sentences of Paragraphs 2–5. Read only the first sentence of each paragraph. Then choose the ideas that you expect.

1. This section will describe the effects of changes in women's   YES   NO
   roles.

2. This section will discuss the causes of the increase in the num-   YES   NO
   ber of women who work outside the home.

3. This section will argue that the feminist movement caused   YES   NO
   women to look for jobs outside the home.

4. This section will identify one main cause for the increase in   YES   NO
   the numbers of working women.

5. This section will show that a large number of jobs were created   YES   NO
in the U.S.

Now read Section I. Complete the Main Ideas Check and the Comprehension Check.

MAIN IDEAS CHECK

Here are the main ideas for the paragraphs in this section. Write the correct paragraph number opposite each main idea.

PARAGRAPH	IDEA
_____	Women began to take work outside the home because many new jobs that men did not want became available.
_____	The experiences of working women led to new interest in the feminist movement.
_____	Many people believe that feminism caused the increase in the numbers of working women. But they are wrong.
_____	Women began to take the jobs which were available outside the home because they needed extra income.

COMPREHENSION CHECK

1. People believe that feminism caused women in the 1960s to   Line(s) _____
go out and look for employment outside the home. What is
the writer's opinion of this idea?
   a. The writer disagrees with it.
   b. The writer accepts it.
   c. The writer believes that it is true.

2. T F   There is one main reason for the increase in the   Line(s) _____
number of women who began to work outside the
home in the 1960s.

3. T F   The population of the U.S. increased in the 1950s   Line(s) _____
and 1960s.

4. T F   Women had to compete with men for the new jobs   Line(s) _____
which were becoming available in the U.S.

5. According to these paragraphs, women wanted to work out-   Line(s) _____
side the home
   a. because housework did not satisfy them.
   b. because they wanted a better standard of living.
   c. because the new household appliances gave them a lot of
   free time.

6. T F   When women began to work outside the home, their   Line(s) _____
           husbands began to take responsibility for some of
           the housework.

7. T F   It was difficult for women to move up to a better job   Line(s) _____
           and earn better money inside the same company or
           office.

8. In this section of the article, you can follow a line of *cause*
   and *effect*. One development leads to another; then this new
   development leads to another, and so on. The picture below
   shows this line of cause and effect. Choose the correct development for each empty box. Write the letter of the correct
   development in the correct box.

   a. Rising costs force women to look for permanent careers.
   b. The U.S. population grows rapidly.
   c. Women want a better standard of living for their families.
   d. Women experience discrimination at work.
   e. Many jobs become available in service industries.

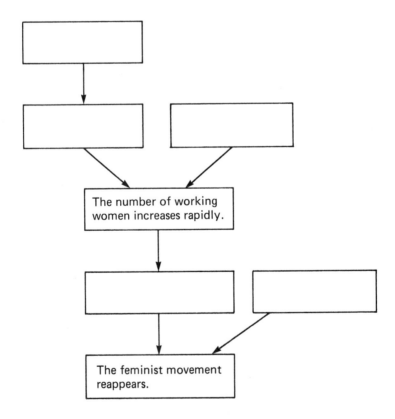

9. What effect did the rising cost of living have on women?　　Line(s) _____
   a. It caused many to give up their jobs.
   b. It caused many to think more seriously about careers.
   c. It caused many to forget about the consumer goods they
      planned to buy.

10. What is the real connection between the feminist movement　　Line(s) _____
    and the increase in the number of working women in the
    1960s?
    a. There is no real connection; the two developments have
       nothing to do with each other.
    b. The feminist movement caused women to be dissatisfied
       with their traditional roles as wives and mothers. As a re-
       sult, more and more women began to take employment
       outside the home.
    c. There was a rapid increase in the number of working
       women; this increase led to the reappearance of feminism.

Now go back to your expectations. How accurate were they?

Section II: Feminism and the Changing Role of Women

EXPECTATIONS

Read only the first sentences of Paragraphs 6–11. Then choose the ideas that you can
expect in this section.

1. This section will discuss the discrimination that women suffer　　YES　NO
   in their jobs.

2. This section will show that women are treated the same as　　YES　NO
   men in their jobs.

3. This section will discuss the goals of the feminist movement.　　YES　NO

4. This section will show that today working women are not　　YES　NO
   treated better than in the past.

5. This section will show that feminists have achieved all their　　YES　NO
   goals.

6. This section will discuss the traditional ideas that society has　　YES　NO
   about the roles of men and women.

7. This section will show that feminists are happy with society's　　YES　NO
   traditional attitudes to the role of women.

Now read this section and complete the Main Ideas Check and the Comprehension Check.

MAIN IDEAS CHECK

Here are the main ideas for the paragraphs in this section. Write the correct paragraph number opposite each main idea.

PARAGRAPH	IDEA
_____	The position of women in certain professions has improved.
_____	According to feminists, women's role in society does not have to be decided by their biological function.
_____	Feminist groups showed that women were treated unfairly at work.
_____	Feminist groups have tried to change traditional attitudes to male and female roles in society.
_____	In many areas of employment, women still have not achieved true equality.
_____	Job discrimination against women can occur because society still expects women to raise children and do the housework.

COMPREHENSION CHECK

1. T F   In the early 1970s it was impossible for a woman to become a doctor or a lawyer in the U.S.   Line(s) _____

2. What difficulties did working women meet in the 1970s?   Line(s) _____
   a. It was difficult for them to win promotions.
   b. It was difficult for them to enter certain professions.
   c. They were often paid less for the same work.

3. Look at lines 73–75. Why does the writer use the example of elementary school teachers and principals?   Line(s) _____
   a. In order to show that women get less pay than men for the same work
   b. In order to show that women's roles were changing in U.S. society
   c. In order to show that women are discriminated against in job promotions

4. T F In the opinion of many people, women's work was not   Line(s) _____
as important as men's work.

5. T F According to feminists, the laws of nature require   Line(s) _____
women to raise any children that are born.

6. T F Since the early 1970s, there has been some improve-   Line(s) _____
ment in the position of women in U.S. society.

7. Look at line 124–125. According to the writer, 99% of all sec-   Line(s) _____
retaries are women. Why does the writer mention this?
   a. To show that a large number of women now have jobs outside the home
   b. To show that there has been a great deal of progress in
   employment for women
   c. To show that women still tend to have low-paying jobs

8. T F Women have achieved full equality in the area of   Line(s) _____
employment.

9. Why does the writer use the example of the banking industry?   Line(s) _____
   a. To show that many women work in banking
   b. To show that there is sex discrimination in promotion
   c. To show that business could not function without women

Now go back to your expectations for this section. How accurate were they?

Section III: Reactions to the Changing Role of Women

EXPECTATIONS

Read only the first sentences of Paragraphs 12–16. Then choose the ideas that you
expect in this section.

1. This section will show that everyone in the U.S. agrees with   YES NO
the goals of the feminist movement.

2. All of the opponents of the feminist movement are men.   YES NO

3. According to some people, feminist ideas threaten traditional   YES NO
family life in the U.S.

4. This section will show that changes in the role of women are   YES NO
causing problems for U.S. society.

5. This section will only discuss the problems that are caused by changes in the role of women; it will not discuss solutions.

YES   NO

6. The writer is a conservative who cannot accept the changes in the role of women.

YES   NO

MAIN IDEAS CHECK

Here are the main ideas for the paragraphs in this section. Write the correct paragraph number opposite each main idea.

PARAGRAPH	IDEA
_____	We need to create more flexible attitudes toward the social roles of men and women.
_____	There is opposition to women's liberation because changes in women's roles necessitate other social changes.
_____	A lot of people disagree with women's liberation because, according to them, it threatens traditional family life in the U.S.
_____	Some people mistakenly believe that society would be better if women went back to their old roles as housewives and mothers.
_____	Opposition to the feminist movement comes from men and women who feel that the movement is a danger to their positions in society.

COMPREHENSION CHECK

1. T F   The writer is surprised that there is opposition to feminist ideas.   Line(s) _____

2. T F   Changes in the role of women only have an effect on the lives of women, not on the lives of anyone else.   Line(s) _____

3. What is *not* given as a reason for the opposition to the feminist   Line(s) _____
movement?
   a. Men are afraid that women will compete with them for jobs.
   b. People are shocked by the behavior of some extremists in the feminist movement.
   c. Women believe that feminism places little importance on traditional women's work.

4. Why do opponents of the feminist movement use statistics   Line(s) _____
which show that divorce is increasing and that many children now live with only one parent?

a. To show the good effects of feminist ideas on family life
b. To show that working mothers can bring economic benefits to their families
c. To show that family life will suffer if women have outside careers

5. T   F   The writer does not believe that feminist ideas are   Line(s) _____
             causing any problems for U.S. society.

6. Some people believe that there will be no more problems if   Line(s) _____
   women give up their struggle for equality and if they accept their
   traditional roles. What is the writer's opinion of this solution?

   a. The writer believes that it is an excellent solution and that
      it will solve many problems in families.
   b. The writer believes that we must turn back the clock of
      history.
   c. The writer believes that this solution ignores reality. It is
      therefore not a good suggestion.

7. What is the writer's attitude toward the role of women in U.S.   Line(s) _____
   society?

   a. We must resist the changes which the feminist movement is
      demanding.
   b. We must accept changes in the roles of men and women.
   c. A woman can have a career if she has no small children
      and if her husband permits it.

Now go back to your expectations for this section. How accurate were they?

Now do the paragraph reading exercise on the next page.

PARAGRAPH READING

These sentences form a paragraph, but they are not in the correct order. Put the sentences into their correct order. The first sentence is already in its correct place.

__1__   Because women now have better opportunities for jobs and for promotion, there is now an increasing number of marriages where the wife's salary is higher than her husband's.

_____   The study also found that heart disease is a much more common occurrence in men when their wives earn more than they do.

_____   If men earn less than their wives, the researchers argue, they begin to feel bad and begin to feel that they are in competition with their wives.

_____   How can we explain these findings?

_____   This situation is the opposite of the traditional situation, where the husband is expected to be the main breadwinner, and it is already having some negative consequences.

_____   This feeling of competition, the researchers conclude, increases pressure on some men, and the pressure leads to the marriage difficulties and the health problems which were found in the study.

_____   According to the researchers, the findings suggest that men tend to measure their importance by the amount of money they earn.

_____   For example, a recent study found that divorce is twice as common when a wife earns more than her husband.

Grammar Study: Explanations and Exercises

Introductory Unit

ACTIONS IN THE PAST

Introduction

You can already understand sentences like these:

1. Carlos plays baseball in the summer.
2. Abdullah lives in an apartment on Market Street.
3. Mike doesn't work on Sundays.

In these sentences the verbs are in the *simple present tense*. They give us information about things *today*. Now let us look at three different examples. They give us information about things in the *past*. Try to understand them.

Examples

4. In 1982 in Colombia, Carlos played soccer in the summer.
5. In 1981, Abdullah lived at home with his family.
6. Mike didn't work last Friday. He was sick.

In these examples we see past time from the following words: **in 1982, in 1981, last Friday.** But we can also see past time from the verbs. Look at them carefully. What differences do you see between Examples 1–3 and Examples 4–6?

Explanation

1. For information about the past, we often use verbs in the simple past tense.
2. Many verbs are *regular:* simple past = **verb** + **ed,** or **verb** + **d.**
3. Some verbs are *irregular;* their simple past is different from verb to verb. A list of these verbs appears in Appendix 2 (see pp. 312–313).
4. In negative sentences, simple past = **did** + **not** + **basic form.**
5. In questions, simple past = **did** + **subject** + **basic form.**
6. Here are some time expressions for past time. You often see verbs in the simple past with these expressions:

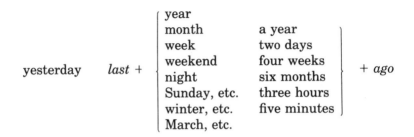

yesterday   *last* +
year	
month	a year
week	two days
weekend	four weeks
night	six months	+ *ago*
Sunday, etc.	three hours
winter, etc.	five minutes
March, etc.	

Exercises

SAME OR DIFFERENT?

Read the two sentences in each example. Pay attention to the verbs. Some are in the *simple present;* others are in the *simple past.* Do the two sentences have the same meaning and tense? Write *S* for sentences with the same meaning; write *D* for sentences with different meanings.

1. a. During the vacation, Mike played soccer every day.   ____
   b. During the vacation, Mike plays soccer every day.

2. a. The student lives with his parents.   ____
   b. The student lives at home with his father and mother.

3. a. Some friends of mine visited me yesterday.   ____
   b. Yesterday some friends of mine visited me.

4. a. The students drove to the university.   ____
   b. The students drive to the university.

5. a. My family drove to Florida.   ____
   b. My family went to Florida by car.

6. a. Mike walks to work on Fridays.   ____
   b. Mike walked to work on Friday.

7. a. Maria wanted to study English; she came to the U.S. _____
   b. Maria came to the U.S. to study English.

8. a. The drive to New York takes eight hours. _____
   b. The drive to New York took eight hours.

9. a. I get up at six o'clock every day. _____
   b. I got up at six o'clock every day.

10. a. I cannot go to that class. _____
    b. I could not go to that class.

PARAGRAPH READING

Read the following paragraphs. Pay attention to the verbs and their tenses. Pay attention to the time words. Use your list of irregular verbs in Appendix 2 to help you. Then answer the questions about each paragraph. Choose *T* for a true (correct) sentence and *F* for a false (wrong) sentence.

Look for the following simple past verbs in Appendix 2: **began, came, taught, was, went.** Then read the paragraph.

```
1        In 1976, José came to the United States from Mexico. He
2    studied English for a year in Pittsburgh. Then he went to Austin,
3    Texas. He started his studies in business. He stayed in Austin for
4    two years. He finished his studies in 1979 and went back to Mex-
5    ico. He worked there for several years. He was the manager of a
6    hotel. He also taught evening classes at the university in his home-
7    town. Two years ago José returned to the U.S. and began to study
8    for his Ph.D. at Harvard University. He is still there today.
```

1. T F   José lived in the U.S. in 1980.   Line(s) _____

2. T F   José now works in a hotel in Mexico.   Line(s) _____

3. T F   José studied in the U.S. from 1976 to 1979.   Line(s) _____

4. T F   José is a student now.   Line(s) _____

Look for the following simple past verbs in Appendix 2: **could, flew, took, were.** Then read the paragraph.

```
1        Fifty years ago, 95% or more of all travelers crossed the Atlan-
2    tic by ship to Europe or America. These ships were very large and
3    comfortable, and the journey took about five days. At that time, not
4    many planes could fly long distances; the flights across the Atlan-
5    tic were expensive and uncomfortable. Not many people wanted to
```

6   spend twelve hours in a small, noisy, uncomfortable plane. They
7   liked the large ships with their good food and comfortable rooms.
8   Today everything is very different. Few people take a ship across
9   the Atlantic. Most people fly, and the flights only last six or seven
10   hours. Of course, people can still travel across the Atlantic by ship,
11   but the journey still takes about five days, and it is very expensive.

1. T F   In the 1930s most travelers flew across the Atlantic.   Line(s) _____

2. T F   In the 1930s the ships were slow. Today the Atlantic   Line(s) _____
        ships are fast.

3. T F   Today a flight across the Atlantic takes about half   Line(s) _____
        the time of the same journey fifty years ago.

4. T F   Fifty years ago, many people did not like to fly across   Line(s) _____
        the Atlantic.

Look for the following simple past verbs in Appendix 2: **came, could, found, met, spoke, understood.** Then read the paragraph.

1   Mayumi came to the U.S. from Japan five weeks ago. She
2   stayed in a hotel for four days. Then she met Maria, a student from
3   Costa Rica. They found an apartment together, and they are now
4   very happy with it. Five weeks ago, Mayumi could not understand
5   a word of English, but now she understands many words and sen-
6   tences. She and Maria are in different classes, but they always
7   speak English at home together.

1. T F   Mayumi spoke English at home in Japan.   Line(s) _____

2. T F   Mayumi met Maria in the U.S.   Line(s) _____

3. T F   Mayumi did not know Maria in Japan.   Line(s) _____

4. T F   Mayumi understood some English five weeks ago.   Line(s) _____

5. When did the two students find their apartment?   Line(s) _____
   a. Two months ago
   b. Yesterday
   c. Four days ago
   d. About four weeks ago

Look for the following simple past verbs in Appendix 2: **began, fell, had, made, slept, was, went, woke.** Then read the paragraph.

1   Ibrahim doesn't watch television very often. In the evenings he
2   makes his dinner and studies his English. Then he visits his

3	friends or talks with them on the telephone. Last night he made
4	dinner and studied for an hour. There was a movie on television,
5	and Ibrahim wanted to see it. He turned on the television at 8:00
6	and started to watch the film. He watched it for an hour or so. It
7	was very interesting, but it was too long, and Ibrahim began to feel
8	tired and sleepy. At 9:30, in the middle of the movie, he fell asleep
9	on his sofa. He slept there all night! At 7:30 this morning, he woke
10	up and had to hurry for his 8:00 class.

1. T F   Ibrahim watches a lot of television in the evenings.   Line(s) _____

2. T F   Last night Ibrahim talked with some friends on the phone.   Line(s) _____

3. T F   Ibrahim watched part of the movie on television last night.   Line(s) _____

4. T F   Ibrahim went to bed after the movie last night.   Line(s) _____

5. T F   Ibrahim often studies English in the evenings.   Line(s) _____

6. T F   Yesterday Ibrahim had dinner in a restaurant.   Line(s) _____

Unit 1

HOW TO IDENTIFY PEOPLE AND THINGS

RELATIVE CLAUSES I

Introduction

Read the following conversation. Mike and John are in a restaurant.

> Mike: Do you know that man?
>
> John: What man do you mean?
>
> Mike: The man at the table beside the window.
>
> John: Oh, yes, that man. Yes. He's a professor at the university.

At first, John does not understand Mike. Mike did not identify the man well enough; he just said "that man." Maybe there are a number of men in the restaurant. Then Mike uses the words

at the table beside the window.

These words identify the man for John. He now understands Mike.

Writers also need to identify people and things for their readers. Now let us look at ways to do this.

Examples

Read the following examples and try to understand them. Pay attention to the words in boxes.

1. Bob thanked the policeman who helped him with his car.

2. I did not see the accident which happened outside my house. But I heard it.

3. The police did not find the car that caused the accident.

Explanation

1. The words in the boxes identify persons (the policeman) or things (the accident, the car).
2. The words in the boxes are *relative clauses*. (A clause is a part of a sentence with a subject and a verb. In Examples 1–3 there are two clauses: a *main clause* and a *relative clause*.)
3. To identify *people,* we use a relative clause with the word **who** at the beginning.
4. To identify *things* and *animals,* we use a relative clause with the word **that** or **which** at the beginning.
5. You can find relative clauses at the end of sentences or in the middle of sentences:

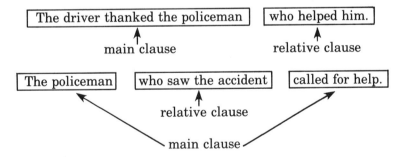

Exercises

Read the following sentences. Find the relative clauses in them. Underline the relative clauses and the person or thing which they identify. Here's an example:

> I didn't see <u>the car</u> <u>which stopped in front of me.</u>

1. She lives in an apartment which is very near the university.
2. I did not know all the students who were at the party.
3. All the snow that fell last week is still on the ground.
4. The plane which leaves at 9:00 A.M. is full. We have to wait for the next plane at 12:30.
5. The students who went to the movie last night really had a good time.
6. Students like professors who can give good explanations.
7. The movie that was on television last night was really good. I watched it from beginning to end.
8. The student who sits next to me in class comes from Japan. Her name is Mayumi.
9. The plane that took us from London to New York was two hours late.
10. What did you say to the policeman who stopped you for driving at 75 miles an hour?

RELATIVE CLAUSES II

Introduction

You can already understand sentences with relative clauses in them. Now let us look at relative clauses which are a little different.

Examples

Read these sentences and try to understand them. Pay attention to the words in the boxes. They are all relative clauses, but they do not look the same.

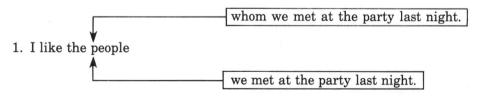

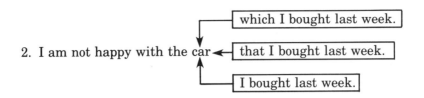

2. I am not happy with the car ← which I bought last week.

that I bought last week.

I bought last week.

Explanation

1. Sometimes we can begin a relative clause *without* **who, whom, which,** or **that**—that is, without a relative pronoun.
2. We can *omit* the relative pronouns in sentences like Examples 1 and 2.
3. In these examples, **the people** and **the car** are also the objects of the verbs in the relative clauses. So we have a choice: We can write the relative pronoun, or we can omit the relative pronoun. The meaning of the sentence stays the same.
4. We omit the object relative pronoun very often in conversation; we do not omit it so often in writing.

Exercises

Read these exercises carefully. Find the relative clauses in them. Be careful: Some relative clauses begin with a clear **who, which,** or **that;** others do not have a clear relative pronoun at the beginning. Underline the relative clauses and the person or thing which they identify.

1. Many people came to the party which we had for Mike last week.
2. I really liked the trip we made to Europe last summer.
3. At the beginning of the year, Mayumi did not understand anything she heard on television. Now she understands almost everything she hears.
4. The car which Maria bought last month is really comfortable.
5. The plane we took from New York to Miami was late. The weather was bad.
6. The books that American students have to buy for their classes are often very expensive.
7. The people Mayumi visited in San Francisco were very nice to her. They showed her places which most visitors do not see.
8. The movie we saw last night was really good.
9. The letter Carlos wrote to his parents in Colombia took two weeks to get there.
10. I really enjoyed the soccer game that was on television last night.

Read the following two passages and answer the questions about them. Pay attention to the relative clauses in the questions.

1	Kate and Susan, two American students, met during the first
2	week of school. Both of them were looking for apartments, so they
3	began to look together. They looked at a number of apartments.
4	Some of them were too small, some were too expensive, and others
5	were not near the university. Then Kate saw an apartment in the
6	student newspaper; it had two bedrooms, and it was near the uni-
7	versity. The girls went to see the apartment; it was clean, comfort-
8	able, and not too expensive. They rented the apartment, and now
9	they are very happy with it.
10	Before the beginning of school, Carlos, Mike, and John saw the
11	same apartment, but they did not take it. It was not suitable for
12	them; they wanted an apartment with three bedrooms. They looked
13	at apartments for several days. They finally found a comfortable
14	one. It was three miles from the university, but the rent was not
15	high. They rented the apartment, and now they take the bus to and
16	from the university every day.

1. T F The three men rented the apartment which the women did not want. Line(s) _____

2. T F The two women took the first apartment they saw. Line(s) _____

3. T F The women rented the apartment which Kate saw in the student newspaper. Line(s) _____

4. T F Kate and Susan now live in the apartment which the men saw before the beginning of school. Line(s) _____

5. T F Carlos, Mike, and John did not rent the first apartment they saw. Line(s) _____

6. T F The apartment which the men rented is near the university. Line(s) _____

7. Which apartment is three miles from the university? Line(s) _____
   a. The apartment which the three men rented
   b. The apartment which the three men did not want
   c. The apartment which Kate and Susan rented

8. Which apartment did Kate and Susan take? Line(s) _____
   a. The apartment which Carlos, Mike, and John rented last year
   b. The apartment which Kate saw in the student newspaper
   c. The apartment which the three men found three miles from the university

1   Mike, Ted, and Joe are three American students. They are
2   good friends, but they do not live together. Mike lives in an apart-
3   ment which is very near the university. It has two bedrooms. Mike
4   shares the apartment with a student from Germany. Mike studies
5   German, and his roommate studies math.
6   Ted lives in a one-bedroom apartment. It is about twenty min-
7   utes on foot from the university. Last year Mike lived in this apart-
8   ment. He told Ted about it.
9   Joe lives with two other American students. Their apartment
10   has three bedrooms; it is in a large apartment building which be-
11   longs to the university. It's about three miles from the university.
12   Joe and his friends read about the apartment in the student news-
13   paper. They lived there last year also.

1. T F   The students who live with Joe are from the U.S.   Line(s) _____

2. T F   The apartment which Mike rented last year was   Line(s) _____
           twenty minutes from the university.

3. T F   Joe has a roommate who comes from Germany.   Line(s) _____

4. Where does Ted live?   Line(s) _____

    a. In the apartment which has two bedrooms
    b. In the apartment which Mike had last year
    c. In the apartment which is three miles from the university

5. Mike has a roommate   Line(s) _____

    a. who studies German.
    b. who teaches math.
    c. who speaks German.

6. Where does Joe live?   Line(s) _____

    a. In an apartment building which belongs to the university
    b. In a one-bedroom apartment which is twenty minutes on
       foot from the university
    c. In an apartment near the university which he shares with a
       student from Germany

Unit 2

ACTIONS IN THE FUTURE

Introduction

You can already understand sentences like the following:

1. Last summer I went to South America for a vacation.

Sentences like this give information about the past. You can understand the verb (in the simple past tense). You can also understand the time expression.

In this unit we will study sentences which give information about the *future*.

Examples

Read these examples and try to understand them. Pay attention first to the time expressions and then to the verbs. (The time expressions and the verbs are in boldface type.)

2. **Next weekend** the students in my class **are having** a party.
3. Perhaps **tomorrow** the weather **will be good.**
4. Carlos **is going to take** his driving test **next week.** But he **won't pass** it. He needs more practice.
5. I **can see** you **tomorrow.**

Explanation

For actions in the future, we can use a number of different verb forms.

1. *will* + *verb* (basic form). The short forms are:

   Positive: *I'll, you'll,* and so on
   Negative: *I won't, you won't,* and so on

2. *am/are/is* + *verb* + *ing* (present continuous). Usually you also see a future time expression with this.
3. *be going to* + *verb* (basic form)
4. Simple present

Here are some future time expressions:

next Monday, etc.	in an hour	tomorrow
next summer, etc.	in two days	the day after tomorrow
next April, etc.	in a week	
next week/weekend/month/year	in three months	
	in six years	

Exercises

Read these exercises. Underline *only* the clauses which talk about the future. Pay attention to time expressions and verbs.

1. At present there are about 600 students from other countries at this university. Next year the number will be about 750.
2. When will we get to London? Well, we left New York two hours ago. We'll be in London in another four hours.
3. You'll need warm clothes for the winter here. It gets very cold here in January and February.
4. I'm going to see the doctor tomorrow. I'm not feeling very well.
5. At present Ibrahim is living in a one-bedroom apartment near the university. His wife is coming to the U.S. next month with their son and daughter. Then he will move to a three-bedroom apartment.
6. Last year Kate took her vacation in Florida, but this year she has no money. She's not going to take a vacation.
7. I'm going to buy a new car sometime in the next twelve months. Right now, I don't have enough money. I won't have enough for another five or six months.
8. Mike and Bob are not happy with the apartment which they rented two months ago. They're going to move out. The building is too noisy, and the rent is going up next month. They're looking for a new apartment at the moment.
9. According to the radio, it's going to snow tomorrow. Perhaps we won't be able to play our soccer game.
10. The math class meets at 11:00 A.M. every Tuesday and Thursday, but the students won't have any classes next week. The professor is going to Europe. He's leaving at the end of this week, and he'll be out of the country for six days.

Read the time expressions carefully. What do you expect after them? Choose the sentence which can follow each time expression. Pay attention to the verbs.

1. At the beginning of next week _____.
   a. I went to London
   b. I was in London
   c. I'll be in London

2. The day after tomorrow _____.
   a. we did a math test
   b. we're going to have a math test
   c. we had a math test

3. At the end of next month _____.
   a. the weather was cold
   b. the weather will get cold
   c. the weather became cold

4. Last summer _____.
   a. José played baseball every Saturday
   b. José is going to play baseball every Saturday
   c. José plays baseball every Saturday

5. Three days ago _____.
   a. Ibrahim went to see the doctor
   b. Ibrahim is going to see the doctor
   c. Ibrahim goes to see the doctor

Now read these sentences and choose the correct time expression which belongs to each sentence. Pay attention to the verbs again.

1. Maria is going to visit some friends _____.
   a. last Friday
   b. next Sunday
   c. yesterday

2. José did not pass his driving test _____.
   a. tomorrow
   b. next week
   c. yesterday

3. According to the radio, the weather will be good _____.
   a. yesterday
   b. last week
   c. tomorrow

4. Mike worked for an airline _____.

   a. now
   b. next year
   c. a year ago

5. Some of Mayumi's friends are having a party _____.

   a. last week
   b. next weekend
   c. yesterday

Some time expressions can be past *or* future. They are:

on + day	today
in + month	this morning/afternoon/evening
at + time	

Read the following sentences carefully. Then complete them with the correct time expressions. There is not only one correct answer. Choose all the correct answers.

1. Did you go to the movies _____?

   a. yesterday   d. last night
   b. next Sunday   e. tomorrow
   c. on Sunday

2. José is flying to Mexico _____.

   a. today   d. tomorrow
   b. this afternoon   e. last weekend
   c. a week ago

3. Kate won't have time to go to the store _____.

   a. yesterday   d. today
   b. this evening   e. next week
   c. on Friday

4. A lot of people will be at the game _____.

   a. last week   d. yesterday
   b. on Sunday   e. next Saturday
   c. three days ago

5. Mike and four of his friends left town _____.

   a. last Saturday   d. a week ago
   b. next week   e. on Sunday
   c. at the end of this week

Read the following two paragraphs and answer the questions about them. Pay attention to the *time* of the sentences and the questions.

1   José is looking for a car. He does not have a lot of money, so he
2   cannot buy a new car. Last weekend he looked at some used cars,
3   but he did not see a car which he liked. Next weekend he is going
4   to try again. He is also going to look at the used car pages in the
5   newspaper.

1. T F   José bought a car last weekend.   Line(s) _____

2. T F   José is going to buy a used car.   Line(s) _____

3. T F   He is going to start looking next weekend.   Line(s) _____

4. T F   The car which he buys will cost a lot of money.   Line(s) _____

5. T F   Perhaps he'll buy a car which he sees in the news-   Line(s) _____
        paper.

1   Abdullah is living with a friend from Kuwait at the moment,
2   but next month he is moving into an apartment which he found
3   last week. His wife and family are coming to the U.S. and they are
4   going to stay with him until the end of his studies. His children are
5   six and seven years old, a boy and a girl. Abdullah is going to send
6   them to an American school. There they'll begin to learn English.
7   At home Abdullah and his wife will speak Arabic with them, so
8   they won't forget their first language.

1. T F   Abdullah is going to live with a friend from Kuwait   Line(s) _____
        next month.

2. T F   Abdullah's wife and children are with him in the U.S.   Line(s) _____

3. T F   Abdullah's children will go to an American school.   Line(s) _____

4. T F   Abdullah's wife and children are going to stay with   Line(s) _____
        him until the end of his studies.

5. T F   Abdullah is going to look for a suitable apartment for   Line(s) _____
        them.

6. T F   Abdullah's children are learning English now.   Line(s) _____

WORD FAMILIES: WAYS TO UNDERSTAND NEW WORDS

Introduction

You now know some English vocabulary. Now let us study some of the words which you already know. Let us think about the following questions: What is a word family? How can I identify words which belong to the same word family? The answers to these questions will help your reading. You will be able to understand words which are new to you without the help of a dictionary.

Examples

Look at the words in these lists. They are all words which you know already. Don't worry about their meanings right now. Do you see anything that is the same in the endings or beginnings of each group of words?

Nouns

player	description	equipment	assistance	ability
teacher	civilization	movement	difference	possibility
driver	decision			

Adjectives

different	skillful	suitable	unusual
important	successful	possible	untrue

Explanation

1. Here are the *noun endings* in the examples:

   -er   (Words with *-er* endings usually describe *people* who do something, but they can also describe *things*.)

   -tion and *-ion*
   -ment
   -ance and *-ence*
   -ility

2. Here are some more *noun endings:*

   -or and *-ar*   (These endings have the same meaning as *-er*. An example is profess*or*.)

   -ness   (Example: sick*ness*)

   -ist   (This ending means a person who studies something. For example, a person who studies science is a scient*ist*.)

3. Here are the *adjective endings* in the examples:

   -ful
   -ent and *-ant*   (Some nouns also have these endings.)
   -able and *-ible*   (These endings mean "people can do something.")

4. Here are some more *adjective endings:*

-less	(This ending usually means *without* something. It is usually the opposite of the *-ful* ending. Example: care*less*.)
-y	(Example: happ*y*. But *-y* can also be a noun ending.)
-al	(Example: origin*al*. But *-al* can also be a noun ending.)

5. Here is the *adjective beginning* in the examples:

un-	(This beginning means "not." *In-* and *im-* mean the same. You can find the same beginnings in nouns.)

6. We can now build some word families. Here are a few examples. Each family begins with a word which you know already.

discover (*verb*)↔discover<u>y</u> (*noun*)↔discover<u>er</u> (*noun*)
origin (*noun*)↔origin<u>al</u> (*adjective*)
explore (*verb*)↔explor<u>er</u> (*noun*)
connect (*verb*)↔connec<u>tion</u> (*noun*)
suitable (*adjective*)↔<u>un</u>suitable (*adjective*)

Exercises

Here are some words. They are not completely new to you. You already know other words in the same word families. Look at the new words and their endings. Then write the words which you know in the same word family.

Adjectives		Nouns		Verbs	
accidental	_____	success	_____	to suit	_____
truthful	_____	destruction	_____	to inform	_____
unsuccessful	_____	certainty	_____	to differ	_____
healthy	_____	exploration	_____	to equip	_____
uncertain	_____	designer	_____	to assist	_____
understandable	_____	arrival	_____	to succeed	_____
useless	_____	suitability	_____	to complete	_____

Use your knowledge of word families for your reading. In each example the word in boldface type is new for you, but it belongs to a word family which is not new. Read each example. Then choose the correct meaning for the sentence.

1. Ali is a very **truthful** person.

    MEANING: a. You can believe everything Ali says.
                   b. Ali likes to help people a lot.
                   c. People like Ali a lot.

2. Columbus tried to find a new way to Asia, but he was **unsuccessful.**

   MEANING: a. Columbus found a new way to Asia.
              b. Columbus was not a successful sailor.
              c. Columbus did not find a new way to Asia.

3. The ancient Egyptians built their boats out of papyrus reeds. Wood was **unavailable.**

   MEANING: a. The wood in Egypt was not suitable for boats.
              b. They could not get any wood for boats.
              c. They did not like wood.

4. This apartment really **suits** us.

   MEANING: a. We want to move from this apartment.
              b. The apartment is just right for us.
              c. We were successful. We found an apartment.

5. Nobody **informed** me about the time of our soccer game yesterday.

   MEANING: a. I was not interested in the game.
              b. No one played soccer on Friday.
              c. No one told me the time of the game.

6. All the students realize the **importance** of the test tomorrow.

   MEANING: a. Tomorrow's test will be impossible. The students know this.
              b. Tomorrow's test matters a great deal. The students know this.
              c. The students will be successful in tomorrow's test.

7. Severin's leather boat was **equipped** with a radio.

   MEANING: a. There was a radio in Severin's boat.
              b. Severin turned on the radio in his boat.
              c. Severin bought some equipment for his boat.

8. Please **complete** this exercise for tomorrow.

   MEANING: a. Do this exercise for tomorrow.
              b. Finish this exercise for tomorrow.
              c. Write this exercise for tomorrow.

9. The new tool which I bought is completely **useless.**

   MEANING: a. The tool does not help me at all.
              b. The tool is very difficult to use.
              c. I have to be careful with the tool.

10. I have doubts about John's **suitability** for the job.

    MEANING: a. In my opinion, John is perhaps not a good person for the job.

                      b. In my opinion, John will be able to do this job very well.

                      c. In my opinion, John will not want to take this job.

Unit 3

SENTENCE CONNECTORS

Introduction

Look at the following example and try to understand it. Think about the *connection* between the ideas of the first sentence and the ideas of the second sentence.

> Many people in the U.S. like to take winter vacations. Last winter 4 million people traveled to Florida, Mexico, and the Caribbean.

The second sentence is an *example,* or *illustration,* which supports the idea in the first sentence. Probably you were able to see this connection. In this unit we will study special words and expressions which can make the connections between sentences very clear.

Examples and Explanations

Read the following examples. Pay attention to the words and expressions in bold-face type. Then read the explanation of each example.

1. Many people in the U.S. like to take winter vacations. Last winter, **for example,** over 4 million people traveled to Florida, Mexico, and the Caribbean.

This expression introduces an *example* or *illustration* of the ideas in the sentence before. A connector with the same meaning as **for example** is **for instance.**

2. It rained all week. **As a result,** we could not play our soccer game yesterday.

This expression introduces the *result* of the ideas or actions in the sentence before. The first sentence contains the cause of the second sentence. Connectors with the same meaning are **therefore, thus,** and **for this reason.**

3. Birth control programs are very successful in some countries. In other countries, **however,** they are complete failures.

This connector introduces ideas which are very *different* from the ideas of the sentence before. Sometimes the ideas are the *opposite* of the ideas in the first sentence. **However** is like **but** between clauses in a sentence.

4. I got home at five o'clock yesterday. I had a lot to do. **First** I made my dinner. **Then** I studied for three hours. **Next** I wrote a letter to a friend. **Finally** at twelve o'clock, I went to bed.

These connectors give a number of actions (or ideas) in their order. Other connectors of this type are **second, third, fourth,** etc.

5. In China, people with one child can get an apartment before people with large families. **In this way** the government hopes to show people the benefits of birth control.

This connector makes a connection between the method (first sentence) and the goal (second sentence).

Exercises

Sentence connectors help you in your reading. They can tell you the connection which you can expect between two sentences. Read the first sentence of each example; then read the beginning of the second sentence. Pay attention to the sentence connectors. Choose the correct ending for the second sentence.

1. There was a lot of ice on the roads. **However,**
   a. the cars moved very slowly.
   b. there were a lot of accidents.
   c. no one was late for class.

2. Maria is making good progress after the accident. **However,** she
   a. is leaving the hospital tomorrow.
   b. has to stay in the hospital for two or three more days.
   c. is feeling very well this afternoon.

3. Some religions are against birth control. **As a result,**
   a. birth control programs are very successful all over the world.

b. a lot of people are planning to use modern methods of birth control.

c. family-planning programs fail in some countries.

4. Some countries today cannot produce enough food for their people. **As a result,**

a. they have to depend on food from other countries.

b. they have weather which does not help the farmers.

c. there are no programs which teach modern farming techniques.

5. Apartments in this part of the town are very expensive, perhaps too expensive for one person. **For this reason,** Mike

a. is going to buy furniture this weekend.

b. is looking for someone who can share an apartment with him.

c. is going to move to this part of town at the end of next week.

6. I usually take my vacation in the summer. This year, **however,**

a. I want to go to some place which is nice and warm.

b. I'm going to Europe for six weeks in June and July.

c. I'm going to spend three weeks in Florida in December.

7. There was a lot of ice on the roads. **As a result**

a. the traffic moved very slowly.

b. everyone drove their cars to work.

c. there were no accidents.

8. Scientists are looking for ways to increase the food that we can grow. **For example,**

a. they are running into a lot of problems with their research.

b. they want to solve the problem of starvation in the world.

c. they are developing plants which can grow without a lot of water.

9. Severin decided to build a leather boat and to sail it across the Atlantic. **In this way,**

a. the boat also had a radio.

b. four other men sailed with him on the journey from Ireland to Newfoundland.

c. he hoped to test the story of St. Brendan's journey to the New World.

10. For many people, Columbus was the first European to reach the New World. According to archaeologists, **however,**

a. in 1492 his three small ships landed in the Bahamas.

b. many European explorers arrived after Columbus.

c. the Vikings were here 400 years before him.

SENTENCES WITH MISSING WORDS

Introduction

You can already understand sentences like this:

The Vikings built a settlement in Newfoundland,

but they did not stay there for long.

The sentence has two clauses; each clause has a subject and verb. In this unit we will look at sentences which do not have all the parts which you expect.

Examples

Read each example. How many verbs do you see in each example? Does each verb have a subject in front of it?

1. Tim Severin built a boat of leather and sailed it to America.
2. I can meet your friends at the airport and drive them to your apartment.
3. Heyerdahl decided to build a reed boat and to sail it across the Atlantic.

Explanation

1. In Example 1, **Tim Severin** is the subject of the two verbs **built** and **sailed.** In a sentence like this, we do not need to repeat the subject. We can omit it:

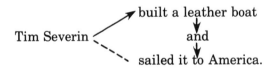

2. In Example 2, **I can** is the subject and auxiliary verb for the two verbs **meet** and **drive.** We can omit **I can** for the second verb.

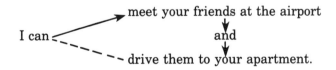

3. In Example 3, **Heyerdahl decided** is the subject and main verb for the two dependent verbs **to build** and **to sail:**

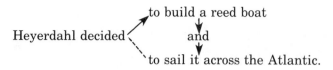

Heyerdahl decided to build a reed boat and to sail it across the Atlantic.

4. In sentences like these, we can also use **or** or **but.** We use **or** as a connection between two negative verbs. Here it means **and not.** We use **but** as a connection between a negative and a positive verb.

Exercises

Read these sentences and try to understand them. Underline the verbs (main verbs, auxiliaries, and basic forms). Then answer the questions about the sentences.

1. Columbus left Spain in August 1492 and landed in the Bahamas in October of the same year.

   Who landed in the Bahamas in October 1492? _____

2. Welfare can help people with no work but cannot solve all their problems.

   Who or what cannot solve all the problems of people with no work?

   _____

3. In the eleventh century, the Vikings came to Newfoundland but did not stay there long.

   Who didn't stay long in Newfoundland? _____

4. They had trouble with the Indians and decided to leave.

   Who decided to leave? _____

5. The governments of some countries are worried about the growth of their populations and are introducing free birth control programs for their people.

   Who are introducing free birth control programs? _____

6. Scientists are spending a great deal of money for medical research but still do not have a cure for the common cold.

   Who do not have a cure for the common cold? _____

7. In the opinion of many people, governments must not control the lives of their people or decide the size of their families.

   Who must not decide the size of people's families? _____

8. Without assistance from wealthy countries, some poor countries will not be able to improve the lives of their people or even to feed them.

Who will not be able to feed their people? _____

9. Doctors know the cause of this disease but cannot cure it.

Can doctors cure this disease? _____

10. Teams of workers go out into the country and teach the country people about birth control.

Who teaches people about birth control? _____

11. The car industry is having serious problems, and many workers are losing their jobs.

Who are losing their jobs? _____

12. The Incas of Peru had a great civilization, but European soldiers destroyed it.

Who destroyed the Incan civilization? _____

13. The ancient Egyptians knew a great deal about the movements of the stars and used this knowledge for their journeys of exploration.

Who used their knowledge of the stars for exploration? _____

14. Some governments give information about birth control on the radio and television, but many poor people still do not accept family planning.

Who do not accept family planning? _____

15. In 1492, Columbus was not looking for a new continent but trying to find a new way to India and China.

What was Columbus planning to do in 1492? _____

Unit 4

COMPARISONS

Introduction

You can already understand sentences like the following.

The film which we saw last night was very interesting, but the film we saw last week was really bad.

This sentence makes a *comparison* between two movies. In this unit we will study other ways to compare people and things.

Examples

Read the following examples and try to understand them. Each example has some information and then comparison sentences which use this information. After each example, read the explanation of the example.

Information	Comparisons
1. Kate is 18 years old. Bob is 18 also, and Mike is 21.	Kate is as old as Bob but she's not as old as Mike.
2. In the math class the students had lots of problems with the first test, but no one had any real problems with the second test.	The second test was easier than the first test. The first test was more difficult than the second test. The second test was less difficult than the first.
3. In 1983 a small Volkswagen cost about $8,000; a Cadillac about $20,000; and a Rolls Royce about $100,000.	The Volkswagen was the cheapest of the three cars. The Rolls Royce was the most expensive. The Volkswagen was the least expensive.

Explanation

1. In Example 1, Kate and Bob are the same age, but Kate and Mike are not. For comparisons like these, we use these constructions:

   Kate is **as**   old   **as** Bob.

       as + adjective + *as*

   Kate is **not** **as**   old   **as** Mike.

       not + *as* + adjective + *as*

2. In Example 2, the two tests are different: The first was difficult, and the second one was easy. For comparisons like this, we use these constructions with the *comparative form* of the adjective.

The second test was **easier** **than** the first test.

adjective + *er* + *than*

The first test was **more difficult than** the second test.

more + adjective + *than*

The second test was **less difficult than** the first test.

less + adjective + *than*

3. In Example 3, we are comparing more than two things. In these comparisons, we use these constructions with the superlative form of the adjective:

The Volkswagen was **the cheapest** of the three cars.

the + adjective + *est*

The Rolls Royce was **the most expensive** of the cars.

the + *most* + adjective

The Volkswagen was **the least expensive** of the cars.

the + *least* + adjective

4. The following table shows how to construct comparative and superlative forms:

Regular

Comparative	Superlative
adjective + *er*	adjective + *est*
or	or
more + adjective	*most* + adjective

Irregular

Basic Form	Comparative	Superlative
good	better	the best
bad	worse	the worst
many/much	more	the most
far	farther/further	the farthest/furthest
little	less	the least

Exercises

Read these sentences. Underline the comparative forms in the sentences. Then choose from (a) and (b) the sentence or sentences with the same meaning. Here is an example.

> <u>More</u> people traveled by plane in 1981 <u>than</u> in 1980.
>
> a. In 1981 not as many people flew as in 1980.
> ⓑ The number of people who traveled by plane was greater in 1981 than in 1980.

You underline *more* and *than*.
You choose *b*.

1. The bus journey from New York to San Francisco is not as expensive as the plane journey.
   a. The bus costs more than the plane.
   b. The bus is cheaper than the plane.

2. According to some people, private schools are better than public schools.
   a. Public schools are not as good as private schools.
   b. Students learn more in public schools than in private schools.

3. In the U.S. there are fewer public schools today than fifteen years ago.
   a. The number of public schools went down in the last fifteen years.
   b. There were more public schools fifteen years ago than there are today.

4. The population of China is greater than the population of the United States.
   a. There are not as many people in China as in the U.S.
   b. There are more people in China than in the U.S.

5. Heyerdahl's second journey across the Atlantic was more successful than his first.
   a. The first journey was less successful than the second.
   b. The first journey was just as successful as the second.

6. Last week the student was seriously ill, but this week he is getting better.
   a. The student is worse this week.
   b. The student's health is improving.

7. Men still make more money than women in their jobs.
   a. Women make less money than men.
   b. Women's pay is lower than men's pay.

8. My new apartment is more expensive than my old apartment.
   a. The rent in my old apartment was higher than the rent in my new apartment.
   b. I paid less rent in my old apartment than I do in my new apartment.

9. Ancient Egyptian sailors of 2,000 years ago were just as skillful as the European sailors of the fourteenth century.
   a. The Europeans of the fourteenth century were better sailors than the ancient Egyptians.
   b. The sailors of ancient Egypt had as much skill as the European sailors of the fourteenth century.

10. For engineering students, good grades in math are more important than good grades in history.
    a. For engineering students, good grades in history do not matter as much as good grades in math.
    b. For engineering students, good math grades are less important than good history grades.

In this exercise, first read the information in the tables. Then read the sentences. Choose only the sentences which agree with the information in the tables.

Numbers of Air Travelers
1980   65 million
1981   73 million
1982   76 million

1. More people flew in 1982 than in 1981.
2. A larger number of people flew in 1980 than in 1981.
3. Fewer people traveled by plane in 1980 than in 1982.
4. 1982 was the best year for the airlines.
5. The increase between 1980 and 1981 was not as large as the increase between 1981 and 1982.

Math Test Scores

Test 1 75%
Test 2 69%
Test 3 68%
Test 4 78%

1. The first math test was easier than the second.
2. The first test was the easiest of the four.
3. The third test was the most difficult of the four tests.
4. The students did better on the second test than on the third test.
5. The students had more problems with Test 1 than with Test 3.
6. The students' scores were higher on Test 3 than on Test 4.
7. The second test was almost as difficult as the third test.
8. Test 4 was less difficult than Test 2.

Apartment Information

	Apt. 1	Apt. 2	Apt. 3
Rent	$355	$275	$500
Size	500 sq. ft.	750 sq. ft.	1300 sq. ft.
Distance	½ mile	2 miles	5 miles
Bedrooms	1	2	3

1. Apt. 1 is less expensive than Apt. 2.
2. Apt. 3 is further from the university than Apt. 1.
3. The rent of Apt. 2 is not as high as the rent of Apt. 3.
4. Apt. 2 is larger than Apt. 1.

Now answer the following questions:

1. Which apartment is the best for a student and his family of four?
   a. Apt. 1   b. Apt. 2   c. Apt. 3

2. Which apartment is worst for a student with no car?
   a. Apt. 1   b. Apt. 2   c. Apt. 3

3. Which apartment is most suitable for two students who do not have a lot of money?
   a. Apt. 1   b. Apt. 2   c. Apt. 3

PASSIVE SENTENCES

Introduction

You can already understand sentences like this one:

1. A lot of people criticize the public schools.

In this section, the subject **a lot of people** are the people who do the action. We call this an *active* sentence. In this unit we are going to study a new way to express the same ideas, but we are going to use new grammar rules.

Examples

Look at the following sentence and compare it with the sentence in the Introduction.

2. The public schools are criticized by a lot of people.

This new sentence has the *same meaning* as Example 1. However, there are *grammar differences*. Look at the two sentences carefully. What differences can you see?

Explanation

1. Example 1 is an *active* sentence. Example 2 has the same meaning, but it is a *passive* sentence. You will often see passive sentences in your reading. You need to be able to understand them without difficulty.
2. You can make a passive sentence from an active sentence. This is a good way to learn about passive sentences. Look at Examples 1 and 2 again:

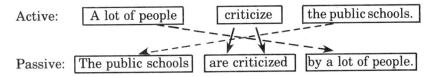

3. Here are the differences between active and passive sentences:
   a. The object of the active sentence (**the public schools**) becomes the subject of the passive sentence.
   b. The subject of the active sentence (**a lot of people**) goes to the end of the passive sentence. We add the word **by** in front of it.
   c. The verb of the active sentence changes its form for the passive sentence. Here we use a new form. We call it the *past participle*.
   d. In the passive sentence we add a form of the verb **to be** in front of the

main verb. This form of **to be** shows the tense of the sentence (**is–was–will be**). It also agrees with the subject for singular or plural (**is–are/was–were**).

4. Sometimes we don't want to mention the person who does the action. In a passive sentence we can omit this information. For example:

> My car was stolen yesterday. (Someone stole my car.)
> The man who stole my car was arrested today. (The police arrested him.)

5. The past participle of *regular* verbs is always the same as the simple past. The past participle of *irregular* verbs is different. There is a list of these irregular verbs on pages 313–14.

Exercises

Read the following examples. Underline *only* the passive verbs in these examples. Then give the tense (present, past, future) of the passive sentence.

1. The public schools of France are controlled by the central government. Local communities have little influence on the schools of their communities.
   Tense: _____

2. State universities in the U.S. are supported by money from the state government. Private universities do not get government support.
   Tense: _____

3. School boards are chosen by the people who live in a community.
   Tense: _____

4. The U.S. Constitution was written at the end of the eighteenth century.
   Tense: _____

5. Fifty years ago, the idea of divorce was not accepted by many people.
   Tense: _____

6. Birth control programs are needed in many countries. Their populations are growing too fast.
   Tense: _____

7. The problem of overpopulation can't be solved just by more birth control programs.
   Tense: _____

8. A great deal of research is being done into ways to increase food production.
   Tense: _____

9. Large increases in the population will have a number of effects. More houses, schools, and hospitals will have to be built; more energy will be needed to heat and cool these new buildings; more jobs will be needed.

    Tense: _____

10. Large amounts of money are being spent for medical research, but we still do not have a cure for the common cold.

    Tense: _____

Read these sentences and then answer the questions about them. Underline the words in each sentence which answer the question. Pay attention to the verbs in the sentences and in the questions. Some verbs are active; some are passive.

1. The police arrested some young people before the soccer game.
   Who were arrested by the police? _____

2. I was invited to a party by a student whom I met last week.
   Who invited me to the party? _____

3. Scientists found the remains of a Viking settlement in Newfoundland.
   What was found in Newfoundland? _____

4. Columbus did not really discover America. America was discovered by people who crossed from Asia more than 20,000 years ago.
   Who really discovered America? _____

5. A new birth control program is being introduced by the government of India.
   What is the Indian government introducing? _____

6. I flew to New York. At the airport I was met by a friend who is studying there.
   Who met me at the airport in New York? _____

7. In some countries, for example, Denmark and West Germany, sex education is taught in the public schools.
   What do Danish and German children learn in school? _____

8. In the U.S. the public schools of a community are controlled by a local school board.
   Who controls the public schools in the U.S.? _____

9. Advertisers are attracted to television by programs with large audiences.
   What attracts advertisers to television? _____

10. Sometimes school classes are disturbed by students who have no interest in learning.
    Who disturbs school classes? _____

SAME OR DIFFERENT?

Read the two sentences in each of these examples. Sometimes the sentences will look different but have the same meaning. Write *S* for sentences with the same meaning. Sometimes the sentences will have different meanings; write *D* for these sentences.

1. a. The bad weather stopped the game.   _____
   b. The game was stopped by the bad weather.

2. a. The police helped the driver.   _____
   b. The police were helped by the driver.

3. a. The warm weather attracts many visitors to Florida in the   _____
      winter.
   b. Many visitors are attracted to Florida in the winter by the
      warm weather.

4. a. Mayumi visited an old friend last weekend.   _____
   b. Mayumi was visited by an old friend last weekend.

5. a. Everybody enjoyed Ali's party last Saturday.   _____
   b. Ali's party last Saturday was enjoyed by everybody.

6. a. Scientists are developing new plants which grow very fast.   _____
   b. New plants which grow very fast are being developed by scientists.

7. a. Carlos invited Maria to a party on Sunday.   _____
   b. Carlos was invited by Maria to a party on Sunday.

8. a. The question of religion in the public schools is being discussed   _____
      by many people in the U.S.
   b. Many people in the U.S. are discussing the question of religion
      in the public schools.

9. a. I took my friend to the airport.   _____
   b. I was taken by my friend to the airport.

10. a. Students in many different countries learn English in school.   _____
    b. Students in many different countries are taught English in
       school.

Unit 5

SENTENCES WITH OBJECT CLAUSES

Introduction

You can already understand sentences like the following:

I really enjoyed the movie, but Mike didn't like it.

In this sentence, **the movie** is the *object* of the verb **enjoyed**; similarly **it** is the *object* of the verb **didn't like.**

You can understand sentences with noun objects and with pronoun objects. In this unit we will study sentences which have a different type of object.

Examples

Read these two examples and compare them. They both have the *same meaning*, but there are *grammar differences*. Look carefully for these differences.

1. The math class was very difficult. The students heard this.
2. The students heard that the math class was very difficult.

Explanation

Example 1 has two sentences; Example 2 has only one. In Example 1 the verb **heard** has a pronoun object **this** (the math class was difficult). Now look at the object of **heard** in Example 2:

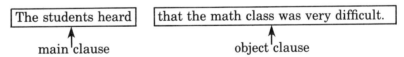

1. In this sentence, the object of the verb heard is a *clause,* with its own subject and verb.
2. The word **that** introduces the *object clause*
3. Object clauses can follow many verbs which you already know:

to believe	to find (out)	to inform someone	to prove
to conclude	to forget	to know	to remember
to discover	to hear	to learn	to say
to explain	to imagine	to predict	to show

| to suggest | to tell someone | to be sure | to be confident |
| to think | to understand | to be certain | |

4. You will also find *that clauses* after some nouns:

belief	information	prediction
conclusion	knowledge	suggestion
fact	message	theory
idea	news	thought

Yesterday we received the news | that an old friend was in the hospital.

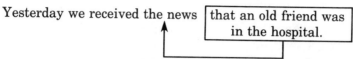

Exercises

Read these sentences. Find the sentences with object clauses. Underline only the object clauses.

1. The officers on the *Titanic* knew that there was ice near the ship, but they did not take any precautions.
2. The people on the *Titanic* did not imagine that anything could happen to the ship.
3. Children who watch television six hours a day often do not learn to read well. Teachers know this, and they are looking for a solution to the problem.
4. Parents who criticize the education system often do not understand that they are possibly also to blame for their children's problems.
5. John did not remember that man at the party.
6. Many people still believe that Columbus was the first European to reach America.
7. However, that idea was proven wrong by the discovery of a Viking settlement in Newfoundland in 1960.
8. Scientists are now certain that the Vikings reached North America about 400 years before Columbus.
9. People who talk about the first people in America often think only of Europeans. They forget that the ancestors of today's native Americans came here over 20,000 years ago.
10. Some people suggest that a strange and terrible power exists in the Bermuda Triangle.

Read the sentences in each example. Do they express the same ideas or different ideas?
  Remember: You can express the **same** ideas with **different** words and **different** grammar!

1. a. According to recent studies, the number of high school students   ———
      who cannot read is increasing.
   b. Recent studies show that the number of high school students
      who cannot read is going up.

2. a. Children have a right to learn about many different ideas in   ———
      school. Many people believe this.
   b. Many people believe that children have the right to learn about
      many different ideas in their school classes.

3. a. A lot of people believe that television has a bad effect on   ———
      children.
   b. Many people think that television does not have a bad effect on
      children.

4. a. The bridge was damaged, and cars could not cross it. The police   ———
      told us this.
   b. The police informed us that the bridge was damaged and that
      cars could not cross it.

5. a. According to experts who examined the *Marie Celeste,* the crew   ———
      left the ship in the lifeboat for some reason.
   b. Experts examined the *Marie Celeste* and concluded that the
      crew left the ship in the lifeboat for some reason.

6. a. According to British law, ships of over 15,000 tons had to have   ———
      sixteen lifeboats for passengers and crew.
   b. British law said that there had to be enough lifeboats for all
      passengers and crew on ships of over 15,000 tons.

7. a. Birth control is the only solution to overpopulation. Some   ———
      people think this.
   b. Some people think that birth control is the only answer to over-
      population.

8. a. According to evidence which was found recently, the owners   ———
      clearly knew about the plan for forty-eight lifeboats on the *Ti-
      tanic.*
   b. Evidence which was discovered recently proves that the owners
      of the *Titanic* knew about the plan for forty-eight lifeboats on
      the ship.

9. a. According to the radio messages which the *Titanic* received, there was a lot of heavy ice in front of the ship. _____

b. The radio messages which were received by the *Titanic* warned that there was a lot of heavy ice in front of the ship.

10. a. Some old Viking tools which scientists discovered in Newfoundland proved that Columbus was not the first European to reach North America. _____

b. Columbus was not the first European to reach North America. This was proven by scientists who discovered some old Viking tools in Newfoundland.

FUTURE IN THE PAST

Introduction

You can already understand sentences like this one:

> I am flying to Europe next week.

In sentences like this one, we look into the future from the present. We see something which is going to happen some time *later than now*. In this unit we will study a different type of future.

Examples

Look at the following example. Pay attention to the verbs and to the times of the actions in the sentence.

> At the beginning of the voyage, the owners of the *Titanic* did not expect that the ship would hit an iceberg.

Explanation

1. The sentence gives information about something in the *past.*
2. The first verb **did not expect** looks forward from the past into the future, to something which will perhaps happen later, to a second action.
3. For the second action, we use **would** + **basic form.** We call this the *future in the past.*
4. This future is different from the future which you saw in the Introduction. It is a future which we imagined *from a time in the past.* We do *not* imagine it from the present.

At the beginning of the voyage, the owners of the *Titanic* did not believe	that the ship would hit an iceberg.

main clause: past   object clause: future in the past

Exercises

In each of these sentences, there are two actions. Look for actions which will perhaps happen in the *future in the past*. Underline only the verbs which describe these actions.

1. Fifteen years ago, family-planning workers in India thought that modern birth control would solve the problem of overpopulation.
2. Fifteen years ago, people thought that overpopulation was the world's most serious problem.
3. Very few people imagined that the *Titanic* would sink in only 2½ hours.
4. The designer of the *Titanic* knew that the ship did not have enough lifeboats.
5. The *Titanic's* officers received warnings that there was ice in the ship's path.
6. No one expected that the *Titanic* would sink on its first voyage across the Atlantic.
7. In 1958 very few people really believed that men would reach the moon only ten years later.
8. Last week the students were told that there would be no classes on the last Friday of the month.
9. In 1940 many people thought that Germany would win the war.
10. At first Columbus did not understand that Cuba and the Bahamas were part of a new continent, not part of Asia.

Read the following sentences. Pay attention to the verb tenses. Then answer the questions about the sentences.

1. Yesterday John told me that he would take me to the airport on Saturday.
   Did John take me to the airport yesterday?   YES   NO

2. Mike told me yesterday that he felt very tired.
   Did Mike feel tired yesterday?   YES   NO

3. Last week the players were very confident that they would win the soccer game tomorrow. Now they aren't so sure.
   Do we know the result of the game?   YES   NO

4. Yesterday Kate told me that she would help me with my math. We're meeting tomorrow.

   Did Kate help me with my math yesterday?   YES   NO

5. Yesterday we got the news that a friend of ours was in the hospital.

   Was our friend in the hospital yesterday?   YES   NO

Choose the clause or clauses which can complete each sentence correctly. Pay attention to the verbs!

1. Before my trip to the U.S., I expected
   a. that I would have problems with the language there.
   b. that English was difficult for me.

2. In 1492, Columbus predicted
   a. that he would find a new way to Asia.
   b. that he discovered a new continent in the west.

3. In 1911 the designer of the *Titanic* informed the ship's owners
   a. that sixteen lifeboats would not be enough to save all the passengers and crew in a disaster.
   b. that the ship does not have enough lifeboats.

4. In 1969 the National Hurricane Center warned people in Louisiana
   a. that the state will be hit by a dangerous hurricane.
   b. that a dangerous hurricane would hit the coast in twenty-four hours.

5. As early as ten years ago, British researchers knew
   a. that sooner or later there would be a disaster with a British lifeboat.
   b. that the old type of lifeboat was unsafe.

6. In 1912, Europe was at peace. Few people imagined
   a. that war began in 1914.
   b. that peace would last only two more years.

7. Welfare was introduced only about forty years ago. At that time, people believed
   a. that it is the best answer to poverty.
   b. that it would solve all the problems of poor people.

8. At the beginning of his journey in 1976, Tim Severin was confident
   a. that he would successfully reach America.
   b. that the leather boat which he designed.

9. Some ships which later disappeared in the Bermuda Triangle reported
   a. that the waves would be 30 feet high.
   b. that they needed assistance badly.

10. At the beginning of their birth control programs, many governments believed
   a. that people would be able to see the benefits of smaller families.
   b. that the programs would solve their population problems.

Unit 6

SUBJECT CLAUSES WITH IT

Introduction

You can already understand the word *it* in sentences like these:

The test was very difficult. Only 30% of the students passed it.

In this example, the word *it* means something which appears in the first sentence of the example, *the test.* In this section we will study a new type of sentence with the word *it*.

Examples

Look at these examples and try to understand them.

1. It is dangerous to drive fast in bad weather.
2. It is becoming more difficult to find good apartments in this part of town.
3. It is possible that the *Titanic's* officers had too much confidence in their ship.

Explanation

In the example in the introduction, you cannot understand the word *it* without the information in the earlier sentence. In Examples 1–3 there are no earlier sentences, but we *can* understand the word *it*. The meaning of *it* comes later in the same sentence:

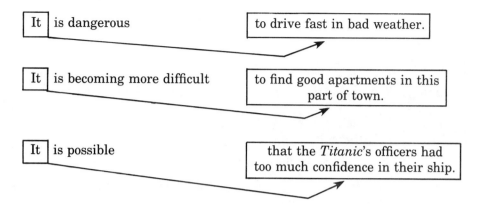

a. In this type of sentence, the word *it* tells the reader: For the real subject of the sentence, for the real meaning of *it,* look later in the sentence (after the verb). The meaning of *it* will be in an infinitive or in a *that clause.*

b. In academic English, you can often find this type of *it* with passive verbs. Here's an example:

It was believed <u>that the *Titanic* was unsinkable.</u>

c. You will also sometimes find **for + noun/pronoun** before the infinitive. Here's an example:

It is difficult for me to get to the university. (Maybe other people don't have problems, but *I* do.)

Exercises

Read these sentences carefully. Underline the words which give you the clear meaning of *it* in each sentence.

1. It was difficult to open the door.
2. It was impossible to do the work without better equipment.
3. It was strange that John did not come to the party.
4. It is not easy for students from other countries to find work in the U.S.
5. It was expected that poor people would immediately understand the benefits of birth control.

Read these sentences carefully. All of them contain the word *it.* Can you understand the word *it* in these sentences without more information? Answer YES or NO for each sentence.

1. It's extremely difficult.   YES   NO

2. It is very interesting.   YES   NO

3. It's wrong.   YES   NO

4. In the U.S. it is necessary.   YES   NO

5. In the nineteenth century, it was possible.   YES   NO

6. It's extremely difficult to run a mile in four minutes.   YES   NO

7. In the U.S. it's necessary for drivers to have insurance.   YES   NO

8. In the nineteenth century, it was impossible to travel from Europe to America in seven hours.   YES   NO

9. It is hoped that the two countries will be able to solve their problems without war.   YES   NO

10. It is very interesting to meet people from other countries.   YES   NO

Read these examples. What is the meaning of the word *it* in each example? Underline the words which give you the meaning of *it*.

1. It is not true that Columbus was the first European to reach America.

2. In 1960, it became clear that the Vikings landed in America 400 years before Columbus.

3. The *Titanic* disaster shocked the world. It also led to a number of important changes in ship design.

4. I'm reading about some new medical research in Germany. Scientists are hoping that it will lead to a cure for heart disease.

5. Who were the first people from the Old World to reach America? It is suggested that the ancient Egyptians sailed to America more than 2,000 years ago.

6. Don't miss the meeting next week. It's extremely important.

7. You can't learn a language just in the classroom, so it's very important to meet Americans and to speak English with them in your free time.

8. I'm sorry. I can't take you to the airport tomorrow. It's just impossible; I have an important test tomorrow at the same time as your plane.

9. There are problems with high school education in the U.S. For example, it is possible for a student to have twelve years of school and still not be able to read.

10. Many people believe that the Vikings were not the first Europeans in America. However, it is not possible to prove that any other people were definitely here earlier. There is no evidence of earlier settlements.

Here are five short paragraphs. Read the first part of each paragraph; then choose the possibility or possibilities which can complete the paragraph. Pay attention to *grammar and meaning*. (000 = nothing; the sentence can stop here.)

1. A lot of people suggest unnatural explanations for the disappearance of ships in the Bermuda Triangle. However, we do not need unnatural explanations. It is possible
   a. to find natural causes for the disappearances.
   b. to find reasons for the ships' problems.
   c. that sudden weather changes caused the disappearances.
   d. 000

2. We have no definite proof that the Irish came to America in the sixth century. However, it is possible
   a. to reach America by boat.
   b. that they, not the Vikings, reached America first.
   c. to cross the Atlantic by plane in eight hours or less.
   d. 000

3. Many people who came to the U.S. from Europe had religious problems in their own countries. Thus, for the writers of the U.S. Constitution, it was important
   a. an official religion for the new country.
   b. to separate the government from all religions.
   c. to protect people's right to practice any religion.
   d. 000

4. Slavery existed in the United States up to the end of the Civil War. After the war, it became illegal
   a. to own slaves.
   b. to treat slaves badly.
   c. slavery.
   d. 000

5. As a young man, Gandhi was very conservative. However, in South Africa, he himself experienced the discrimination and the bad treatment which were part of life for nonwhites. As a result of these experiences, he realized that it would be necessary
   a. racial discrimination and injustice.
   b. to organize opposition to the system which treated nonwhites so badly.
   c. to struggle actively for equal rights for all people.
   d. 000

CONDITIONAL SENTENCES

Introduction

You already can understand sentences like the following:

1. Without water this plant will die.
2. Without penicillin we would not be able to cure many diseases.

These sentences describe things which are possible. They also give the *conditions* which are necessary for the things to happen.

Sometimes the conditions are *real* (they are possible). In Example 1, **without water** means no one gives the plant water.

Sometimes the conditions are *unreal* (they cannot exist in this world). In Example 2, **without penicillin** means in an *unreal* world where penicillin does not exist.

In this unit we will examine other ways to write these two types of conditional sentences.

Examples

Look at the following examples. They have the same meanings as Examples 1 and 2. However, the grammar is different. What differences can you see?

3. If you don't water this plant, it will die.
4. If we didn't have penicillin, we would not be able to cure many diseases.

Explanation

1. We express the condition in a clause which begins with the word **if.**
2. We show that the condition is real or unreal with the verb tenses which we use.
   a. The condition in Example 3 is real (perhaps you will, perhaps you won't water the plant), so we use the present in the if clause; in this main clause, you see the future, but you will also see the present in other sentences.

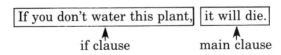

   b. The condition in Example 4 is *unreal* (we have to imagine an unreal world where penicillin does not exist), so we use past in the if clause; in the main clause we use **would** + **basic form**. However, the sentence is still talking about the present, *not* the past!

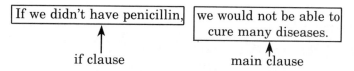

If we didn't have penicillin, ↑ if clause   we would not be able to cure many diseases. ↑ main clause

3. In your examples, the if clause comes at the beginning of the sentence. However, you will also see sentences with the main clause first and the if clause second.
4. **unless** = **if** + **not**. Examples 5 and 6 have the same meaning.

> 5. You'll be late for your plane if you don't leave before 8:00 A.M.
> 6. You'll be late for your plane unless you leave before 8:00 A.M.

Exercises

Read these conditional sentences. Pay careful attention to the verb tenses. Then answer the questions about them.

1. If it rains tomorrow, we will not go to the game.

    Will it rain tomorrow?   YES   NO   MAYBE

2. If I had one million dollars, I would buy myself a Rolls Royce.

    Do I have a million dollars?   YES   NO   MAYBE

3. Many more babies would die in this country if we didn't have a good medical system.

    Do we have a good medical system here?   YES   NO   MAYBE

4. There will not be enough food for everyone if the world's population continues to increase at its present speed.

    Will the population continue to grow at its present speed?   YES   NO   MAYBE

5. More people would go to soccer games in England if the stadiums were clean and comfortable.

    Are the soccer stadiums in England clean and comfortable?   YES   NO   MAYBE

6. Ali, if you choose a university in the northern U.S., you will need to buy warm clothes for the winters.

    Will Ali go to a university in the north?   YES   NO   MAYBE

7. If my apartment were close to the university, I would stay there. It's comfortable, and the rent isn't bad.

Is my apartment near the university?   YES   NO   MAYBE

Am I going to move?   YES   NO   MAYBE

8. If Mike and Kate were wearing their winter clothes—their hats, gloves, and heavy coats—they would not feel so cold.

Do Mike and Kate feel cold?   YES   NO   MAYBE

Are they wearing suitable clothes for the weather?   YES   NO   MAYBE

Read the first part of each exercise. What do you expect at the end? Choose the correct ending or endings. Pay attention to the conditional sentences and the verbs in them.

1. Mike is worried about his math test next week, but he really doesn't need to worry. He's good in math. If he studies for the test,
   a. he'll fail it.
   b. he would pass it.
   c. he'll have no difficulty with it.

2. According to many people, the problems in U.S. schools are the fault of the teachers and teacher-training programs. There would be fewer problems if
   a. better teachers in the schools.
   b. the teachers had better training.
   c. the teachers are better.

3. The F.D.A. is the government department which controls new substances in food and medicine. If research shows that a substance is dangerous, then the department
   a. can stop its production.
   b. will not allow its use.
   c. would not allow it.

4. Some countries cannot feed their own people. However, they often grow food that they sell to the wealthy industrial countries. According to some economists, if these countries used their land to grow basic foods,
   a. their people are not hungry.
   b. they would be able to feed their own people.
   c. there will be less hunger and starvation among their own people.

Unit 7

OBJECTS AND INFINITIVE AFTER VERBS

Introduction

You already know these verbs. If you are unsure about their meanings, look them up in the earlier units of the book.

to allow	to encourage	to order	to tell
to ask	to expect	to permit	to want
to cause	to forbid	to teach	to warn

You can understand these verbs in sentences like these:

1. I can drive. My brother taught me.
2. No one expected that the *Titanic* would sink so fast.

In this unit we will study a new type of sentence with these verbs.

Examples

Read these sentences carefully and try to understand them. In addition, try to find the grammar rule which the sentences have in common. Something in the grammar remains the same for both sentences.

3. The law forbids us to drive at more than 55 miles an hour.
4. Scientists did not expect DDT to damage the environment so much.

Explanation

1. In Examples 3 and 4, you can see the same grammar construction:

   subject + verb + person/thing + to + basic verb, etc.

2. After the main verb, there is an object. But it is not the *that clause* which we saw in Unit 5. It is a new construction. Here it is:

Subject	Verb	Object		
		Person/Thing	To + verb	
The law	forbids	us	to drive	at more than 55 MPH.
Scientists	did not expect	DDT	to damage	the environment so much.

3. In this construction the person or thing after the main verb really becomes the subject of the second action (the action of the basic verb).
4. The verbs in the Introduction often have this type of grammar construction after them. In this unit you will also learn three new verbs with the same construction: **to force, to require, to enable.**

Exercises

Read the sentences and underline the *person/thing* + *to* + *verb* constructions. Then answer the questions about the sentences.

1. My brother taught me to drive.
   Who learned to drive? _____

2. Ali's parents encouraged him to come to America.
   Who came to America? _____

3. This new equipment will allow the workmen to finish the job quickly.
   Who or what will finish the job? _____

4. The *Titanic*'s captain ordered the crew and passengers to abandon ship.
   Who had to abandon the ship? _____

5. The police did not allow drivers to use the bridge.
   Who could not use the bridge? _____

6. The weather office warned drivers not to use the roads during the snowstorm.
   Who gave the warning? _____

7. The doctor told my father to give up cigarettes.
   Who should give up cigarettes? _____

8. The ice on the road caused the car to hit a tree.
   What hit the tree? _____

Here are eight short exercises. Choose the phrase or phrases that can complete the exercise correctly. Pay attention to the grammar *and* the meaning of the exercises.

1. The designer of the *Titanic* realized that the ship needed forty-eight lifeboats. He warned
   a. the owners not to reduce the number of lifeboats.
   b. to increase the number from sixteen to forty-eight.

2. After the *Titanic* disaster, the British government changed the law about the number of lifeboats on ships. The new law ordered
   a. to make available enough lifeboats for all passengers and crew.
   b. builders to equip every ship with enough lifeboats for all passengers and crew.

3. The government is trying to solve the economic problems of the country. For example, it is trying to encourage
   a. companies to open new factories here.
   b. the development of new industries.

4. Everyone was surprised to see Mike at the party. They did not expect
   a. to come to the party.
   b. him to be there.

5. Early in U.S. history, the government did not ignore the rights of the Indians. For example, a law of 1789 forbade
   a. settlers to take land which belonged to Indians.
   b. the Indians to stay on land which belonged to them.

6. In the U.S. slaves had no rights. For example, they were not even allowed
   a. to learn to read.
   b. black people to educate themselves.

7. In most states of the U.S. drivers must have car insurance. Without insurance, legally you are not permitted
   a. a person to drive a car.
   b. to drive a car.

8. Environmentalists are not satisfied with the present laws against pollution. They want
   a. stricter laws.
   b. the government to introduce stricter laws against pollution.

MORE SENTENCES WITH SUBORDINATE CLAUSES

Introduction

You can already understand sentences with more than one clause. For example:

If we leave early, we'll get to the airport in time.
Some people still claim **that smoking doesn't damage your health.**

The sentences contain a main clause and a subordinate clause (the subordinate clauses are in boldface type). In this unit we are going to study other types of subordinate clauses.

Examples and Explanations

1. *Subordinate clauses of time* give information about the *time* of the action in the main clause. They are introduced by the words: **before, after, when, while, until.**

   > The Vikings reached America **before Columbus landed there in 1492.**
   > **After the game finished,** all the people went home.
   > The government decided to ban the chemical **when its effects on human health became clear.**
   > Mike broke his leg **while he was playing soccer.**
   > Please stay in your seats **until the plane stops at the arrivals building.**

2. *Subordinate clauses of reason* give information about the *reason for* or the *cause of* the action in the main clause. Clauses of reason are introduced by the word **because.**

   > The government plans to ban this chemical **because it is clearly a danger to human health.**

3. *Subordinate clauses of concession* contain information which *contrasts* with the action of the main clause. The action of the main clause seems *unexpected* because of the subordinate clause. Concession clauses are introduced by the word **although** (in spite of).

   > **Although the weather was cold,** we enjoyed our vacation.

4. *Subordinate clauses of purpose* explain the *purpose* of the action in the main clause:

   > Mike left his apartment at 8:00 A.M. **so that he would not miss his plane at 10:00 A.M.**

   There are two other common ways to express purpose without a full clause:

   > I came here **to learn English.**
   > I came here **in order to learn English.**

Exercises

Read the two sentences in each example. Do they express the same ideas or different ideas? Pay attention to subordinate clauses.

1. a. We have to wait here until Mike arrives.   _____
   b. We can't leave before Mike arrives.

2. a. While he was driving to New York, Ali had a minor automobile   _____
      accident.
   b. Ali had a minor car accident on his way to New York.

3. a. Although it was snowing heavily, the students decided to go for   _____
      a drive.
   b. The students decided to go for a drive because it was snowing
      heavily.

4. a. So that he is not late for his classes, Mike has to get up at 6:30.   _____
   b. Mike has to get up at 6:30 in order to be in time for his classes.

5. a. In spite of a number of warnings about ice, the *Titanic*'s officers   _____
      did not reduce speed or change direction.
   b. The *Titanic*'s officers did not reduce speed or change direction
      although they received a number of warnings about ice.

6. a. Segregation in the U.S. only ended when the federal govern-   _____
      ment used soldiers to enforce the law.
   b. Segregation in the U.S. did not stop until the federal govern-
      ment used soldiers to enforce the law.

7. a. When the *Titanic* hit the iceberg, it was traveling at nearly 25   _____
      miles an hour.
   b. After it hit the iceberg, the *Titanic* traveled 25 miles.

8. a. The government did not ban 2,4,5-T until doctors began to re-   _____
      port serious health problems in people who were exposed to it.
   b. The government did not ban 2,4,5-T although doctors reported
      serious health problems in people who were exposed to it.

9. a. After people began to use the chemical, scientists discovered   _____
      that it was dangerous to human health.
   b. People began to use the chemical after scientists discovered
      that it was dangerous to human health.

10. a. Chemical companies should always prove that a chemical is   _____
       safe before it is sold to the public.

b. A chemical should be sold to the public only after the producers prove that it is safe.

Read the first part of these exercises. What do you expect at the end? Choose the correct ending or endings. Pay attention to the words which introduce the subordinate clauses.

1. The owners of the *Titanic* decided to equip the ship with only sixteen lifeboats in order
   a. to save money.
   b. British law said that sixteen lifeboats were enough.
   c. they believed that the ship was unsinkable.

2. Although it is clear that certain chemicals are extremely dangerous,
   a. governments are often reluctant to stop their use.
   b. people who use them should be very careful.
   c. the government is going to ban them.

3. Although there is no doubt that acid rain is a danger to the environment,
   a. people are beginning to take the problem seriously.
   b. lakes and rivers in parts of the country are already contaminated.
   c. governments are still trying to ignore the problem.

4. Because diseases like cancer often need many years to develop,
   a. it is difficult to prove that they are caused by exposure to chemicals.
   b. they are often caused by dangerous chemicals in the environment.
   c. they are not connected with pollution.

5. When Severin saw that there was already a great deal of ice in the sea between Iceland and America,
   a. he decided to continue his journey.
   b. he realized that it would be too dangerous to continue the journey that year.
   c. he realized that his leather boat would be able to reach America.

SENTENCES WITH PRESENT PERFECT VERBS

Introduction

You can already understand a number of verb tenses in English. You can understand verbs in the present, in the past, and in the future. In this unit we will study another tense which is common in English.

Examples

Read these examples and try to understand them. Pay special attention to the time of the actions and to the verbs (in boldface type).

1. Mike **has been** a student here for three years. He plans to finish his studies next year.
2. My car was stolen three days ago. So far the police **haven't found** it.
3. Many people **have written** books about the *Titanic* disaster.

Explanation

1. In all the examples, you see verbs with this form: **has/have + past participle.**
2. We call this tense the *present perfect.*
3. We use the present perfect
   a. for actions which began in the past and which continue until the present (Examples 1 and 2), and
   b. for actions which happened in a period of time which continues until the present (Example 3).
4. Writers often use the present perfect to show that a past action has important effects in the present.
5. There are several time expressions which usually go with verbs in the present perfect: **until now, until the present, up to the present, since + time** (from then to now), **in the last/past two years/days** (etc.).
6. You will also see the present perfect in passive sentences. Here's an example:

   Many illegal chemical dumps **have been discovered** in the last five years in the U.S.

Exercises

Read the sentences and pay attention to verbs in the present perfect. Underline only the verbs in the present perfect.

1. John has been ill for the last four days. He's not getting any better. I think that he should see his doctor.
2. I can't get into my apartment. I've lost my keys.
3. There has been a lot of criticism of the government's new pollution laws. According to many people, they are not strict enough.

4. John: Have you taken your driving test yet?

   Maria: Yes, I took it last Friday.

   John: Well, did you pass?

5. John: How long have you been in the U.S.?

   Maria: Almost seven months. I came here late last year.

6. In spite of all the research which has been conducted, scientists still have not found a cure for the common cold.

7. The position of black people has improved since World War II, but racial discrimination hasn't completely disappeared in the U.S.

8. No one has ever given a satisfactory explanation for the disappearance of the people on the ship *Marie Celeste.*

You now know three uses for the English verb **to have:**

   1. Do you have time? (**Have** is a full verb.)
   2. I have to leave now. (**Have** means must.)
   3. I haven't seen that movie. (**Have** is a part of the present perfect.)

It is important to see the difference quickly between (1), (2), and (3) when you are reading. Here is some practice. Use the examples above and choose the correct meaning—(1), (2), or (3)—for each **has/have** in these sentences.

   1. Black people in America still have not achieved true equality with whites.   1 2 3

   2. However, their lives have improved in the past thirty years.   1 2 3

   3. They don't have to attend separate schools or travel in a special part of the bus or train.   1 2 3

   4. However, many don't have jobs.   1 2 3

   5. According to many people, if we really want stricter laws against pollution, we will have to put pressure on the government.   1 2 3

   6. The chemical industry has grown rapidly since World War II.   1 2 3

   7. We don't have 100% definite proof that chemical pollution causes cancer in humans.   1 2 3

   8. But a number of studies have shown that certain chemicals can cause cancer in experimental animals.   1 2 3

   9. The E.P.A has the authority to ban dangerous chemicals.   1 2 3

   10. In order to solve the problem of acid rain, we'll have to reduce the pollution from power plants which use coal.   1 2 3

Read the first part of these sentences. What do you expect at the end? Choose the correct ending or endings. Pay attention to the verb tenses and the time expressions.

1. Ali has been in the U.S. _____.
   a. since 1983
   b. two years ago
   c. for six months now

2. There has been a great increase in the number of working women _____.
   a. in the last fifteen years
   b. last year
   c. in the 1960s

3. Abdullah has to go to the airport _____.
   a. since last Monday
   b. tomorrow
   c. up to now

4. The government has done nothing to protect the environment _____.
   a. since it was elected
   b. up to now
   c. until 1980

5. In 1960 a scientist wrote a book about the long-term effects of DDT on the environment. Since that time _____.
   a. more and more people have realized that chemicals are a serious problem
   b. governments ignored the problem of chemical pollution
   c. much more research has been conducted into DDT

6. The present government claims that it is very concerned about pollution. So far, however, _____.
   a. it has spent a great deal of money to protect the environment
   b. it decided not to punish companies which were polluting the environment
   c. it has done very little to solve the problem

Irregular Verbs

SIMPLE PAST

Simple Past	Basic Form	Simple Past	Basic Form
ate	eat	grew	grow
became	become	had	have
began	begin		(Present tense: has/have)
bore	bear		
bought	buy	heard	hear
broke	break	held	hold
brought	bring	hit	hit
built	build	hurt	hurt
came	come	kept	keep
caught	catch	knew	know
chose	choose	laid	lay
cost	cost	lay	lie
could	be able to	learnt	learn
	(Present tense: can)	led	lead
		left	leave
cut	cut	let	let
did	do	lost	lose
drank	drink	made	make
drove	drive	meant	mean
fed	feed	met	meet
fell	fall	paid	pay
felt	feel	put	put
flew	fly	ran	run
forbade	forbid	rang	ring
forgot	forget	read	read
fought	fight	(Say like "red")	
found	find	rose	rise
gave	give	said	say
got	get	sang	sing

Simple Past	Basic Form	Simple Past	Basic Form
sank	sink	thought	think
sat	sit	threw	throw
saw	see	told	tell
sent	send	took	take
shot	shoot	tore	tear
shut	shut	understood	understand
slept	sleep	was/were	be
sold	sell		(Present tense:
spent	spend		am/is/are)
spoke	speak	went	go
stole	steal	woke	wake
stood	stand	won	win
swam	swim	wore	wear
taught	teach	wrote	write

PAST PARTICIPLES FOR PASSIVE AND PRESENT PERFECT VERBS

Past Participle	Basic Form (Infinitive)	Past Participle	Basic Form (Infinitive)
beaten	beat	forgotten	forget
become	become	fought	fight
been	be	found	find
begun	begin	given	give
borne	bear	gone	go
bought	buy	got/gotten	get
broken	break	grown	grow
brought	bring	had	have
built	build	heard	hear
come	come	held	hold
caught	catch	hit	hit
chosen	choose	hurt	hurt
cost	cost	kept	keep
done	do	known	know
driven	drive	laid	lay
drunk	drink	lain	lie
eaten	eat	learnt	learn
fallen	fall	led	lead
fed	feed	left	leave
felt	feel	let	let
flown	fly	lost	lose
forbidden	forbid	made	make

Past Participle	Basic Form (Infinitive)	Past Participle	Basic Form (Infinitive)
meant	mean	spoken	speak
met	meet	stolen	steal
paid	pay	stood	stand
put	put	sung	sing
read	read	sunk	sink
(Say like "red")		swum	swim
risen	rise	taken	take
run	run	taught	teach
rung	ring	thought	think
said	say	thrown	throw
sat	sit	told	tell
seen	see	torn	tear
sent	send	understood	understand
shut	shut	woken	wake (up)
slept	sleep	won	win
sold	sell	worn	wear
spent	spend	written	write

Entry-Level Specifications

ENTRY-LEVEL GRAMMAR

Present simple and present progressive

Negation

Yes/no and *wh* questions (with *what, when, where, why, which, how, who*)

Existential *there*

Regular noun plurals

Determiners (*the, a/an, some/any/no, each, every, this/these, that/those*)

Possessives (all)

Personal pronouns (all)

Adjectives (in attributive and predicative use)

Adverbs

Prepositional phrases (as adverbials and as post-nominal modifiers) with the following prepositions:

about	before	down	for	in	of	through	under	with
across	behind	during	from	into	off	to	until	without
after	beside				on		up	
against	between				out of			
at	by							

Simple sentences with (a) transitive verbs, (b) intransitive verbs, (c) linking verbs (*be, become*).

ENTRY-LEVEL VOCABULARY (CLOSED SETS)

Days of the week

Months of the year

Numbers 1–99, hundred, thousand, million

ENTRY-LEVEL VOCABULARY

ability/able
action
address
again
age
airline
airport
already
alright
also
always
and
angry
animal
to answer
apartment
to ask
asleep
attention
away

baby
bad
ball
banana
baseball
to be
beard
to become
to begin
to belong to
bill
black
boat
body
book
boot
to borrow
bottle
to bring
brother
to build

building
business
but
to buy

cafeteria
can (=be able)
car
careful
to carry
chair
cheap
child/children
choice/to choose
city
class
close
clothes
coal
coast
coat
cold
to come
comfortable
computer
continent
conversation
to cook
cool
correct
country
culture
to cut

day
different
to die
difficult/difficulty
dinner
distance
to divide
to do

doctor
dog
to drink
to drive/driver

early
earth
east
easy
to eat
electric
end
to enjoy
enough
even
evening
every
example
to exist
exit
to expect
expensive
to explain/explanation
to express

fact
factory
to fall
family
famous
far
fast
father
to feed
to feel
field
to find
to finish
fire
first
to fix
flight

floor
to fly
to follow
food
football
to forget
free
friend
full
furniture

game
garden
gas
general
to get
to get up
to give
to go
good
green
ground

hand
to happen
happy
to have
to have to
to hear
to heat
to help
here
history
home
to hope
horse
hospital
hot
hour
house
hunger
hurt
husband

ice
idea
ill/illness
industry/industrial
to inform/information
intelligent
interesting

job
journey

to keep
to kill
kind (=type)
kitchen
to know

land
language
large
late
law
leaf
to learn
left
leg
to let
letter
library
to lie
life
light (n., adj.)
to like
line
to live
long
to look (=appear)
to look for
to lose
a lot
lunch

machine
to make

many
married
math
to matter
to mean
to meet/meeting
middle
mile
million
minute
mistake
money
month
morning
mother
movie
music

name
near
necessary
to need
new
newspaper
next
night
no
north
not
now
number

ocean
to offer
office
often
oil
old
only
to open
opposite
to own

page
painting
parents
part
to pay
to pay attention
people
person
picture
piece
place
to plan
plane
plant
to play/player
police
political
poor
possible
practice
present (=now)
price
professor
program

question

to rain
to read
reason
religion
to remember
to rent
restaurant
to return
rich
right
to ring
river
road
roof
room
rule
to run

safe
salt
same
to say
school
scientist
sea
seat
to see
to sell
sentence
ship
shirt
shoe
short
shorts
to show
sick
side
to sleep
slow
small
to smoke
snow
soccer
some
someone
something
south
to speak
to spend
sports
stadium
stairs
to stand
star
to start
to stay
still
to stop
story
street
strength/strong
student

to study
stupid
subject
suit
suitcase
summer
sun/sunny
sure

table
to take
to teach
team
telephone
television
to tell
test
to thank
there
thing
to think
ticket
time
tired
today
together
tomorrow
tonight
too
top
town
to travel
tree
trip
true
to try
type

to understand
unhappy
university
use
to use

vacation
very
to visit/visitor

to wake
to wait
to walk
wall
to want
war
warm
to watch

water
to wear
weather
week
well (=healthy)
west
white
whole
wife
to win
wind
window

winter
wonderful
word
to work
world
to write/writer
wrong

year
yes
young

Vocabulary Index

Page numbers refer to the page on which a word is defined and exemplified. A small number of morphologically related words are introduced in the readings; for them line numbers have also been provided. Grammatical categories are specified only in cases which would otherwise be ambiguous.

conclusion, 112
condition, 102
to conduct, 179
confidence, 131 (l. 107)
confident, 124
to connect, 14
connection, 14
consequence, 185
consequently, 206 (l. 113)
conservative, 82
constitution, 85
consumer, 225
to contain, 20
to contaminate, 178
contaminated, 178
to continue, 3
control, 49
to control, 49
to create, 240
creation, 245 (l. 63)
crew, 123
crime, 153
criminal, 153
critic, 79
to criticize, 79
crops, 191
cure, 50
to cure, 50

damage, 111
to damage, 111
damaged, 111
danger, 22
dangerous, 22
deadly, 199
deal, a great ___ of, 25
to decide, 12
decision, 12
to decrease, 92
defect, 186
defective, 186
definite, 21
deliberate, 111
demand, 167 (l. 102)
to demand, 137
to demonstrate, 153
demonstration, 153
demonstrator, 167 (l. 82)
to deny, 137
department, 103
to depend, 43
descendant, 162

to describe, 19
description, 19
design, 14
to design, 14
designer, 130 (l. 60)
to destroy, 19
destruction, 190 (l. 29)
to develop, 50
developing, 50
development, 95 (l. 3)
to disagree, 49
disagreement, 65 (l. 26)
to disappear, 111
disappearance, 111
disaster, 102
disastrous, 190 (l. 35)
to discover, 10
discovery, 10
to discriminate, 138
discrimination, 138
to discuss, 84
discussion, 84
disease, 50
disobedience, 141 (l. 10)
dissatisfaction, 96 (l. 48)
dissatisfied, 81
to disturb, 91
divorce, 81
divorced, 81
domestic, 241
doubt, 14
to doubt, 14
dump, 180
duty, 116

ecological, 189
ecologist, 190 (l. 34)
ecology, 189
economic, 61
economics, 65 (l. 50)
economy, 205 (l. 84)
to educate, 70
educated, 151 (l. 9)
education, 70
effect, 43
to elect, 72
election, 72
elementary, 70
to employ, 137
employment, 137
to enable, 304
to encourage, 193

to endanger, 36 (l. 61)
energy, 41
to enforce, 179
to entertain, 78
entertaining, 78
entertainment, 80
environment, 177
environmental, 190 (l. 30)
environmentalist, 178 (l. 14)
equal, 137
equality, 137
to equip, 168 (l. 153)
equipment, 26
to escape, 124
especially, 188
evidence, 116
excellent, 84
experience, 114
to experience, 204 (l. 58)
experienced, 114
experiment, 199
to explode, 168 (l. 125)
exploding, 64 (title)
exploration, 36 (l. 42)
to explore, 13
explorer, 13
explosion, 66 (l. 84)
to expose, 185
exposure, 186 (l. 11)
extreme, 141
extremely, 141
extremist, 142 (l. 20)

facility, 161
factor, 200
to fail, 42
failure, 42
familiar, 124
family planning, 49
fault, 79
fear, 149
to fear, 149
feature, 231
federal, 146
federation, 146
female, 218
feminism, 217
feminist, 217
figure, 226
finally, 276
fine (n.), 185
flexible, 240

therefore, 275
to threaten, 189
thus, 275
tool, 25
toxic, 199
tradition, 219
traditional, 219
to train, 73
training (n.), 73
to transport, 60
to treat, 136
treatment, 136
trouble, 2
truth, 11
tuition, 71

uncertainty, 205 (l. 86)
undamaged, 117 (l. 5)
unemployed, 137

unemployment, 137
unhealthy, 151 (l. 12)
unimportant, 166 (l. 55)
unjust, 145
unless, 301
unlike, 23
unpleasant, 53
unpredictable, 118 (l. 24)
unprepared, 131 (l. 118)
unproductive, 190 (l. 2)
unsinkable, 125
unstable, 229
unsuitable, 5
until, 306
unusual, 33
usual, 33

variety, 241
various, 245 (l. 68)

violence, 139
violent, 139
to vote, 136
voyage, 123

wage, 240
to warn, 101
warning, 101
waste, 180
to waste, 180
wave, 105
way, 2
wealthy, 59
welfare, 43
when (conj.), 306
while (conj.), 306
wood, 23
worried, 52
to worry, 52